The Golden Book of
DESSERTS

The Golden Book of
DESSERTS

First English language edition for the United States and Canada published in 2010
by Barron's Educational Series, Inc.

Copyright © McRae Books s.r.l. 2009
Via Umbria, 36-Florence, Italy

The Golden Book of Desserts
was created and produced by McRae Books Srl
Via Umbria, 36 – 50145 Florence, Italy
info@mcraebooks.com
www.mcraebooks.com
Publishers: Anne McRae, Marco Nardi

Project Director Anne McRae
Art Director Marco Nardi
Photography Brent Parker Jones, Paul Nelson (RRPHOTOSTUDIO)
Introduction Carla Bardi
Texts Rachel Lane, Carla Bardi
Editing Anne McRae
Food Styling Lee Blaylock, Michelle Finn
Stylist Lee Blaylock
Food Preparation Rebecca Quinn, Michelle Finn
Layouts Aurora Granata
Pre-press Filippo Delle Monache, Davide Gasparri

All inquiries should be addressed to:
Barron's Educational Series, Inc.
250 Wireless Boulevard
Hauppauge, New York 11788
www.barronseduc.com

ISBN-13: 978-0-7641-6361-6
ISBN-10: 0-7641-6361-2

Library of Congress Control Number: 2009940366

Printed in China

9 8 7 6 5 4 3 2 1

NOTE TO OUR READERS
Eating eggs or egg whites that are not completely cooked poses the possibility of
salmonella food poisoning. The risk is greater for pregnant women, the elderly, the
very young, and persons with impaired immune systems. If you are concerned about
salmonella, you can use reconstituted powdered egg whites or pasteurized eggs.

The level of difficulty for each recipe is given on a scale from
1 (easy) to 3 (complicated).

CONTENTS

INTRODUCTION

A scrumptious dessert makes the perfect finish to any meal, whether it be a week-night or weekend lunch or supper for family and friends or an elegant formal dinner party. In this book, we have selected more than 250 dessert recipes, ranging from simple custards, pies, and fruit desserts, to more challenging dishes, such as layer cakes, savarins, and dacquoise. Here you will find the perfect dessert for every occasion. We have graded each recipe 1, 2, or 3 for level of difficulty, with most falling into the first or second categories.

Like good music, successful dessert-making is based on a secure knowledge of technique tempered by discipline and a touch of inspiration. Since many desserts can only be made successfully by following exact measurements and methods, in this book we have included 19 step-by-step sequences to help you with many of the basic techniques. These range from showing you how to line a pie pan with pastry and how to roll a jelly roll (Swiss roll), to correct frying methods for fritters and how to prepare a basic sponge cake. A full list of the techniques featured with step-by-step photography is provided in the index.

Ingredients

Butter: Butter is high in fat (most commercial brands contain 80–85 percent butter fat). Higher fat gives baked goods better flavor, texture, and a flakier, more tender crumb. Always use softened butter at room temperature when creaming with sugar. Beat by hand or with an electric mixer until pale and creamy.

Chocolate: We have used three different types of chocolate: dark, milk, and white. Dark chocolate comes in many varieties and each brand has different amounts of sugar. Generally bittersweet chocolate has less sugar (about 46 percent), while semisweet is sweeter (about 56 percent sugar). Experiment and choose the best-quality chocolate that most suits your taste buds.

Cocoa Powder: Is made from unsweetened chocolate. It will often benefit from sifting—to remove the lumps rather than to add air.

Cream: We have indicated either heavy (double) or light (single) cream. Heavy cream has more fat (up to 48 percent), while light cream has less (about 18 percent). Fat levels can vary, but remember that if you want to whip the cream to finish a dessert you will need a cream with at least 30–35 percent fat.

Eggs: Eggs contribute flavor, structure, richness, and texture to many desserts and should always be as fresh as possible. We have specified large eggs throughout. Large eggs weigh about 2 ounces (60 g) each. Eggs should be at room temperature; cold eggs can curdle the batter. Take them out of the refrigerator an hour or two before you start.

Flour: Unless otherwise specified, we have used all-purpose (plain) flour throughout (since that is what most people have in their kitchens). We found the results more than satisfactory. Modern flour is all pre-sifted, so there is no need to sift it before adding to the batter.

Milk: While not specified in the recipes, we suggest you use whole milk for best results.

Sugar: When the recipes list sugar, we mean ordinary granulated sugar; all other sugars are indicated by name—superfine (caster) sugar, confectioners' (icing) sugar, light brown sugar, and dark brown sugar.

Carla Bardi

CUSTARDS & CREAMS

LIGHT CRÈME BRÛLÉE

Preheat the oven to 300°F (150°C/gas 2). • Oil four
³/₄-cup (180-ml) ramekins. • Spilt the vanilla pod in
half lengthwise and use a knife to scrape out the
seeds. Combine the seeds in a saucepan with the
cream and milk. Place over medium heat and bring
to a boil. • Remove from the heat and set aside for
1 hour to allow the flavors to infuse. • Beat the egg
yolks and superfine sugar in a medium bowl with
an electric mixer on high speed until pale and
creamy. Gradually beat in the cream and milk.
Step 1: Strain through a fine-mesh sieve into a
pitcher (jug) and then pour into the ramekins.
Step 2: Place the ramekins in a deep baking pan.
Pour enough boiling water into the baking pan to fill
halfway up the sides of the ramekins. • Bake for
35–45 minutes, or until the custard has set but is
still a little wobbly in the center. Let cool to room
temperature, about 1 hour. Chill in the refrigerator
for at least 4 hours. • Sprinkle the brown sugar
evenly over the top of each ramekin, ensuring that
the cream is completely covered. Wipe the rims.
Step 3: Light a chef's blowtorch and caramelize the
sugar until melted and golden brown. **Step 4:** If you
don't have a chef's blowtorch, preheat a broiler
(grill) on high. Place the ramekins 3–4 inches
(8–10 cm) below the broiler and broil until the
sugar begins to melt and turns a golden caramel,
3–5 minutes. • Serve at once or chill in the
refrigerator and serve later.

1	vanilla pod
1¼	cups (300 ml) light (single) cream
¼	cup (60 ml) milk
3	large egg yolks
¼	cup (50 g) superfine (caster) sugar
½	cup (100 g) firmly packed light brown sugar

Serves: 4
Preparation: 20 minutes
  + 6 hours to infuse
  and chill
Cooking: 40–50 minutes
Level: 2

PREPARING CRÈME BRÛLÉE

Classic crème brûlée (often called "burnt cream" in English) is traditionally made with rich, heavy (double) cream. In this recipe we have used light (single) cream to lighten the dish a little.

1. STRAIN the egg and cream mixture through a fine-mesh sieve into a pitcher (jug). Pour into the ramekins.

2. PLACE the ramekins in a deep baking pan. Pour enough boiling water into the baking pan to fill halfway up the sides of the ramekins.

3. CARAMELIZE the sugar using a blowtorch until the sugar begins to melt and turns a golden caramel.

4. Alternatively, preheat a broiler (grill) on high. Broil until the sugar begins to melt and turns a golden caramel, 3–5 minutes.

CLASSIC CRÈME BRÛLÉE

Preheat the oven to 300°F (150°C/gas 2). • Oil six ½-cup (125-ml) ramekins. • Spilt the vanilla pod in half lengthwise and use a knife to scrape out the seeds. Combine the seeds in a saucepan with the cream. Place over medium heat and bring to a boil. • Remove from the heat and set aside for 1 hour to allow the flavors to infuse. • Beat the egg yolks and superfine sugar in a medium bowl with an electric mixer on high speed until pale and creamy. • Gradually pour the cream into the egg mixture, stirring with a wooden spoon until incorporated. Strain through a fine mesh sieve into a small bowl or pitcher (jug). • Pour in the custard mixture into the ramekins. • Place the ramekins in the baking pan. Pour enough boiling water into the baking pan to come halfway up the sides of the ramekins. • Bake for 35–45 minutes, or until the custard has set but is still a little wobbly in the center. • Remove the ramekins from the pan and let cool to room temperature, about 1 hour. Cover and refrigerate for at least four hours, or until required. • Just before serving, light a chef's blowtorch or preheat a broiler (grill) on high heat. • Sprinkle the Demerara sugar evenly over the top of the custards. Wipe the rims clean. Sit the ramekins in a pan of ice water. Caramelize the tops under the grill or with a chef's blow torch. • Serve at once or chill in the refrigerator and serve later.

1	vanilla pod
2	cups (500 ml) heavy (double) cream
5	large egg yolks
½	cup (100 g) superfine (caster) sugar
½	cup (100 g) Demerara sugar

Serves: 6
Preparation: 20 minutes
 + 6 hours to infuse
 and chill
Cooking: 40–50 minutes
Level: 2

RASPBERRY CRÈME BRÛLÉE

Preheat the oven to 300°F (150°C/gas 2). • Oil six ½-cup (125-ml) ramekins. • Spilt the vanilla pod in half lengthwise and use a knife to scrape out the seeds. Combine the seeds in a saucepan with the cream. Place over medium heat and bring to a boil. • Remove from the heat and set aside for 1 hour to allow the flavors to infuse. • Beat the egg yolks and superfine sugar in a medium bowl with an electric mixer on high speed until pale and creamy. • Gradually pour the cream into the egg mixture, stirring with a wooden spoon until incorporated. Strain through a fine mesh sieve into a small bowl or pitcher (jug). • Combine the raspberries and liqueur in a small bowl. Spoon the raspberries evenly into the base of the ramekins and pour the custard in over the top. • Place the ramekins in a deep baking pan. Pour enough boiling water into the baking pan to come halfway up the sides of the ramekins. • Bake the custards for 35–45 minutes, or until the custard has set but is still a little wobbly in the center. Remove the ramekins from the pan and let cool to room temperature, about 1 hour. Cover and refrigerate for at least four hours, or until required. • Just before serving, light a chef's blowtorch or preheat a broiler (grill) on high heat. Sprinkle the Demerara sugar evenly over the top of the custards. Wipe the rims clean. Sit the ramekins in a pan of ice water. Caramelize the tops under the broiler or with the blow torch. • Serve immediately.

1   vanilla pod

2   cups (500 ml) heavy (double) cream

5   large egg yolks

½   cup (100 g) superfine (caster) sugar

1   cup (150 g) fresh raspberries

3   tablespoons raspberry liqueur

¼   cup (50 g) Demerara sugar

Serves: 6
Preparation: 20 minutes + 6 hours to infuse and chill
Cooking: 40–50 minutes
Level: 2

BAKED NUTMEG CUSTARDS

Preheat the oven to 300 F (150 C/gas 2). • Oil four 1-cup (250-ml) ramekins. • Place the milk in a medium saucepan over medium heat and bring to a boil. Remove from the heat and set aside. • Whisk the eggs, egg yolk, sugar, and vanilla in a medium bowl until just combined. • Gradually pour the hot milk into the egg mixture, stirring with a wooden spoon until incorporated. Strain the custard mixture through a fine mesh into a small bowl or pitcher (jug). • Place the ramekins in a deep baking pan. Pour the custard mixture into the ramekins and dust with the nutmeg. Pour enough boiling water into the baking pan to come halfway up the sides of the ramekins. • Bake for 30 minutes, or until the custard has set but is still a little wobbly in the center. • Serve warm or chilled.

2½ cups (625 ml) milk

3 large eggs + 1 large egg yolk

⅓ cup (70 g) superfine (caster) sugar

1½ teaspoons vanilla extract (essence)

½ teaspoon ground nutmeg

Serves: 4
Preparation: 20 minutes
Cooking: 30 minutes
Level: 1

■ ■ ■ *These pretty little custards are equally delicious dusted with ground cinnamon or ginger. Serve them warm with cookies during the winter and well chilled with fresh fruit during the hot summer months.*

CRÈME CARAMEL

Preheat the oven to 350°F (180°C/gas 4). • Rinse six $^1/_2$-cup (125-ml) ramekins with cold water. • Place $^3/_4$ cup (150 g) of sugar and the water in a small heavy-based saucepan over medium heat. Cook, stirring occasionally, until the sugar dissolves and turns into a golden caramel, 5–10 minutes. Pour the caramel into the ramekins and leave to cool. • Place the milk in a medium saucepan over medium heat and bring to a boil. Remove from the heat and set aside. • Whisk the eggs, egg yolks, the remaining $^1/_2$ cup (100 g) of sugar, and vanilla in a medium bowl until just combined. • Gradually pour the milk into the egg mixture, stirring with a wooden spoon, until incorporated. Strain the custard mixture through a fine mesh into a small bowl or pitcher (jug). • Place the ramekins in a deep baking pan and fill with the custard mixture. Pour enough hot water into the baking pan to come halfway up the sides of the ramekins. • Bake for 30–35 minutes, or until the custard has set but is still a little wobbly in the center. • Remove from the pan and let cool to room temperature, about 1 hour. Refrigerate until chilled, at least 4 hours. • Turn the crème caramels onto individual serving plates, allowing the caramel to drizzle down the sides.

1¼ cups (250 g) superfine (caster) sugar

2 tablespoons water

2½ cups (625 ml) milk

3 large eggs + 3 large egg yolks

1½ teaspoons vanilla extract (essence)

Serves: 6
Preparation: 30 minutes + 5 hours to cool and chill
Cooking: 35–45 minutes
Level: 1

ORANGE & TEQUILA FLAN

Heat the milk, vanilla pod, and orange zest in a medium pan over medium-low heat. Bring to a gentle simmer then remove from the heat and set aside. Let the flavors infuse for 1–2 hours (or overnight in the refrigerator). • Preheat the oven to 300°F (150°C/gas 2). • Rinse six $3/4$-cup (180-ml) ramekins with cold water. • To prepare the caramel, place $3/4$ cup (150 g) of sugar with the water and 2 tablespoons of tequila in a small saucepan over low heat. When the sugar has melted turn the heat up to medium and simmer until the mixture turns a deep caramel color. Stir in the remaining 2 tablespoons of tequila and pour the caramel into the ramekins. • Beat the eggs, egg yolks, and remaining sugar with an electric mixer on medium-high speed until pale and creamy. • Remove the vanilla pod and orange zest from the infused milk and reheat to boiling point. Gradually whisk the hot milk into the egg mixture. Pour the custard into the ramekins. • Place the ramekins in a deep baking pan and fill the dish with enough boiling water to come halfway up the sides of the ramekins. • Bake for 30–35 minutes, or until the custard has set but is still a little wobbly in the center. • Let cool to room temperature. Turn out onto plates to serve.

3	cups (750 ml) milk
1	vanilla pod, split in half
5	strips untreated orange zest
1	cup (200 g) semifine (caster) sugar
$1/3$	cup (90 ml) water
$1/4$	cup (60 ml) tequila
4	large eggs + 4 large egg yolks

Serves: 6
Preparation: 20 minutes
  + 2–3 hours to infuse
  and cool
Cooking: 30–35 minutes
Level: 2

■ ■ ■ *This is a delicious Mexican variation on baked custard. Serve at the end of a dinner party for a light and elegant finish.*

ORANGE PANNA COTTA

32

Place the cream and sugar in a medium saucepan over medium heat and bring to a boil. Decrease the heat and simmer until reduced by about a third, about 5 minutes. • Meanwhile, pour the water into a small cup. Sprinkle the gelatin over the water and leave to soak for 5 minutes. • Remove the cream from the heat and add the orange liqueur and gelatin, stirring until incorporated. • Strain the cream through a fine mesh sieve into a small bowl or pitcher (jug). Stir in the orange zest and set aside until cooled, about 15 minutes. • Pour the cream mixture into six ³/₄-cup (180-ml) plastic molds and refrigerate until set, at least 6 hours. • To serve, gently pull the side of each panna cotta away from the molds and invert onto individual serving plates. Decorate with the orange segments and serve.

4	cups (1 liter) heavy (double) cream
³/₄	cup (150 g) sugar
2	tablespoons water
3	teaspoons unflavored gelatin powder
2	tablespoons orange liqueur, such as Cointreau
2	oranges, zest finely grated, peeled, and segmented

Serves: 6
Preparation: 15 minutes
  + 6–7 hours to cool
  and chill
Cooking: 5 minutes
Level: 1

■ ■ ■ *Panna cotta (baked cream) is a classic Italian dessert. Try this one with Chocolate Crème Anglaise spooned over the top (see variations, page 586).*

BLACKBERRY PANNA COTTA

Panna Cotta: Place the cream and sugar in a medium saucepan over medium heat and bring to a boil. Decrease the heat and simmer until reduced by about a third, about 5 minutes. • Meanwhile, pour the water into a small cup. Sprinkle the gelatin over the water and leave to soak for 5 minutes.
• Place the blackberries and cassis in a small saucepan over medium heat. Gently simmer until the blackberries have softened, 3–5 minutes.
• Strain the blackberries through a fine mesh sieve into a small bowl. • Remove the cream from the heat and add the gelatin and blackberry purée, stirring until incorporated. • Strain the cream through a fine mesh sieve into a small bowl or pitcher (jug). Set aside until cooled, about 15 minutes. • Pour the cream mixture into six $3/4$-cup (180-ml) plastic molds and refrigerate until set, at least 6 hours. • Blackberry Compote: Combine the blackberries, cassis, and sugar in a small saucepan over medium heat. Simmer until the berries just begin to soften and release their juices, about 5 minutes. • To serve, gently pull the side of each panna cotta away from the molds and invert onto individual serving plates. Spoon the blackberry compote over the top and serve.

Panna Cotta

4   cups (1 liter) heavy (double) cream
$3/4$ cup (150 g) sugar
2   tablespoons water
3   teaspoons unflavored gelatin powder
$2/3$ cup (100 g) fresh blackberries
1   tablespoon cassis liqueur

Blackberry Compote

1   cup (150 g) fresh blackberries
1   tablespoon cassis liqueur
1   tablespoon sugar

Serves: 6
Preparation: 15 minutes + 6–7 hours to cool and chill
Cooking: 5 minutes
Level: 2

CHILLED LEMON SOUFFLÉ

To prepare the soufflé dishes, tie parchment paper around six 1/2-cup (125-ml) ramekins, so that 3/4 inch (2 cm) collars are created above the rim of the dishes. • Place the lemon juice in a small saucepan. Sprinkle with the gelatin and set aside for 5 minutes. Gently warm over low heat, stirring until the gelatin has dissolved. Remove from the heat and set aside. • Put the egg yolks, sugar, and lemon zest in a small heatproof bowl and place over a saucepan of barely simmering water. Beat using an electric mixer on medium speed until pale and thick. • Add the gelatin mixture and whisk to combine. Remove from the heat and place the bowl in a container of iced water, stirring occasionally until cooled and almost at setting point. • Beat the egg whites in a small bowl with an electric mixer on high speed until soft peaks form. • Add a large spoonful to the egg yolk mixture and stir to combine. Gently fold the remaining whites into the egg yolk mixture. • Whip the cream in a medium bowl with an electric mixer on high speed until soft peaks form. Fold into the lemon mixture. • Spoon into the prepared ramekins, filling 1/2 inch (1 cm) above the rim. • Chill in the refrigerator for at least 3 hours, or until required. • To serve, remove the paper collars and press toasted coconut onto the exposed ring of soufflé that stands above the dish.

3/4 cup (180 ml) freshly squeezed lemon juice, strained

2½ teaspoons unflavored powdered gelatin

4 large eggs, separated

3/4 cup (150 g) sugar

1 teaspoon finely grated lemon zest

1 cup (250 ml) heavy (double) cream

1/4 cup (30 g) shredded (desiccated) coconut, lightly toasted

Serves: 6
Preparation: 30 minutes
+ 3 hours to chill
Cooking: 10 minutes
Level: 2

CHILLED CHOCOLATE SOUFFLÉ

To prepare the soufflé dishes, tie parchment paper around eight $1/2$-cup (125-ml) ramekins, so that $3/4$ inch (2 cm) collars are created above the rims of the ramekins. • Place the milk in a small saucepan over medium heat and bring to a boil. Remove from the heat and add the chocolate, stirring until melted. • Beat the egg yolks, sugar, and vanilla in a medium bowl with an electric mixer on high speed until pale and thick. • Gradually pour in the chocolate milk, beating until combined. • Return the mixture to the pan and place over low heat. Cook, stirring continuously with a wooden spoon, until the mixture thickens to a custard consistency. • Strain through a fine mesh sieve into a medium bowl. Set aside to cool. • Place the coffee in a small saucepan. Sprinkle with the gelatin and set aside for 5 minutes. Gently warm over low heat, stirring until the gelatin has dissolved. • Add the gelatin mixture to the chocolate custard, stirring to combine. Place the bowl in a container of iced water, stirring occasionally until cooled and almost at setting point. • Beat the egg whites in a small bowl with an electric mixer on high speed until soft peaks form. Add a large spoonful to the chocolate custard and stir to combine. Gently fold in the remaining whites. • Whip the cream in a small bowl with an electric mixer on high speed until soft peaks form. Fold into the chocolate mixture. • Spoon into the ramekins, filling $1/2$ inch (1 cm) above the rim. Refrigerate for at least 3 hours. • To serve, remove the paper collars and press grated chocolate onto the exposed ring of soufflé that stands above the dish.

$3/4$ **cup (180 ml) milk**

8 **ounces (250 g) dark chocolate, coarsely chopped + extra, grated, to serve**

4 **large eggs, separated**

$1/2$ **cup (100 g) sugar**

1 **teaspoon vanilla extract (essence)**

$1/3$ **cup (90 ml) strong black coffee**

3 **teaspoons unflavored gelatin powder**

1 **cup (250 ml) heavy (double) cream**

Serves: 8
Preparation: 30 minutes + 3 hours to chill
Cooking: 5–10 minutes
Level: 2

MOCHA POTS DE CRÈME

Preheat the oven to 300°F (150°C/gas 2). • Line the base of a deep baking pan with a kitchen towel and place six 1/2-cup (125-ml) ramekins or molds on top. • Place the light cream in a small saucepan over medium-low heat and bring to a gentle simmer. Remove from the heat and add the chocolate and coffee granules, stirring until smooth. • Beat the egg yolks and sugar in a medium bowl using an electric mixer on high speed until pale and thick. • Gradually pour in the hot chocolate cream, stirring with a wooden spoon until combined. • Strain through a fine mesh sieve into a medium bowl or pitcher (jug). Skim off any froth from the top with a spoon. • Divide the chocolate custard evenly among the ovenproof dishes. Pour enough boiling water into the baking pan to come halfway up the sides of the dishes. Cover the pan with aluminum foil • Bake for 30–35 minutes, until the pots are set but still slightly wobbly in the center. • Remove from the oven and set aside to cool for 1 hour. Refrigerate for at least 4 hours, or until required. • To serve, top each pot with whipped cream and a few chocolate-coated coffee beans.

1½ **cups (375 ml) light (single) cream**

5 **ounces (150 g) dark chocolate, coarsely chopped**

2 **teaspoons freeze-dried coffee granules**

5 **large egg yolks**

1/3 **cup (70 g) superfine (caster) sugar**

1/2 **cup (125 ml) heavy (double) cream, whipped**

Chocolate-coated coffee beans, to serve

Serves: 6
Preparation: 20 minutes
  + 5 hours to cool
  and chill
Cooking: 30–35 minutes
Level: 2

CHOCOLATE & HAZELNUT POTS DE CRÈME

Pots de Crème: Preheat the oven to 300°F (150°C/gas 2). • Line the base of a deep baking pan with a kitchen towel and place six $^1/_2$-cup (125-ml) ramekins or molds on top. • Place the light cream, liqueur, and cinnamon in a small saucepan over medium-low heat and bring to a gentle simmer. Remove from the heat and add the chocolate, stirring until smooth. • Beat the egg yolks and brown sugar in a medium bowl with an electric mixer on high speed until thick. • Gradually pour in the hot chocolate cream, stirring with a wooden spoon until combined. • Strain through a fine mesh sieve into a medium bowl or pitcher (jug). Skim off any froth from the top with a spoon. • Divide the chocolate and hazelnut custard evenly among the ramekins. Pour enough hot water into the baking pan to come halfway up the sides of the dishes. Cover the pan with aluminum foil. • Cook for 30–35 minutes, until the pots are set but still slightly wobbly in the center. • Remove from the oven and set aside to cool for 1 hour. Refrigerate for at least 4 hours, or until required. • Hazelnut Praline: Line a baking sheet with parchment paper. • Put the sugar in a small pan and gently heat until melted and pale gold, about 5 minutes. Add the hazelnuts and cook, stirring, for 30 seconds. Pour onto the prepared baking sheet and leave to harden. Break into small pieces. • To serve, top each pot with whipped cream and shards of hazelnut praline.

Pots de Crème

$1^1/_2$ cups (375 ml) light (single) cream

2 tablespoons hazelnut liqueur

$^1/_4$ teaspoon ground cinnamon

8 ounces (250 g) dark chocolate, coarsely chopped

5 large egg yolks

$^1/_4$ cup (50 g) firmly packed light brown sugar

$^1/_2$ cup (125 ml) heavy (double) cream, whipped

Hazelnut Praline

$^1/_3$ cup (70 g) superfine (caster) sugar

$^1/_4$ cup (40 g) blanched hazelnuts, coarsely chopped

Serves: 6
Preparation: 45 minutes
  + 5 hours to cool
  and chill
Cooking: 35–40 minutes
Level: 2

CARAMEL POTS DE CRÈME

Preheat the oven to 300°F (150°C/gas 2). • Line the base of a deep baking pan with a kitchen towel and place six 1/2-cup (125-ml) ramekins or molds on top. • Place the cream and vanilla pod in a small saucepan over medium-low heat and bring to a gentle simmer. • Remove from the heat and add the chocolate, stirring until smooth. Set aside. • Place half of the sugar and the water in a small saucepan and gently heat until melted and pale gold, 3–5 minutes. Pour the caramel into the hot cream and stir to combine. • Beat the egg yolks and the remaining sugar in a medium bowl with an electric mixer on high speed until pale and thick. • Gradually pour in the hot caramel cream, stirring with a wooden spoon until combined. Strain through a fine mesh sieve into a medium bowl or pitcher (jug). Skim off any froth from the top with a spoon. • Divide the caramel custard evenly among the ramekins. Pour enough boiling water into the baking pan to come halfway up the sides of the dishes. Cover the pan with aluminum foil. • Cook for 30–35 minutes, until the pots are set but still slightly wobbly in the center. • Remove from the oven and set aside to cool for 1 hour. Refrigerate for at least 4 hours, or until required. • Serve with the biscotti to the side.

■ ■ ■ *Biscotti are Italian-style cookies usually made with coarsely chopped nuts. As their name suggests, they are cooked twice and are often quite hard. They are available in Italian food stores and supermarkets.*

1½ cups (375 ml) half-and-half (single) cream

1 vanilla pod, split lengthwise

3½ ounces (100 g) white chocolate, coarsely chopped

½ cup (100 g) sugar

1 tablespoon water

5 large egg yolks

Biscotti, to serve

Serves: 6
Preparation: 30 minutes
  + 5 hours to cool
  and chill
Cooking: 35–40 minutes
Level: 2

CHOCOLATE BAVAROIS

46

Custard Base: Combine the milk and cream in a
heavy-bottomed saucepan over medium-low heat.
Scrape in the vanilla seeds, add the pod, and slowly
heat almost to boiling point. • Beat the egg yolks
and sugar in a large bowl with an electric mixer on
high speed until pale and creamy. • Discard the
vanilla pod. Whisk the hot milk mixture into the egg
and sugar a little at a time. Return the mixture to
the saucepan and simmer over very low heat,
stirring constantly, until the custard thickens and
coats the back of a spoon, about 5 minutes.
Do not let the custard boil. • If you are using the
leaf gelatin, fill a small bowl with cold water. Add
the leaf gelatin and leave to soak until softened,
about 5 minutes. If you are using powdered gelatin,
sprinkle it over the 3 tablespoons of cold water and
leave to soften for 5 minutes • If you are using leaf
gelatin, remove the gelatin from the water, squeeze
gently, and stir into the warm custard. If you are
using powdered gelatin, stir the gelatin mixture into
the warm custard. • Strain the custard through a
fine-mesh sieve into a bowl and leave to cool.
Stir occasionally to prevent a skin from forming.
Flavoring: Melt the chocolate in a double boiler over
barely simmering water. Let cool. • Stir the cooled
chocolate into the custard, cover, and chill. • When
the custard starts to set around the edges, whip the
cream in a medium bowl until thick but not stiff.
Fold the cream into the chocolate bavarois. (If the

Custard Base
- 1/3 cup (90 ml) milk
- 1/3 cup (90 ml) heavy (double) cream
- 1 vanilla pod, split lengthwise
- 3 large egg yolks
- 1/4 cup (50 g) sugar
- 2 sheets leaf gelatin or 1 1/2 teaspoons unflavored gelatin powder + 3 tablespoons water

Flavoring
- 8 ounces (250 g) dark chocolate, coarsely chopped
- 3/4 cup (200 ml) heavy (double) cream

Decoration
- 1 ounce (30 g) dark chocolate, coarsely grated
- 1/2 cup (100 g) fresh mixed berries (blueberries, red currants, raspberries), optional

Serves: 4
Preparation: 30 minutes
+ 1 hour to cool
+ 3–4 hours to chill
Cooking: 20 minutes
Level: 2

custard is too stiff, set it in a bowl over hot water and whisk until soft enough to fold in the cream.) • Lightly oil four ½-cup (125-ml) ramekins or molds and spoon in the mixture. Chill in the refrigerator until firmly set, 3–4 hours. • To serve, gently pull the side of each bavarois away from the molds and invert onto individual serving plates. Decorate with the grated chocolate and berries.

47

■ ■ ■ *Bavarois, or Bavarian cream, is a classic dessert. It has an egg custard base which is usually mixed with a flavoring and whipped cream and then set with gelatin in a mold. Food historians are not sure if it was actually invented in Bavaria in southern Germany, or if this is just a name given to it by the French chefs who made it famous in the 19th century.*

CINNAMON & ORANGE BAVAROIS

Place the milk, 1/2 cup (125 ml) of cream, and 1/4 cup (50 g) of sugar in a small saucepan over medium heat and bring to a boil. Remove from the heat and set aside. • Beat the egg yolks, remaining sugar, and cinnamon in a small bowl with an electric mixer on high speed until pale and thick.
• Gradually pour the hot milk mixture into the yolk mixture, stirring with a wooden spoon until incorporated. Return the mixture to the pan and place over low heat. Cook, stirring continuously, until the mixture thickens to a custard consistency. Set aside to cool. • Soak the gelatin sheets in cold water until soft, about 5 minutes. Drain and gently squeeze to remove excess water. • Add to the hot custard, stirring until dissolved. Strain the custard through a fine mesh sieve into a medium bowl and set aside. • Meanwhile, place the orange juice in a small saucepan over medium heat and bring to a boil. Decrease the heat and gently simmer until reduced by half, 4–5 minutes. Strain through a fine mesh sieve and stir into the custard mixture. Refrigerate until chilled and almost at setting point, about 15 minutes. • Whip the remaining cream in a small bowl with an electric mixer on high speed until soft peaks form. Fold into the custard mixture. • Lightly oil eight 1/2-cup (125-ml) bavarois molds. Fill with the mixture and chill in the refrigerator until set, about 4 hours. • To serve, gently pull the side of each bavarois away from the molds and invert onto individual serving plates. Dust with extra cinnamon.

1	cup (250 ml) milk
1¼	cups (300 ml) heavy (double) cream
½	cup (100 g) sugar
6	large egg yolks
1	teaspoon ground cinnamon + extra, to dust
4	sheets leaf gelatin
1	cup (250 ml) freshly squeezed orange juice

Serves: 8
Preparation: 30 minutes + 4 hours to chill
Cooking: 5–10 minutes
Level: 2

COFFEE BAVAROIS

Place the milk, $1/2$ cup (125 ml) of cream, and $1/4$ cup (50 g) of sugar in a small saucepan over medium heat and bring to a boil. Remove from the heat and set aside. • Beat the egg yolks and remaining sugar in a small bowl with an electric mixer on high speed until pale and thick. • Gradually pour the hot milk mixture into the yolks, stirring with a wooden spoon until incorporated. Return the mixture to the pan and place over low heat. Cook, stirring continuously, until the mixture thickens to a custard consistency. Set aside to cool. • Soak the gelatin leaves in cold water until soft, about 5 minutes. Drain and gently squeeze to remove excess water. Add to the hot custard, stirring until dissolved. Stir in the coffee. • Strain the custard through a fine mesh sieve into a medium bowl. Refrigerate until chilled and almost at setting point, 10–15 minutes. • Whip the remaining cream in a small bowl with an electric mixer on high speed until soft peaks form. Fold into the custard mixture. • Lightly oil eight $1/2$-cup (125-ml) bavarois molds. Fill with the prepared mixture and refrigerate until set, about 4 hours. • To serve, gently pull the side of each bavarois away from the molds and invert onto individual serving plates.

1	cup (250 ml) milk
1¼	cups (300 ml) heavy (double) cream
½	cup (100 g) sugar
6	large egg yolks
4	sheets leaf gelatin
½	cup (125 ml) strong espresso coffee, cooled

Serves: 8
Preparation: 20 minutes
+ 4 hours to cool
and chill
Cooking: 5–10 minutes
Level: 2

WHITE CHOCOLATE & PASSION FRUIT MOUSSE

Place the chocolate and passion fruit pulp in a double boiler over barely simmering water and stir until melted and smooth. Remove from the heat and set aside for 3 minutes to cool. Add the egg yolks, stirring to combine. • Beat the egg whites in a small bowl with an electric mixer on high speed until soft peaks form. Add a large spoonful to the passion fruit mixture and stir to combine. Gently fold in the remaining whites. • Whip 1 cup (250 ml) of the cream in a small bowl with an electric mixer on high speed until soft peaks form. Fold into the passion fruit mixture. • Spoon the mousse evenly into 4 serving glasses or bowls. Cover and chill in the refrigerator for at least 3 hours, or until required. • To serve, whip the remaining cream with the confectioners' sugar until soft peaks form. Spoon into a pastry bag fitted with a star-shaped nozzle. Pipe rosettes on top of each mousse and drizzle with the extra passion fruit pulp.

8 ounces (250 g) white chocolate, coarsely chopped

3/4 cup (180 ml) passion fruit pulp, strained, + extra, to serve

4 large eggs, separated

1½ cups (375 ml) heavy (double) cream

1 tablespoon confectioners' (icing) sugar

Serves: 4
Preparation: 20 minutes
 + 3 hours to chill
Cooking: 10 minutes
Level: 2

■ ■ ■ *This is an elegant dish to serve at the end of a dinner party. The cool tropical flavors make it an ideal dessert if you have served hot and spicy Asian food beforehand.*

LAYERED COCONUT & MANGO MOUSSE

Reserve 6 tablespoons of mango. Place the remaining mango in a food processor and chop until smooth. Remove half of the mango pulp and set aside. • Add the coconut milk and confectioners' sugar to the remaining mango and process until combined. Transfer to a medium bowl. • Place the lime juice and water in a small saucepan. Sprinkle with the gelatin and set aside for 5 minutes. Gently warm over low heat, stirring until the gelatin has melted. Remove from the heat and add to the coconut and mango mixture, stirring to combine. • Whip the cream in a small bowl with an electric mixer on high speed until soft peaks form. Fold the cream and lime zest into the coconut and mango mixture. • To assemble, place a spoonful of mango pulp in the bottom of 6–8 serving glasses. Spoon half of the coconut and mango mousse over the top. Repeat the process with the remaining mango purée and mousse. • Cover and refrigerate for at least 3 hours, or until required. • To serve, top each mousse with the reserved mango and shaved coconut.

1½ pounds (750 g) mango flesh, canned or fresh, coarsely chopped

1 cup (250 ml) coconut milk

3 tablespoons confectioners' (icing) sugar

3 limes, zest finely grated and juiced

2 tablespoons water

3 teaspoons unflavored gelatin powder

1 cup (250 ml) heavy (double) cream

¼ cup (30 g) shaved coconut, lightly toasted

Serves: 6–8
Preparation: 20 minutes
  + 3 hours to chill
Cooking: 5 minutes
Level: 1

WHITE CHOCOLATE MOUSSE WITH STRAWBERRY COMPOTE

White Chocolate Mousse: Put ½ cup (125 ml) of the cream, the chocolate, and vanilla in a double boiler over barely simmering water, stirring occasionally, until melted and smooth. • Remove from the heat and set aside for 3 minutes to cool. • Whisk in the egg yolks until well combined. • Beat the egg whites in a small bowl with an electric mixer on high speed until soft peaks form. Add a large spoonful to the white chocolate mixture and stir to combine. Gently fold in the remaining whites. • Whip the remaining cream in a small bowl with an electric mixer on high speed until soft peaks form. Fold into the white chocolate mixture. • Spoon the mousse evenly into 6 serving glasses or dishes. Cover and chill in the refrigerator for at least 3 hours, or until required.
Strawberry Compote: Combine the strawberries, brandy, and brown sugar in a small saucepan over medium heat. Simmer until the berries just begin to soften and release their juices, about 5 minutes. • To serve, spoon a little of the strawberry compote over each mousse.

White Chocolate Mousse

1½ cups (375 ml) heavy (double) cream

8 ounces (250 g) white chocolate, coarsely chopped

1 teaspoon vanilla extract (essence)

4 large eggs, separated

Strawberry Compote

2 cups (300 g) strawberries, quartered

2 tablespoons brandy

1 tablespoon light brown sugar

Serves: 6
Preparation: 30 minutes
   + 3 hours to chill
Cooking: 15–20 minutes
Level: 1

■ ■ ■ *Make an equally delicious berry compote by replacing the strawberries in this recipe with the same quantity of raspberries or red currants.*

CHOCOLATE & COINTREAU MOUSSE

Melt the chocolate in a double boiler over barely simmering water, stirring occasionally, until smooth. Gradually pour in the oil, stirring to combine. Remove from the heat and set aside. • Beat the egg yolks and half the sugar in a medium bowl with an electric mixer on high speed until pale and thick. • Gradually pour in the chocolate mixture and Cointreau, whisking until combined. • Beat the egg whites and remaining sugar in a small bowl with an electric mixer on high speed until soft peaks form. Add a large spoonful to the chocolate mixture and stir to combine. Gently fold in the remaining whites. • Spoon the mousse evenly into 4 serving dishes. Cover and chill in the refrigerator for at least 3 hours, or until required. • Top with the extra chocolate and serve.

8 ounces (250 g) dark chocolate, coarsely chopped, + extra, to serve

½ cup (125 ml) light extra-virgin olive oil

4 large eggs, separated

½ cup (100 g) superfine (caster) sugar

¼ cup (60 ml) Cointreau or other orange liqueur

Serves: 4
Preparation: 15 minutes + 3 hours to chill
Cooking: 5 minutes
Level: 2

■ ■ ■ *Lighten this dessert up by serving each portion topped with fresh mandarins divided into segments or a few fresh raspberries.*

ORANGE AND LEMON SYLLABUB

Place the wine, confectioners' sugar, and lemon juice and zest in a small bowl, stirring until the sugar has dissolved. • Whip the cream in a medium bowl with an electric mixer on high speed until soft peaks form. Gradually pour in the wine and lemon mixture, beating until combined. • Spoon half of the lemon cream into 6–8 serving glasses and cover with half of the orange segments. Repeat with the remaining cream and orange segments. • Cover and chill in the refrigerator for 1 hour, or until required.

½ cup (125 ml) sweet dessert wine

¼ cup (30 g) confectioners' (icing) sugar

¼ cup (60 ml) freshly squeezed lemon juice

2 teaspoons finely grated lemon zest

2 cups (500 ml) heavy (double) cream

4 oranges, peeled and segmented

Serves: 6–8
Preparation: 15 minutes
+ 1 hour to chill
Cooking: 1 hour
Level: 1

SUGAR SNAP BASKETS WITH STRAWBERRY RICOTTA CREAM

Preheat the oven to 350°F (180°C/gas 4).
• **Step 1:** <u>Sugar Snap Baskets:</u> Line a large baking sheet with parchment paper. Butter the paper. • Set out 6 medium-size water glasses. • **Step 2:** Melt the butter in a small saucepan over low heat. Add the sugar and honey and stir until the sugar has melted and the mixture is smooth. Remove from the heat and stir in the flour. • **Step 3:** Divide the mixture into 6 small balls. Place the balls on the prepared baking sheet. Do not flatten them, they will spread out by themselves in the oven. Bake for 7–8 minutes. • **Step 4:** Let cool until you can just handle them then, working quickly, wrap them over the bottoms of the glasses to form a basket shape and leave to cool and harden. • **Step 5:** <u>Strawberry Ricotta Cream:</u> Cook 2 cups (300 g) of the strawberries with the sugar in a medium saucepan over medium-low heat until tender, about 10 minutes. Chop in a food processor until smooth.
• **Step 6:** Beat the ricotta with the confectioners' sugar until smooth. Add the strawberry mixture, stirring only a little to obtain a marbled red-and-white cream. • Spoon the cream into the sugar snap baskets. Top with the remaining strawberries and serve immediately.

Sugar Snap Baskets

3	tablespoons butter
¼	cup (50 g) sugar
2	tablespoons honey
⅓	cup (50 g) all-purpose (plain) flour

Strawberry Ricotta Cream

3	cups (450 g) fresh strawberries, sliced
½	cup (100 g) sugar
14	ounces (400 g) fresh creamy ricotta cheese, drained
⅓	cup (50 g) confectioners' (icing) sugar

Serves: 6
Preparation: 45 minutes
Cooking: 10 minutes
Level: 3

■ PREPARATION STEP-BY-STEP

These pretty little desserts are fun to make and striking to serve. For a change, try filling the sugar snap baskets with Vanilla Pastry Cream (see page 590) or Chantilly Cream (see page 600) and top with red currants or raspberries. Remember to fill the baskets just before serving, so that they don't become soggy.

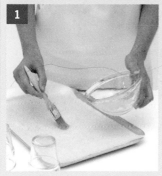

1. LINE a large baking sheet with parchment paper. Butter the paper. Set out 6 medium-size water glasses.

2. MELT the butter in a small saucepan over low heat. Add the sugar and honey and stir until smooth. Stir in the flour.

3. DIVIDE the mixture into 6 small balls. Place the balls on the prepared baking sheet and bake as directed.

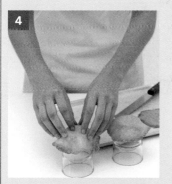

4. LET COOL until you can just handle. Wrap over the bottoms of the glasses in basket shapes and let cool and harden.

5. COOK 2 cups (300 g) of strawberries with the sugar until tender, about 10 minutes. Chop in a food processor.

6. BEAT the ricotta with the confectioners' sugar. Add the strawberry mixture, stirring to obtain a marbled cream.

LEMON CREAM
WITH CITRUS SALAD

68

Lemon Cream: Heat the cream and sugar in a small saucepan over medium-low heat until the sugar has dissolved. Increase the heat to medium-high and boil the cream mixture for 5 minutes. Remove from the heat. • Place the lemon juice and water in a small saucepan. Sprinkle with the gelatin and set aside for 5 minutes. Gently warm over low heat, stirring until the gelatin has melted. Remove from the heat let cool a little before adding to the cream mixture. • Strain the lemon cream through a fine mesh sieve into a small bowl or pitcher (jug). Pour the lemon cream evenly into 6 dessert glasses or bowls. Place the glasses on a tray and chill in the refrigerator overnight. • **Citrus Salad:** Combine the lemon juice and sugar in a medium bowl. Add the blood orange, orange, tangerines, and lime segments to the sweetened juice and toss well to coat. Chill in the refrigerator for 20 minutes to allow the flavors to infuse. • To serve, top each serving of lemon cream with a decorative pile of citrus salad.

Lemon Cream

2   cups (500 ml) heavy (double) cream

½   cup (100 g) sugar

⅓   cup (90 ml) freshly squeezed lemon juice

2   tablespoons water

2   teaspoons unflavored gelatin powder

Citrus Salad

Freshly squeezed juice of 1 lemon

½   cup (100 g) sugar

1   blood orange, peeled and segmented

1   orange, peeled and segmented

2   tangerines (mandarins), peeled and segmented

1   lime, peeled and segmented

Serves: 6
Preparation: 25 minutes
    + overnight to chill
Cooking: 10 minutes
Level: 1

LEMON CREAM

Pour the cream into a saucepan and add the sugar and half the zest. Bring to a boil over medium heat, stirring constantly. Reduce the heat to low and simmer, stirring all the time, for 3 minutes. Do not let the cream bubble up and boil. • Remove from the heat. • Place the lemon juice and water in a small saucepan. Sprinkle with the gelatin and set aside for 5 minutes. Gently warm over low heat, stirring until the gelatin has melted. Remove from the heat let cool a little before stirring into to the cream mixture. • Leave the cream to cool for 15 minutes. • Stir once and pour into 6–8 small ramekins, liqueur glasses, or espresso cups. Sprinkle with the remaining zest and chill in the refrigerator until set, 4 hours (or overnight). • Decorate with fresh sprigs of mint.

2   **cups (500 ml) heavy (double) cream**

2/3   **cup (125 g) superfine (caster) sugar**

Finely grated zest of 2 large lemons

1/3   **cup (90 ml) freshly squeezed lemon juice**

2   **tablespoons water**

2   **teaspoons unflavored gelatin powder**

Sprigs of mint, to decorate

Serves: 6–8
Preparation: 15 minutes
    + 15 minutes to cool
    + 4 hours to chill
Cooking: 10 minutes
Level: 1

■ ■ ■ *Replace the lemon in this recipe with lime for a slightly different flavor and color.*

MANGO CREAM

Combine the mango, lemon juice, lime juice, and
1 tablespoon of the orange juice in a blender and
purée until smooth. If it is too stiff, add more
orange juice, 1 tablespoon at a time, until a thick
sauce consistency is achieved. Press through a fine
mesh sieve into a bowl with a wooden spoon.
Refrigerate until chilled, about 1 hour. • Whip the
mascarpone with an electric mixer at low speed
until smooth. Stir into the mango mixture. • Beat
the cream with the confectioners' sugar in another
bowl until thick. Fold into the mango mixture.
Spoon into 6 dessert glasses. • Chill for
1–2 hours before serving.

1   ripe mango, peeled,
    and coarsely chopped

1   tablespoon freshly
    squeezed lemon juice

1   tablespoon freshly
    squeezed lime juice

1–3 tablespoons freshly
    squeezed orange juice

1   cup (250 g)
    mascarpone cheese

1   cup (250 g) heavy
    (double) cream

2   tablespoons
    confectioners' (icing)
    sugar

Serves: 6
Preparation: 10 minutes
    + 1–2 hours to chill
Level: 1

LEMON & BERRY CREAM

Place the mascarpone, condensed milk, and lemon juice and zest in a medium bowl and stir to combine. • Purée the berries in a food processor. Strain through a fine mesh sieve and stir into the lemon mixture. • Whip the cream in a small bowl with an electric mixer on high speed until soft peaks form. Fold into the lemon and berry mixture. • Spoon the lemon and berry cream evenly into 6–8 serving glasses or dishes. Cover and chill in the refrigerator for 2 hours, or until required. • Top with the extra berries and serve.

1 cup (250 g) mascarpone cheese

$3/4$ cup (180 ml) sweetened condensed milk

2 lemons, zest finely grated and juiced

$1^{1/2}$ cups (250 g) mixed fresh berries, + extra, to serve

$1^{1/2}$ cups (375 ml) heavy (double) cream

Serves: 6–8
Preparation: 15 minutes
    + 2 hours to chill
Level: 1

TRIFLES & CHARLOTTES

CHOCOLATE TIRAMISÙ

78

Combine ³/₄ cup (180 ml) of cream, the chocolate, and liqueur in a double boiler over barely simmering water. Stir occasionally until melted and smooth. Chill in the refrigerator until cooled, about 15 minutes. • Whip the remaining cream in a small bowl with an electric mixer on high speed until soft peaks form. Fold into the mascarpone until combined. • Line the base of four 1¹/₂-cup (375–ml) serving glasses with half of the sponge fingers, breaking them into pieces to fit. Spoon half of the chocolate sauce over the top, followed by the cream. Repeat with the remaining fingers, sauce, and cream. Dust the tops with cocoa. • Cover and chill in the refrigerator for 4 hours, or until required.

1½ **cups (375 ml) heavy (double) cream**

5 **ounces (150 g) dark chocolate, coarsely chopped**

2 **tablespoons coffee liqueur**

1 **cup (250 g) mascarpone cheese**

16 **Italian ladyfinger (sponge finger biscuits)**

Unsweetened cocoa powder, to dust

Serves: 4
Preparation: 30 minutes + 4 hours to chill
Cooking: 5 minutes
Level: 1

■ ■ ■ *There are many variations on this famous Italian dessert. Served in small glasses or cups, this one is particularly attractive.*

BERRY TIRAMISÙ

80

Whip the cream in a small bowl with an electric mixer on high speed until soft peaks form. • Fold into the mascarpone until combined. Stir in the berries. • Dip half of the sponge fingers one at a time into the dessert wine to soften. Line the base of four 1½-cup (375–ml) serving glasses with the ladyfingers, breaking them into pieces to fit. Spoon half of the berry cream over the top. Repeat with the remaining ladyfingers and cream. Dust the tops with cinnamon. • Cover and refrigerate for 4 hours, or until required.

1   cups (250 ml) heavy (double) cream

1   cup (250 g) mascarpone cheese

2   cups (300 g) fresh berries, mashed with a fork

½   cup (125 ml) dessert wine

16   Italian ladyfingers (sponge finger biscuits)

     Ground cinnamon, to dust

Serves: 4
Preparation: 20 minutes
   + 4 hours to chill
Level: 1

CLASSIC TIRAMISÙ

Beat the egg yolks and sugar with an electric mixer on high speed until pale and creamy. • Carefully fold in the mascarpone. • Beat the egg whites with the salt until stiff and fold them into the mixture. • Spread a thin layer of this cream over the bottom of a large oval serving dish. • Soak the ladyfingers briefly in the coffee and place a layer over the cream on the bottom of the dish. Cover with another layer of the cream and sprinkle with a little chocolate. Repeat this layering process until all the ingredients are in the dish. • Finish with a layer of cream and chocolate, and dust with cocoa.

82

5 **large eggs, separated**
1 **cup (150 g) sugar**
2 **cups (500 g) mascarpone**
  Pinch of salt
  About 30 Italian ladyfingers (sponge finger biscuits)
1 **cup (250 ml) strong black coffee**
5 **ounces (150 g) dark chocolate, grated**
1 **tablespoon unsweetened cocoa (cocoa powder)**

Serves: 6–8
Preparation: 20 minutes + 3 hours to chill
Level: 1

■ ■ ■ *This is the classic version of this much-loved Italian dessert. Be aware that it contains raw eggs which can sometimes carry salmonella. If you do decide to consume raw eggs, always buy organic or free-range eggs from well-known farms. To avoid any risk, either use pasteurized eggs or heat the yolks and whites to 160°F (80°C) in a double boiler for 15 seconds.*

BLACK FOREST TRIFLE

84

Drain the cherries into a small bowl. Combine half of the cherry syrup and the liqueur in a separate bowl and set aside. • Whip the cream, confectioners' sugar, and vanilla in a small bowl with an electric mixer on high speed until soft peaks form. • Dip six of the chocolate cookies into the cherry liquid and place in the base of six 1-cup (250-ml) serving glasses. Top with one-third of the cherries and spoon a little of the liquid over the top. Spread with one-third of the cream. Repeat this layering process with the remaining cookies, cherries, liquid, and cream. Top each trifle with shaved chocolate. • Cover and chill in the refrigerator for 4 hours, or until required.

1 cup (250 g) pitted dark sweet cherries in syrup, coarsely chopped

¼ cup (60 ml) cherry liqueur

1¼ cups (300 ml) heavy (double) cream

1 tablespoon confectioners' (icing) sugar

1 teaspoon vanilla extract (essence)

18 plain chocolate cookies (biscuits)

3 ounces (100 g) dark chocolate, shaved

Serves: 6
Preparation: 20 minutes
   + 4 hours to chill
Level: 1

RASPBERRY & PEACH TRIFLE

Custard: Place the milk and vanilla bean in a medium saucepan over medium heat and bring to a boil. Remove from the heat and set aside. • Beat the egg yolks and sugar in a small bowl with an electric mixer on high speed until pale and creamy. • Gradually pour the hot milk mixture into the yolks, stirring with a wooden spoon until incorporated. Strain through a fine mesh sieve and return to the pan. Place over low heat and cook, stirring continuously, until the mixture thickens to a thin custard consistency. Set aside to cool. • Trifle: Place 2 cups (300 g) of raspberries, the peach slices, 1/4 cup (60 ml) of peach juice, and the sherry in a medium bowl and set aside for the flavors to infuse, about 1 hour. • Whip the cream in a medium bowl with an electric mixer on high speed until soft peaks form. • To assemble the trifles, divide the fruit evenly among ten 1-cup (250-ml) serving glasses. Place two sponge fingers (broken in half or in thirds) on top and spoon the sherry liquid over the top. Pour the custard over the top. Cover with whipped cream and decorate with the remaining raspberries. • Cover and chill in the refrigerator for 4 hours, or until required.

Custard

4	cups (1 liter) milk
1	vanilla bean, halved lengthwise
6	large egg yolks
1	cup (200 g) sugar

Trifle

3	cups (450 g) raspberries
1	(14-ounce/400-g) can peach halves in juice, sliced, juice reserved
3/4	cup (180 ml) sweet sherry
20	Italian ladyfingers (sponge finger biscuits)
2	cups (500 ml) heavy (double) cream

Serves: 10
Preparation: 30 minutes
+ 5 hours to infuse
and chill
Cooking: 10 minutes
Level: 1

TROPICAL FRUIT TRIFLE

Coconut Custard: Place the milk, coconut milk, and vanilla bean in a medium saucepan over medium heat and bring to a boil. Remove from the heat and set aside. • Beat the egg yolks and sugar in a small bowl with an electric mixer on high speed until pale and creamy. • Gradually pour the hot milk mixture into the yolks, stirring with a wooden spoon until incorporated. Strain through a fine mesh sieve and return to the pan. Place over low heat and cook, stirring continuously, until the mixture thickens to a custard consistency. Set aside to cool. • Trifle: Place the mango, passion fruit, and Malibu in a medium bowl and set aside for flavors to infuse, about 1 hour. • Whip the cream in a small bowl with an electric mixer on high speed until soft peaks form. • To assemble the trifles, divide the fruit evenly among ten 1-cup (250-ml) serving glasses. Place two sponge fingers on top (broken in half or in thirds) and spoon the fruit and coconut liqueur mixture over the top. Spoon in the custard. Cover with whipped cream and top with the coconut shavings. • Cover and chill in the refrigerator for 4 hours, or until required.

Coconut Custard

2	cups (500 ml) milk
2	cups (500 ml) coconut milk
1	vanilla bean, halved lengthwise
6	large egg yolks
1	cup (200 g) sugar

Trifle

4	mangoes, peeled, seeded, and diced
6	passion fruit, pulp removed
3/4	cup (180 ml) Malibu or coconut liqueur
20	Italian ladyfingers (sponge finger biscuits)
2	cups (500 ml) heavy (double) cream
1/3	cup (40 g) shaved coconut, lightly toasted

Serves: 10
Preparation: 30 minutes
  + 5 hours to infuse
  and chill
Cooking: 10 minutes
Level: 1

LEMON & BLUEBERRY TRIFLE

Place half of the blueberries and the water in a small saucepan over low heat. Cook until the blueberries begin to soften, 5–10 minutes, then mash with a fork. • Remove from the heat, stir in the remaining blueberries and set aside to cool. • Place the lemon curd, mascarpone, and confectioners' sugar in a medium bowl and beat to combine. Set aside. • Whip the cream in a small bowl with an electric mixer on high speed until soft peaks form. • To assemble, divide the sponge cake evenly among 6 serving glasses. Spoon the blueberries on top and drizzle with limoncello and any remaining liquid. Top with the lemon curd mixture and finish with whipped cream. Decorate with the extra blueberries. • Cover and chill in the refrigerator for 4 hours, or until required.

1½ cups (375 g) fresh blueberries, + extra, to decorate

3 tablespoons water

1 cup (250 g) lemon curd

1 cup (250 g) mascarpone cheese

4 tablespoons confectioners' (icing) sugar

1½ cups (375 ml) heavy (double) cream

⅓ cup (90 ml) limoncello

12 ounces (350 g) storebought sponge cake or homemade (Basic Génoise, see page 260 or Basic Sponge Cake, see page 592), cut into small cubes

Serves: 6
Preparation: 25 minutes
  + 4 hours to chill
Cooking: 5–10 minutes
Level: 1

■ ■ ■ *Limoncello is an Italian lemon liqueur. Very strong, and very sweet, it is usually kept in the freezer and served as an after-dinner drink.*

90

SUMMER PUDDING

Line four 1-cup (250-ml) dariole molds or individual pudding basins with plastic wrap (cling film), allowing extra to hang over the sides. • Cut four rounds of bread to fit the base of the molds and another four to fit the tops. Slice the remaining bread into ³/₄-inch (2-cm) strips. Set aside. • Place the berries, sugar, and water in a small saucepan over medium-low heat. Simmer until the berries are tender and releasing their juices, 5–10 minutes. • Dip the four smaller bread disks into the berry syrup and place in the base of the molds. Dip the bread strips and line the sides of the molds, overlapping slightly so there are no gaps. Fill with the berry mixture, packing well. Place the remaining disks of bread on top of the fruit and spoon a little syrup over the top. • Cover with plastic wrap, place on a tray, and weigh down the puddings with a board. Refrigerate overnight, along with any remaining syrup. • To serve, invert the puddings onto individual serving plates. Remove the plastic wrap and spoon the remaining syrup over the top. Serve with the crème fraîche passed separately.

18 slices white sandwich bread, crusts removed

3 cups (500 g) mixed berries (strawberries, blueberries, raspberries, redcurrants)

¹/₂ cup (100 g) sugar

¹/₂ cup (125 ml) water

³/₄ cup (180 ml) crème fraîche, to serve

Serves: 4
Preparation: 30 minutes
  + 12 hours to chill
Cooking: 10 minutes
Level: 2

STRAWBERRY CHARLOTTE

94

Put the boiling water in a small cup, sprinkle the gelatin over the top, and stir until dissolved. • Place the strawberries and confectioners' sugar in a food processor and blend until smooth. • Add the gelatin mixture and blend to combine. Strain through a fine mesh sieve into a medium bowl. • Whip the cream and vanilla in a small bowl with an electric mixer on high speed until soft peaks form. • Fold the cream into the strawberry purée and set aside. • To assemble, dip the ladyfingers into the liqueur one at a time to soften. Line the sides of four 1-cup (250-ml) molds with the ladyfingers, placing the rounded ends down first. Brush with any remaining liqueur. • Fill the sponge-lined molds with strawberry cream. Cover and chill in the refrigerator until set, about 6 hours. • To serve, run a knife around the edge of the molds and invert the charlottes onto individual serving plates. Dust with confectioners' sugar.

2 tablespoons boiling water

2 teaspoons unflavored gelatin powder

2 cups (300 g) strawberries, + extra

4 tablespoons confectioners' (icing) sugar, + extra, to dust

3/4 cup (180 ml) heavy (double) cream

1 teaspoon vanilla extract (essence)

16 Italian ladyfingers (sponge finger biscuits), broken in half to fit molds

1/2 cup (125 ml) orange liqueur, such as Cointreau or Grand Mariner liqueur

Serves: 4
Preparation: 25 minutes
+ 6 hours to chill
Level: 1

BLUEBERRY CHARLOTTE

96

Put the boiling water in a small cup, sprinkle the gelatin over the top, and stir until dissolved. • Place the blueberries, confectioners' sugar, and lemon juice in a food processor and blend until smooth. • Add the gelatin mixture and blend to combine. Strain through a fine mesh sieve into a medium bowl. • Whip the cream in a small bowl with an electric mixer on high speed until soft peaks form. • Fold the cream into the blueberry purée and set aside. • To assemble, dip the ladyfingers into the sherry one at a time to soften. • Line the sides of four 1-cup (250-ml) molds with the ladyfingers, placing the rounded ends down first. Brush with any remaining sherry. • Fill the sponge-lined molds with blueberry cream. Cover and refrigerate until set, about 6 hours. • To serve, run a knife around the edge of the molds and invert the charlottes onto individual serving plates. Decorate with the remaining blueberries and dust with confectioners' sugar.

2   **tablespoons boiling water**

2   **teaspoons unflavored gelatin powder**

2   **cups (300 g) blueberries, + extra, to serve**

4   **tablespoons confectioners' (icing) sugar, + extra, to dust**

2   **tablespoons freshly squeezed lemon juice**

3/4   **cup (180 ml) heavy (double) cream**

1/2   **cup (125 ml) sweet sherry**

16   **Italian ladyfingers (sponge finger biscuits), broken in half to fit molds**

Serves: 4
Preparation: 25 minutes + 6 hours to chill
Level: 1

PLUM CHARLOTTE

98

Put the boiling water in a small cup, sprinkle the gelatin over the top, and stir until dissolved. • Place the plums, confectioners' sugar, and cinnamon in a food processor and blend until smooth. • Add the gelatin mixture and blend to combine. Strain through a fine mesh sieve into a medium bowl. • Whip the cream in a small bowl with an electric mixer on high speed until soft peaks form. • Fold the cream into the plum purée and set aside. • Combine ¼ cup (60 ml) of the reserved syrup and the sherry in a small bowl. • To assemble, dip the sponge fingers into the reserved sherry syrup one at a time to soften. • Line the sides of four 1-cup (250-ml) molds with the fingers, placing the rounded ends down first. Brush with any remaining syrup. • Fill the sponge-lined molds with the plum cream. • Cover and chill in the refrigerator until set, about 6 hours. • To serve, run a knife around the edge of the molds and invert the charlottes onto individual serving plates.

2 tablespoons boiling water

2 teaspoons unflavored gelatin powder

1 (14-ounce/400-g) can whole plums, pitted and drained, syrup reserved

4 tablespoons confectioners' (icing) sugar, + extra

1 teaspoon ground cinnamon

¾ cup (180 ml) heavy (double) cream

¼ cup (60 ml) sweet sherry

16 Italian ladyfingers (sponge finger biscuits), broken in half to fit molds

Serves: 4
Preparation: 25 minutes + 6 hours to chill
Level: 1

PEACH CHARLOTTE

Put the boiling water in a small cup, sprinkle the gelatin over the top, and stir until dissolved. • Place the peaches and confectioners' sugar in a food processor and blend until smooth. • Add the gelatin mixture and blend to combine. Strain through a fine mesh sieve into a medium bowl. • Whip the cream and vanilla in a small bowl with an electric mixer on high speed until soft peaks form. • Fold the cream into the peach purée and set aside. • Combine 1/4 cup (60 ml) of the reserved syrup and the sherry in a small bowl. • To assemble, dip the sponge fingers into the sherry syrup one at a time to soften. • Line the sides of four 1-cup (250-ml) molds with the sponge fingers, placing the rounded ends down first. Brush over any remaining syrup. • Fill the sponge-lined molds with the peach cream. Cover and chill in the refrigerator until set, about 6 hours. • To serve, run a knife around the edge of the molds and invert the charlottes onto individual serving plates.

2   tablespoons boiling water

2   teaspoons unflavored gelatin powder

1   (14-ounce/400-g) can peach halves, drained, syrup reserved

4   tablespoons confectioners' (icing) sugar

3/4 cup (180 ml) heavy (double) cream

1   teaspoon vanilla extract (essence)

1/4 cup (60 ml) sweet sherry

16 Italian ladyfingers (sponge finger biscuits), broken in half to fit molds

Serves: 4
Preparation: 25 minutes + 6 hours to chill
Level: 1

MANGO & AMARETTI PARFAIT

Place the mango, passion fruit pulp, and lime juice in a food processor and blend until puréed. Transfer to a medium bowl. • Whip the cream and sugar in a small bowl with an electric mixer on high speed until soft peaks form. • To assemble, spoon half of the mango purée into the base of four tall serving dishes. Layer with half of the amaretti cookies and spoon in half of the cream. Repeat with the remaining mango, amaretti, and cream. Decorate with the flaked almonds. • Cover and chill in the refrigerator for 4 hours, or until required.

14 ounces (400 g) fresh mango, peeled and coarsely chopped

2 tablespoons passion fruit pulp, strained

Freshly squeezed juice of 1 lime

1¼ cups (300 ml) heavy (double) cream

2 tablespoons confectioners' (icing) sugar

4 ounces (120 g) amaretti cookies, crumbled

⅓ cup (50 g) flaked almonds, lightly toasted

Serves: 4
Preparation: 15 minutes
+ 4 hours to chill
Level: 1

■ ■ ■ *Originally, the French term parfait was used to refer to a frozen dessert. Nowadays, especially in North America, it is used to describe a dessert made by layering cream, ice cream, or flavored gelatin with ingredients such as granola, nuts, yogurt, syrups, liqueurs, or fresh fruit. A parfait is normally made in a tall clear glass so that all the layers are visible.*

APRICOT & GINGER PARFAIT

Place the apricots, ginger wine, and stem ginger in a food processor and blend until puréed. Transfer to a medium bowl. • Whip the cream and sugar in a small bowl with an electric mixer on high speed until soft peaks form. • Combine 1/4 cup (60 ml) of the reserved apricot syrup with 1 tablespoon of the ginger syrup in a small bowl. • To assemble, spoon half of the apricot purée into the base of four tall serving glasses. Layer with half of the gingersnap cookies, drizzle with half of the apricot syrup, then spoon in the half of the cream. Repeat with the remaining apricot, syrup, gingersnaps, and cream. • Cover and chill in the refrigerator for 4 hours, or until required.

1   (14-ounce/400-g) can apricot halves, drained, syrup reserved

2   tablespoons ginger wine

2   pieces stem ginger in syrup, finely sliced, syrup reserved

1¼ cups (300 ml) heavy (double) cream

2   tablespoons confectioners' (icing) sugar

4   ounces (125 g) gingersnap cookies (gingernuts), crumbled

Serves: 4
Preparation: 15 minutes
   + 4 hours to chill
Level: 1

CHILLED CHOCOLATE RASPBERRY DESSERT

Place $\frac{1}{3}$ cup (90 ml) of the cream, the chocolate, and 2 tablespoons of the liqueur in a double boiler over barely simmering water and melt, stirring occasionally, until smooth. Refrigerate until cooled, about 15 minutes. • Whip the remaining cream in a small bowl with an electric mixer on high speed until soft peaks form. Fold into the cooled chocolate mixture. • Place the remaining liqueur, raspberries, and macaroons in a small bowl and stir to combine. • To assemble, fill four serving glasses with half of the raspberry and macaroon mixture. Spoon in half of the chocolate cream. Repeat with the remaining macaroon mixture and chocolate cream. Decorate with the coconut. • Chill in the refrigerator for 4 hours, or until required.

$1\frac{1}{4}$ **cups (300 ml) heavy (double) cream**

4 **ounces (125 g) dark chocolate, coarsely chopped**

$\frac{1}{3}$ **cup (90 ml) Malibu, or other coconut liqueur**

1 **cup (150 g) fresh raspberries**

4 **ounces (125 g) coconut macaroon cookies, crumbled**

$\frac{1}{3}$ **cup (40 g) shredded (desiccated) coconut, lightly toasted**

Serves: 4
Preparation: 20 minutes + 4 hours to chill
Level: 1

CHILLED RHUBARB
& VANILLA DESSERT

108

Place the rhubarb, sugar, water, and vanilla in a small saucepan over low heat. Cook until the rhubarb is softened, 5–10 minutes. • Transfer to a small bowl and refrigerate until chilled, about 15 minutes. Discard the vanilla bean. • Whip the cream in a small bowl with an electric mixer on high speed until soft peaks form. • Mix in the yogurt and cinnamon. • To assemble, spoon half of the rhubarb into the base of four serving glasses. Sprinkle with half of the amaretti cookies and spoon in half of the vanilla cream. Repeat with the remaining rhubarb, amaretti, and cream. Dust with cinnamon. • Cover and chill in the refrigerator for 4 hours, or until required.

1   **bunch rhubarb (about 12 ounces/350 g), trimmed and coarsely chopped**

4   **tablespoons sugar**

2   **tablespoons water**

1   **vanilla bean, split lengthwise**

½   **cup (125 ml) heavy (double) cream**

¾   **cup (180 ml) vanilla yogurt**

1   **teaspoon ground cinnamon, + extra, to dust**

4   **ounces (125 g) amaretti cookies, crumbled**

Serves: 4
Preparation: 30 minutes
   + 4 hours to chill
Cooking: 5–10 minutes
Level: 1

ALMOND CRUNCH WITH RASPBERRY COMPOTE

Almond Crunch: Toast the almonds in a heavy-bottomed pan over medium heat, stirring until golden, about 5 minutes. Sprinkle with the sugar and continue stirring until caramelized. Remove from the heat before the sugar turns too dark.
• Transfer to a plate and let cool, stirring frequently, to prevent the almonds from clumping together.
• Beat the cream in a large bowl with an electric mixer on high speed until it stands in soft peaks.
• Fold in the coarsely ground almonds, candied orange peel, liqueur, and roasted sugar almonds.
• Spoon into 6 serving glasses and chill for 1–2 hours. • Raspberry Compote: Combine the raspberries and sugar in a saucepan with 1 tablespoon of water. Bring to a boil over low heat. If the raspberries stick to the pan, add the remaining water. Simmer for 2–3 minutes. The raspberries should soften and release their juices but still hold their shape. Set aside to cool. • Serve the almond crunch with the raspberry compote spooned over the top.

Almond Crunch

3/4 cup (75 g) blanched almonds, finely chopped

2 tablespoons sugar

1 1/4 cups (300 ml) heavy (double) cream

2 tablespoons coarsely ground almonds

1 tablespoon finely chopped candied (glacé) orange peel

2 tablespoons amaretto or Cointreau liqueur

Raspberry Compote

2 cups (300 g) fresh raspberries

2 tablespoons sugar

1-2 tablespoons water

Serves: 6
Preparation: 30 minutes
    + 1–2 hours to chill
Cooking: 5–10 minutes
Level: 2

WINTER FRUIT
& MASCARPONE TRIFLE

112

Syrup: Bring the water to a boil in a medium saucepan and add the brown sugar. Reduce the heat to very low and add the cloves, cinnamon, and nutmeg. Simmer for 30 minutes. • Fruit: Combine the prunes, apricots, and figs in a large bowl and pour the syrup on top. Let cool for 10 minutes. Cut the orange zest into thin strips and finely grate the lime zest. Add orange and lime zest and juice. Cover with plastic wrap (cling film) and leave to macerate overnight. • Toast the almonds in a dry frying pan, coarsely chop, and set aside. • To assemble the trifle, drain the fruit, reserving the soaking liquid, and discard the cinnamon stick and cloves. Line the bottom of a large glass serving bowl with well over half of the sponge cake. Pour about $^2/_3$ cup (150 ml) of the soaking liquid over the cake, sprinkle with 1 tablespoon of almonds, and spoon half the fruit on top. Make a second layer with the remaining cake pieces. Pour over another $^2/_3$ cup (150 ml) of the syrup, sprinkle with 1 tablespoon of almonds, and top with the rest of the fruit. At this point it should look quite juicy. If not, add more liquid. Reserve any remaining liquid for later. • Place the trifle in the refrigerator to soak up the juices for at least 2 hours, or overnight. • Cream Topping: Whisk together the mascarpone and sugar. Add the Cointreau, lemon zest, and juice. Add the vanilla and whisk again. If it is very stiff, whisk in 1 or 2 teaspoons of the reserved soaking syrup.

Syrup

4	cups (1 liter) water
$^3/_4$	cup (150 g) firmly packed light brown sugar
4	cloves
1	cinnamon stick
$^1/_4$	teaspoon freshly grated nutmeg
	Zest and freshly squeezed juice of 1 orange
	Zest and freshly squeezed juice of 1 lime

Fruit

$^1/_2$	cup (100 g) pitted (stoned) prunes
1	cup (200 g) dried apricots
$^1/_2$	cup (100 g) dried figs, halved
3	tablespoons blanched almonds
12	ounces (350 g) storebought sponge cake or homemade (Basic Génoise, see page 260 or Basic Sponge Cake, see page 592), cut into small cubes

Cream Topping

1¼ cups (300 g) mascarpone

2 tablespoons superfine (caster) sugar

1 tablespoon Cointreau or freshly squeezed orange juice

Finely grated zest of ½ lemon

1 tablespoon freshly squeezed lemon juice

½ teaspoon vanilla extract (essence)

¾ cup (200 g) heavy (double) cream

2 tablespoons sesame seeds, toasted, to decorate

1 tablespoon finely grated orange zest

Serves: 8
Preparation: 40 minutes
+ 12 hours to soak fruit
+ 3 hours to rest
Cooking: 30 minutes
Level: 2

• Whip the cream until it stands in soft peaks. Fold into the mascarpone mixture. The topping should be light enough to spread easily. • Spoon the cream topping over the trifle, smoothing with the back of the spoon. Sprinkle lightly with orange zest. Refrigerate for at least 1 hour before serving. Decorate with sesame seeds and the remaining almonds.

113

■ ■ ■ *Serve this hearty trifle during the cold winter months. It makes a great dessert for hungry skiers after a day on the slopes.*

CLASSIC TRIFLE

Trifle: Combine the raspberries, sugar, lemon zest, and lemon juice in a bowl. Stir and leave to macerate for about 1 hour. • Custard: Heat the cream, milk, and vanilla seeds in a heavy pan over low heat until just below boiling point. • Whisk the egg yolks and sugar in a medium heatproof bowl. Whisk one-third of the warm cream and milk into the yolks. Whisk in the rest. • Place the bowl over a saucepan of barely simmering water. Cook, stirring constantly, until the custard coats the back of a wooden spoon. • Strain into a bowl, cover with plastic wrap (cling film), and refrigerate. • Spread the sponge fingers with raspberry preserves. • Fill the bottom third of a large glass bowl with a layer of sponge fingers. Drizzle with the sherry. Top with the raspberries and juices. Pour the custard over the top, cover, and chill in the refrigerator for at least 4 hours. • Whip the cream with the sugar in a small bowl with an electric mixer on high speed until soft peaks form. • Spread over the custard. Sprinkle with almonds and top with the extra raspberries.

Trifle

3 cup (500 g) raspberries, + extra, to decorate

2 tablespoons sugar

½ teaspoon finely grated lemon zest

2 tablespoons freshly squeezed lemon juice

20 ladyfingers (sponge finger biscuits)

⅓ cup (100 g) raspberry preserves (jam)

½ cup (125 ml) sherry

Custard

1 cup (250 ml) heavy (double) cream

1 cup (250 ml) milk

1 vanilla pod

4 large egg yolks

½ cup (100 g) sugar

Topping

1 cup (250 ml) heavy (double) cream

2 teaspoons sugar

2 tablespoons flaked almonds, toasted

Serves: 6
Preparation: 45 minutes + 5 hours to rest and chill
Cooking: 15 minutes
Level: 2

ZUPPA INGLESE

Whisk the egg yolks and sugar until straw-colored and then stir in the flour. • Heat the milk with the vanilla extract until fairly hot, but not boiling. • Pour the milk into the egg mixture and then cook for 7–8 minutes in a heavy-bottomed saucepan over a low heat, stirring continuously to prevent lumps forming. • Pour half the custard into a bowl and cover with plastic wrap touching the surface to prevent a skin forming. • Melt the chocolate in a double boiler over barely simmering water. • Return the remaining custard to the heat and stir in the melted chocolate. Cook for 2 minutes, stirring continuously. • Pour the chocolate custard into a bowl and cover with plastic wrap touching the surface to prevent a skin forming. • Set the custards aside to cool before using. • Mix the Alchermes, rum, and water together in a bowl. • Dip the ladyfingers into the water and liqueur mixture, then use one-third of them to line a 2-quart (2-liter) glass bowl or soufflé dish. • Pour the chocolate custard over the top, cover with another layer of dipped ladyfingers, and spread the plain custard on top. • Finish with the remaining ladyfingers, cover with foil and refrigerate for about 12 hours. • Just before serving, decorate with plenty of whipped cream and, if liked, a little more grated chocolate.

■ ■ ■ *This Italian trifle comes from Florence, Italy. Alchermes is a bright red liqueur made by the monks of San Marco in Florence. Replace with any light liqueur colored with red food coloring.*

5 large egg yolks

3/4 cup (150 g) sugar

1/3 cup (50 g) all-purpose (plain) flour

2 cups (500 ml) milk

Few drops of vanilla extract (essence)

4 ounces (125 g) grated dark chocolate, + extra, to serve (optional)

1/2 cup (125 ml) Alchermes liqueur

1/2 cup (125 ml) rum

1/4 cup (60 ml) water

20 Italian ladyfingers (sponge finger biscuits)

Whipped cream, to serve

Serves: 8–10
Preparation: 45 minutes + 12 hours to chill
Cooking: 10 minutes
Level: 1

CHOCOLATE CREAM MILLEFEUILLE

Melt the chocolate in a double boiler over barely simmering water. • Pour the melted chocolate over a large sheet of parchment paper and spread to 1/8-inch (3-mm) thick. Let stand until set, at least 30 minutes. • Cut the chocolate into 18 rectangles of equal size. • Finely chop the mint, reserving a few leaves to garnish. • Beat the cream and sugar in a large bowl until stiff. Mix in the chopped mint. • Refrigerate until ready to use. • Place a rectangle of chocolate on each serving plate. Top with a spoonful of cream and a few raspberries. Cover with another piece of chocolate, more cream and raspberries, and finish with another layer of chocolate. • Decorate with the reserved mint leaves and raspberries. Dust with the confectioners' sugar. Serve immediately.

14 ounces (400 g) dark chocolate

1 sprig fresh mint leaves

1½ cups (375 ml) heavy (double) cream

4 tablespoons sugar

2 cups (300 g) raspberries

⅓ cup (50 g) confectioners' (icing) sugar

Serves: 6
Preparation: 35 minutes + 30 minutes to set
Cooking: 5–10 minutes
Level: 2

FROZEN DESSERTS

VANILLA ICE CREAM

Place a medium bowl in the freezer to chill. • **Step 1:** Place 3½ cups (875 ml) of milk in a heavy-based saucepan with the coffee beans, cinnamon stick, lemon zest, vanilla pod, and salt over medium-low heat. Mix well and bring to a boil. Lower the heat and simmer gently for 5 minutes. • **Step 2:** Beat the egg yolks, sugar, and cornstarch in a medium bowl with an electric mixer on high speed until pale and creamy. • **Step 3:** With mixer on low speed, add the remaining cold milk followed by the hot milk mixture. Return to the saucepan and simmer over very low heat, stirring constantly, for 2 minutes. Do not let the mixture boil. • **Step 4:** Remove from the heat and filter into the chilled bowl. Let cool completely, stirring often. Chill in the refrigerator for 30 minutes. • **Step 5:** Beat 2 egg whites until stiff peaks form and fold them into the mixture just before you transfer it to your ice cream machine. Freeze following the manufacturer's instructions. • Transfer to a freezer-proof container and freeze until required.

4	cups (1 liter) milk
6	coffee beans
1	small (about 1-inch/2.5-cm long) cinnamon stick
	Small piece of lemon zest, removed using a sharp knife
1	large vanilla pod
⅛	teaspoon salt
1	cup (200 g) sugar
5	large egg yolks
½	teaspoon cornstarch (cornflour)
2	large egg whites

Serves: 6
Preparation: 20 minutes + 30 minutes to chill + time to churn
Cooking: 5–10 minutes
Level: 1

Making ice cream at home is simple, especially if you own an ice cream machine. The method is the same for all flavors; first you make a milk- or cream-based custard, then flavoring is added, before being tipped into the machine to churn. By making ice cream at home you can be sure that there are no preservatives or additives —just wholesome eggs, sugar, milk, and cream.

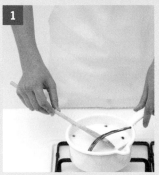

1. SIMMER 3$\frac{1}{2}$ cups (875 ml) of milk with the coffee, cinnamon, lemon zest, vanilla, and salt over medium-low heat.

2. BEAT the egg yolks, sugar, and cornstarch in a bowl with an electric mixer on high speed until pale and creamy.

3. ADD the remaining cold milk to the egg mixture then the hot milk mixture. Return to the pan and simmer over low heat, stirring constantly, for 2 minutes. Do not let the mixture boil.

4. REMOVE from the heat and filter into a chilled bowl. Let cool, stirring often. Refrigerate for 30 minutes.

5. BEAT 2 egg whites until stiff peaks form. Fold into the mixture. Transfer to an ice cream machine and churn.

LIME & GINGER MASCARPONE ICE CREAM

Place a medium bowl in the freezer to chill. • Beat the egg yolks, sugar, and lime zest in a small bowl with an electric mixer on high speed until pale and creamy. • Place the milk and ginger in a small saucepan over medium heat and bring to a boil.
• Gradually pour the milk into the egg yolk mixture, stirring to combine. • Return the mixture to the pan and simmer over low heat, stirring until thickened slightly. Do not allow the mixture to boil. • Remove from the heat and pour into the chilled bowl. Chill in the refrigerator for 30 minutes. • Add the lime juice and mascarpone to the yolk mixture, stirring to combine. • Pour into an ice cream machine and churn according to the manufacturer's instructions.
• Transfer to a freezer-proof container and freeze until required.

4   large egg yolks
1   cup (150 g) sugar
1½ teaspoons finely grated lime zest
⅓ cup (90 ml) milk
3   tablespoons candied (glacé) ginger, finely chopped
¾ cup (180 ml) freshly squeezed lime juice
1¼ cups (300 g) mascarpone cheese

Serves: 4
Preparation: 20 minutes + 30 minutes to cool + time to churn
Cooking: 5–10 minutes
Level: 1

BANANA ICE CREAM

Place a medium bowl in the freezer to chill. • Beat the egg yolks and sugar in a medium bowl with an electric mixer on high speed until pale and creamy. • Add the banana and honey stir to combine. • Place the cream, milk, and nutmeg in a medium saucepan over medium heat and bring to a boil. • Gradually pour into the egg yolk mixture, stirring to combine. • Return the mixture to the pan and simmer over low heat, stirring until thickened slightly. Do not allow the mixture to boil. • Remove from the heat and pour into the chilled bowl. Chill in the refrigerator for 30 minutes. • Pour into an ice-cream machine and churn according to the manufacturer's instructions. • Transfer to a freezer-proof container and freeze until required.

6   large egg yolks

$\frac{1}{3}$ cup (70 g) sugar

3   large ripe bananas, mashed

3   tablespoons honey

$1\frac{1}{4}$ cups (300 ml) heavy (double) cream

1   cup (250 ml) milk

1   teaspoon ground nutmeg

Serves: 4
Preparation: 20 minutes
    + 30 minutes to cool
    + time to churn
Cooking: 5–10 minutes
Level: 1

TURKISH DELIGHT ICE CREAM

Place a medium bowl in the freezer to chill. • Beat the egg yolks, sugar, and rose water in a medium bowl with an electric mixer on high speed until pale and creamy. • Place the cream and milk in a medium saucepan over medium heat and bring to a boil. • Gradually pour into the egg yolk mixture, stirring to combine. • Return the mixture to the pan and simmer over low heat, stirring until thickened slightly. Do not allow the mixture to boil. • Remove from the heat and pour into the chilled bowl. Chill in the refrigerator for 30 minutes. • Stir in the Turkish delight. • Pour into an ice cream machine and churn according to the manufacturer's instructions. • Transfer to a freezer-proof container and freeze until required.

6   large egg yolks

⅓   cup (70 g) sugar

1   teaspoon rose water

1¼ cups (300 ml) heavy (double) cream

1   cup (250 ml) milk

3   ounces (90 g) Turkish delight, coarsely diced

Serves: 4
Preparation: 20 minutes
  + 30 minutes to cool
  + time to churn
Cooking: 5–10 minutes
Level: 1

MALAGA ICE CREAM

Rinse the raisins. Drain well and place in a small bowl. Cover with the wine or rum and let plump while you prepare the ice cream. • Place a medium bowl in the freezer to chill. • Place the milk and cream in a heavy-based saucepan over medium heat and bring to a boil. • Beat the egg yolks and sugar in a medium bowl with an electric mixer on high speed until pale and creamy. • Pour the hot milk mixture into the bowl with the egg yolk mixture, beating constantly with a wooden spoon. Return to the saucepan and simmer over very low heat, beating constantly, until it just coats the back of the spoon. Do not let the mixture boil. • Remove from the heat and pour into the chilled bowl. Chill in the refrigerator for 30 minutes. • Transfer the mixture to your ice cream machine and freeze according to the manufacturer's instructions. Add the raisins and their liquid 1–2 minutes before the ice cream is ready. • Transfer to a freezer-proof container and freeze until required.

½ cup (90 g) Malaga or other plump tasty raisins

¼ cup (60 ml) Moscato dessert wine (or rum)

2 cups (500 ml) milk

¾ cup (200 ml) heavy (double) cream

6 large egg yolks

¾ cup (150 g) sugar

Serves: 4–6
Preparation: 20 minutes
  + 30 minutes to cool
  + time to churn
Cooking: 5–10 minutes
Level: 1

GELATO WITH VIN SANTO AND ALMOND BISCOTTI

Place a medium bowl in the freezer to chill. • Place the milk and cream in a heavy-based saucepan over medium heat and bring to a boil. • Beat the egg yolks and sugar in a medium bowl with an electric mixer on high speed until pale and creamy. • Pour the hot milk mixture over the egg mixture, beating constantly with a wooden spoon. Return the mixture to the saucepan. Simmer over very low heat, stirring constantly, until it just coats the back of the spoon. Do not let the mixture boil. • Remove from the heat and pour into the chilled bowl. Chill in the refrigerator for 30 minutes. • Stir in the Vin Santo. Transfer the mixture to your ice cream machine and freeze according to the manufacturer's instructions. • Divide three-quarters of the biscotti evenly among 6 serving glasses or bowls and top with the ice cream. Sprinkle with the remaining biscotti and serve.

2 cups (500 ml) milk
¾ cup (200 ml) heavy (double) cream
6 large egg yolks
¾ cup (150 g) sugar
5 tablespoons (75 ml) Vin Santo (or sherry or port)
20 biscotti di Prato, coarsely chopped

Serves: 6
Preparation: 20 minutes + 30 minutes to cool + time to churn
Cooking: 5–10 minutes
Level: 1

■ ■ ■ Biscotti di Prato are very crisp Italian almond biscotti from the city of Prato, near Florence. Substitute with any other Italian biscotti. Vin Santo, literally "holy wine," is a Tuscan dessert wine. Substitute with sherry or port, if preferred.

CHOCOLATE CHERRY ICE CREAM BOMBE

Line an 8-cup (2 liter) pudding basin with plastic wrap (cling film), leaving a 2-inch (5-cm) overhang. • Beat the egg yolks and sugar in a medium bowl with an electric mixer on high speed until pale and creamy. • Place the cream, milk, vanilla beans, and seeds in a large saucepan over medium heat and bring to a boil. • Gradually pour into the egg yolk mixture, stirring to combine. • Return the mixture to the pan and simmer over low heat, stirring until thickened slightly. Do not allow the mixture to boil. Remove from the heat. • Place the white chocolate in a large heat-proof bowl. Pour in about 2 cups (500 ml) of the hot cream mixture, stirring until melted. Add the remaining liquid, stirring to combine. • Strain through a fine mesh sieve and discard the vanilla beans. Refrigerate until cooled, about 30 minutes. • Pour into an ice cream machine and churn according to the manufacturer's instructions until almost frozen. • Add the cherries, pistachios, and coconut and churn for 1 more minute. • Spoon the ice cream into the prepared basin, cover with plastic wrap, and freeze overnight. • Melt the dark chocolate in a double boiler over barely simmering water until smooth. Let cool a little. • Remove the bombe from the freezer, invert onto a serving plate and remove the plastic wrap. • Drizzle the cooled, melted chocolate over the bombe and return to the freezer until set. • Slice into portions using a hot knife and serve immediately.

12	large egg yolks
¾	cup (150 g) sugar
2½	cups (625 ml) heavy (double) cream
2	cups (500 ml) milk
2	vanilla beans, split lengthwise and seeds scraped
4	ounces (125 g) white chocolate, coarsely chopped
1	cup (250 g) fresh or canned cherries, pitted and halved, drained if canned
½	cup (75 g) pistachios, toasted and coarsely chopped
½	cup (30 g) shredded (desiccated) coconut
4	ounces (125 g) dark chocolate, coarsely chopped

Serves: 8–10
Preparation: 30 minutes
   + 30 minutes to cool
   + time to churn
   + 12 hours to freeze
Cooking: 5–10 minutes
Level: 2

LEMON & PASSION FRUIT PARFAIT

Line a 3 x 9-inch (8 x 23-cm) loaf pan with plastic wrap (cling film), leaving a 2-inch (5-cm) overhang. • Beat the egg yolks in a medium bowl with an electric mixer on high speed until pale and creamy. • Strain ³/₄ cup (180 ml) of passion fruit pulp through a fine mesh sieve. Combine with the sugar and lemon juice in a medium saucepan over medium-low heat and gently simmer until thickened to a syrup consistency, 3–4 minutes. • Gradually pour the syrup into the egg yolks, beating until thick and cool, 4–5 minutes. • Place both types of cream in a medium bowl and beat with an electric mixer on high speed until soft peaks form. • Stir half of the cream mixture into the egg yolk mixture then gently fold in the rest. • Pour into the prepared pan, cover with plastic wrap, and freeze overnight. • Remove the parfait from the freezer, invert onto a serving plate and remove the plastic wrap. • Slice into portions using a hot knife and drizzle with the remaining passion fruit pulp. Serve immediately.

8   **large egg yolks**

1   **cup (250 ml) passion fruit pulp (about 20 passion fruit)**

1   **cup (200 g) sugar**

¼   **cup (60 ml) freshly squeezed lemon juice**

1¼ **cups (300 ml) heavy (double) cream**

½   **cup (125 ml) half-and-half (single) cream**

Serves: 6–8
Preparation: 30 minutes + 12 hours to freeze
Cooking: 5–10 minutes
Level: 2

WHITE CHOCOLATE & STRAWBERRY PARFAIT

Line a 3 x 9-inch (8 x 23-cm) loaf pan with plastic wrap (cling film), leaving a 2-inch (5-cm) overhang. • Beat the egg yolks in a medium bowl with an electric mixer on high speed until pale and creamy. • Place ¼ cup (60 ml) of the heavy cream in a small saucepan over low heat and bring to a boil. • Place the chocolate in a small heatproof bowl and pour the hot cream over the top, stirring until smooth. Set aside. • Place the sugar, strawberries, and lemon juice in a small saucepan over medium-low heat and gently simmer until the strawberries are soft and the liquid is syrupy, 3–4 minutes. • Transfer to a food processor and blend until puréed. Pass through a fine mesh sieve. • Gradually pour the strawberry syrup into the egg yolks, beating until thick and cool, 4–5 minutes. Add the melted chocolate mixture and stir to combine. • Place the remaining heavy cream and half-and-half in a medium bowl and beat with an electric mixer on high speed until soft peaks form. • Stir half of the cream into the strawberry mixture and then gently fold in the remaining cream. • Pour into the prepared pan, cover with plastic wrap, and freeze overnight. • Remove the parfait from the freezer, invert onto a serving plate and remove the plastic wrap. • Slice into portions using a hot knife. Halve the extra strawberries and use them to decorate each portion. • Serve immediately.

8 large egg yolks

1¼ cups (300 ml) heavy (double) cream

4 ounces (125 g) white chocolate, coarsely chopped

1 cup (200 g) sugar

2½ cups (375 g) strawberries, + 6–8 extra, to decorate

2 tablespoons freshly squeezed lemon juice

½ cup (125 ml) half-and-half (single) cream

Serves: 6–8
Preparation: 30 minutes + 12 hours to freeze
Cooking: 5–10 minutes
Level: 2

FROZEN RASPBERRY SOUFFLÉ

To prepare the soufflé dishes, tie a strip of parchment paper or aluminum foil around four $3/4$-cup (180-ml) ramekins, so that 1-inch (2.5-cm) collars extend above the rim of the dishes. • Beat the egg yolks, $1/4$-cup (50 g) of sugar, and lemon zest in a small bowl with an electric mixer on high speed until pale and creamy. • Place the raspberries in a food processor and blend until puréed. Pass through a fine mesh sieve and discard the seeds. • Add to the egg yolk mixture and stir to combine. • Whip the cream in a small bowl with an electric mixer on high speed until soft peaks form. Fold into the raspberry mixture. • Beat the egg whites in a small bowl with an electric mixer on high speed until foamy. • Gradually add the remaining 2 tablespoons of sugar and beat until soft peaks form. • Add a large spoonful to the raspberry mixture and stir to combine. Gently fold in the remaining whites. • Spoon the mixture into the prepared ramekins, filling $1/2$ inch (1 cm) above the rim. Cover loosely with plastic wrap (cling film) and freeze for 4 hours, or until firm. • Remove the paper collars, decorate with raspberries, and dust with confectioners' sugar. • Serve immediately.

3　large eggs, separated

$1/4$　cup (50 g) + 2 tablespoons superfine (caster) sugar

1　teaspoon finely grated lemon zest

2　cups (300 g) raspberries + extra, to decorate

1　cup (250 ml) half-and-half (single) cream

　Confectioners' sugar, to dust

Serves: 4
Preparation: 30 minutes + 4 hours to freeze
Level: 2

RASPBERRY SORBET

Place the sugar and water in a small saucepan over medium heat and bring to a boil. Remove from the heat and set aside to cool. • Place the raspberries and lemon juice in a food processor and blend until puréed. • Pass through a fine mesh sieve and discard the seeds. • Add the sugar syrup and stir to combine. Refrigerate until cooled, about 30 minutes. • Pour into an ice cream machine and churn according to the manufacturer's instructions. • Transfer to a freezer-proof container and freeze until required.

3/4 **cup (150 g) sugar**

1/2 **cup (125 ml) water**

2 **pounds (1 kg) raspberries**

1/4 **cup (60 ml) freshly squeezed lemon juice**

Serves: 6–8
Preparation: 10 minutes
  + 30 minutes to cool
  + time to churn
Cooking: 5 minutes
Level: 1

STRAWBERRY YOGURT SORBET

Place the sugar and water in a medium saucepan over medium heat. Bring to a boil and simmer, stirring constantly, until the sugar has completely dissolved, 2–3 minutes. Remove from the heat and set aside to cool, about 30 minutes. • Add the strawberries to the cooled sugar syrup. Stir in the yogurt then chop the mixture in a food processor until smooth. • Transfer to an ice cream machine and freeze according to the manufacturer's instructions. • Transfer to a freezer-proof container and freeze until required.

½ cup (100 g) sugar
2 cups (500 ml) water
3 cups (500 g) ripe strawberries, chopped
1¼ cups (300 g) plain yogurt

Serves: 4
Preparation: 10 minutes
  + 30 minutes to cool
  + time to churn
Cooking: 2–3 minutes
Level: 1

PEACH SORBET WITH CREAM AND AMARETTI

Place the sugar and water in a medium saucepan over medium heat. Bring to a boil and simmer, stirring constantly, until the sugar has completely dissolved, 2–3 minutes. Remove from the heat and set aside to cool, about 30 minutes. • Chop the peaches in a food processor until smooth. You should have just over 1 pound (500 g) of peach purée. • Stir the peach purée and lemon juice into the cooled sugar syrup. • Beat the egg white with an electric mixer on high speed until stiff. Fold into the peach mixture. • Transfer to an ice cream machine and freeze according to the manufacturer's instructions. • Transfer to a freezer-proof container and freeze until required. • Serve with whipped cream and amaretti cookies.

1¾ cups (350 g) sugar

1½ cups (375 ml) water

1½ pounds (750 g) ripe white peaches, peeled, pitted, and sliced

Freshly squeezed juice of 2 lemons

1 large egg white

Whipped cream, to serve

Amaretti cookies, to serve

Serves: 8
Preparation: 30 minutes + 30 minutes to cool + time to churn
Cooking: 2–3 minutes
Level: 1

MELON SORBET WITH BASIL

Place 1 pound (500 g) of the melon cubes and basil in a blender with the orange juice, sugar, and salt. Chop until the sugar has dissolved and the mixture is smooth, about 30 seconds. Transfer to a bowl and chill in the refrigerator for 1 hour. • Transfer to an ice cream machine and freeze according to the manufacturer's instructions. • Place the remaining melon cubes in 6 serving glasses. Pipe or scoop the frozen sorbet over the top. Decorate with the extra fresh basil leaves and serve.

152

1½ pounds (750 g) cantaloupe (rock) melon flesh, peeled weight, cut in cubes

6 fresh basil leaves + extra, to garnish

⅓ cup (90 ml) freshly squeezed orange juice

¾ cup (150 g) sugar

¼ teaspoon salt

Serves: 6
Preparation: 15 minutes
+ 1 hour to chill
+ time to churn
Level: 1

CHOCOLATE SPUMONE

Place 6 glasses or serving bowls in the freezer to chill. • Place the chocolate in a medium bowl and pour in the boiling water. Stir until the chocolate has melted completely. Let cool completely, about 30 minutes. Chill in the refrigerator for 30 minutes. • Beat the cream in a large bowl with an electric mixer on high speed until thick. Fold the cream into the chilled chocolate mixture. Stir in the sugar, vanilla, and salt. • Transfer the mixture to an ice cream machine and freeze according to the manufacturer's instructions until creamy and almost frozen, 20–25 minutes (this time will depend on your machine). • Pipe or spoon the spumone into the chilled glasses. Top with the extra whipped cream, chocolate, and strawberries and serve immediately.

5   ounces (150 g) dark chocolate, chopped

3/4   cup (200 ml) boiling water

2   cups (500 ml) heavy (double) cream

1   cup (200 g) superfine (caster) sugar

1   teaspoon vanilla extract (essence)

1/8   teaspoon salt

Whipped cream, to serve

Grated chocolate, to serve

Fresh strawberries, sliced, to serve

Serves: 6
Preparation: 20 minutes
    + 1 hour to cool and chill
    + time to churn
Cooking: 5 minutes
Level: 2

PINK GRAPEFRUIT & CAMPARI GRANITA

Place the grapefruit juice, water, sugar, and mint in a small saucepan over low heat and bring to a boil. Decrease the heat to low and gently simmer until the sugar has dissolved, 2–3 minutes. • Remove from the heat and transfer to a medium bowl. Discard the mint. • Add the Campari and lemon juice and refrigerate until cooled, about 30 minutes. • Pour the liquid into a plastic or stainless steel container about 10 inches (25 cm) square. Cover with plastic wrap (cling film) and freeze for 2 hours. • Remove from the freezer and use a fork to break up the granita into large crystals. Return the container to the freezer for 1 hour, then break up with a fork again. Repeat three more times, until the crystals are completely frozen. • Spoon the granita into serving glasses and serve immediately.

1   cup (250 ml) freshly squeezed pink grapefruit juice, strained
1   cup (250 ml) water
1   cup (200 g) sugar
1   sprig fresh mint
3   tablespoons Campari
2   tablespoons freshly squeezed lemon juice

Serves: 4
Preparation: 15 minutes
    + 30 minutes to chill
    + 6 hours to freeze
Cooking: 5–10 minutes
Level: 2

■ ■ ■ *Campari is an Italian aperitif made by infusing bitter herbs and aromatic plants and fruit in a mixture of alcohol and water. First made in Italy in the 1860s, the exact recipe has been kept secret for almost 150 years. Campari is made or exported all over the world.*

LIMONCELLO GRANITA

Place the water and sugar in a heavy-based saucepan over low heat and stir until the sugar is completely dissolved. Remove from the heat and let cool to room temperature. • Stir in the Limoncello and lemon juice then pour the syrup into a plastic or stainless steel container about 10 inches (25 cm) square. • Place in the freezer and leave for 1 hour. Use a fork or hand blender to break the granita up into large crystals. If using an ice cream machine, transfer to the machine at this point and follow the instructions. To continue by hand, replace the container in the freezer for 30 minutes, then break up again with a fork. Repeat 3 or 4 times, until the crystals are completely frozen. • Scoop into 4–6 wine goblets or glasses and garnish with the strawberries.

2 cups (500 ml) water
½ cup (100 g) sugar
½ cup (125 ml) Limoncello liqueur
¼ cup (60 ml) freshly squeezed lemon juice
2 fresh strawberries, sliced, to garnish

Serves: 4–6
Preparation: 15 minutes
  + 5 hours to freeze
Cooking: 5 minutes
Level: 2

■ ■ ■ *Limoncello is a lemon liqueur made by infusing lemon peel with pure alcohol. It originally comes from the Amalfi Coast and the island of Capri, near Naples, but is now a favorite all over Italy and many other parts of the world. It should be kept in the freezer (it contains enough alcohol to prevent it from freezing solid) and is usually served icy cold as an after-dinner drink.*

BLACKBERRY GRANITA

Place the blackberries in a large bowl and mash well with a fork. Press through a fine mesh strainer to eliminate the seeds. • Place the sugar and water in a saucepan over medium-low heat and stir until the sugar is completely dissolved. Remove from the heat and let cool to room temperature. • Stir the blackberry purée into the sugar syrup. Pour the mixture into a plastic or stainless steel container about 10 inches (25 cm) square. • Place in the freezer and leave for 1 hour. Use a fork or hand blender to break the granita up into large crystals. If using an ice cream machine, transfer to the machine at this point and follow the manufacturer's instructions. To continue by hand, replace the container in the freezer for 30 minutes, then break up again with a fork. Repeat 3 or 4 times, until the crystals are completely frozen. • Scoop into 4–6 wine goblets and serve.

1½ **pounds (750 g) fresh ripe blackberries**

¾ **cup (150 g) sugar**

1¼ **cups (300 ml) water**

Serves: 4–6
Preparation: 20 minutes
 + 5 hours freeze
Cooking: 5 minutes
Level: 2

■ ■ ■ *Use the same quantity of raspberries or strawberries for an equally delicious raspberry or strawberry granita.*

ZUCCOTTO

Step 1: Cut the sponge cake into thin slices.
• **Step 2:** Place the sugar and water in a saucepan over medium heat and simmer until the sugar is dissolved, 2–3 minutes. Remove from heat, add the brandy and rum, and let cool. • **Step 3:** Moisten the sides of a domed 1¹/₂-quart (1.5-liter) pudding mold with a little sugar syrup. • **Step 4:** Line the mold with three-quarters of the sliced sponge cake. Make sure there are no gaps between the pieces of sponge cake. Brush with the remaining syrup. • **Step 5:** Beat the cream in a large bowl with an electric mixer on high speed until thick. Mix the confectioners' sugar, nuts, candied fruit, and chocolate into the whipped cream. • **Step 6:** Spoon the cream mixture into the mold and cover with the remaining sponge slices. • Freeze overnight. Turn out onto a serving dish and serve in wedges.

½ **Italian Sponge Cake (see page 594)**
¾ **cup (150 g) sugar**
1   **cup (200 ml) water**
3   **tablespoons brandy**
3   **tablespoons rum**
2   **cups (500 ml) heavy (double) cream**
⅓ **cup (50 g) confectioners' (icing) sugar**
⅓ **cup (30 g) almonds, toasted and chopped**
⅓ **cup (30 g) hazelnuts, toasted and chopped**
4   **tablespoons candied (glacé) fruit, chopped**
5   **ounces (150 g) dark chocolate, chopped**

Serves: 6
Preparation: 30 minutes + 12 hours to freeze
Cooking: 2–3 minutes
Level: 2

■ ■ ■ *This Florentine dessert is served all over Italy. Its shape is said to mirror the outline of Brunelleschi's famous dome on the city's cathedral.*

PREPARING ZUCCOTTO

Zuccotto is an Italian dessert from Florence. This recipe uses half an Italian sponge cake–freeze the rest for the next time you make zuccotto, or serve with fresh fruit and whipped cream as a family dessert. If short of time, use storebought sponge.

1. CUT the sponge cake into thin slices.

2. SIMMER the sugar and water over medium heat until dissolved, 2–3 minutes. Remove from heat, add the brandy and rum, and let cool.

3. MOISTEN Moisten the sides of a domed 1$\frac{1}{2}$-quart (1.5-liter) pudding mold with a little sugar syrup.

4. LINE the mold with three-quarters of the cake. Make sure there are no gaps between the pieces of sponge cake.

5. BEAT the cream until thick. Mix in the confectioners' sugar, nuts, candied fruit, and chocolate.

6. SPOON the cream mixture into the mold and cover with the remaining sponge slices.

TWO-TONED ZUCCOTTO

Line a 1$\frac{1}{2}$-quart (1.5-liter) domed pudding mold or a stainless steel domed bowl with plastic wrap (cling film). • Slice the sponge cake thinly and dip in the rum until moist. Line the prepared mold with the cake slices. • Melt the chocolate with 2 tablespoons of rum and the coffee in a double boiler over barely simmering water. • Set aside to cool. • Beat 1$\frac{1}{2}$ cups (375 ml) of the cream with the confectioners' sugar and vanilla in a large bowl until stiff. • Gently fold half the cream into the melted chocolate. • Fold the candied fruit and almonds into the remaining cream. • Spoon the chocolate mixture into the mold. Spoon the candied fruit cream over the top, smoothing the top. Cover with a layer of cake. • Cover with a sheet of parchment paper and refrigerate for 12 hours, or overnight. • Invert and turn out of the mold onto a serving plate. • Beat the remaining cream in a medium bowl until stiff. Spread the cream over the top and dust with the cocoa.

$\frac{1}{2}$ **Italian Sponge Cake (see page 594)**

$\frac{1}{4}$ **cup (60 ml) rum**

4 **ounces (125 g) dark chocolate, chopped**

2 **tablespoons freeze-dried instant coffee granules**

2 **cups (500 ml) heavy (double) cream**

2 **tablespoons confectioners' (icing) sugar**

1 **teaspoon vanilla extract (essence)**

$\frac{2}{3}$ **cup (60 g) chopped mixed candied fruit**

$\frac{1}{2}$ **cup (50 g) chopped almonds**

$\frac{1}{3}$ **cup (50 g) unsweetened cocoa powder**

Serves: 6–8
Preparation: 1 hour
   + 12 hours to chill
Cooking: 5 minutes
Level: 2

FROZEN RASPBERRY LIQUEUR CAKE

Beat the egg and egg yolks, sugar, flour, vanilla, and salt in a large bowl with an electric mixer on high speed until well blended. • With the mixer on low speed, gradually beat in the milk. Transfer the mixture to a large saucepan. Cook over low heat, stirring constantly with a wooden spoon, until the mixture lightly coats a metal spoon or registers 160°F (80°C) on an instant-read thermometer. • Sprinkle the gelatin over the water in a saucepan. Let soften 1 minute. Stir the gelatin over low heat until it has completely dissolved. Stir the gelatin mixture into the egg mixture. • Brush the sides of an 8-cup (2-liter) domed pudding bowl with liqueur. Moisten slices of sponge cake with liqueur and spread with preserves. Stick the slices, preserve-side facing inward, onto the sides of the bowl. Spread with cream. Moisten the remaining cake with liqueur and spread with preserves and layer it into the pudding bowl, alternating with the cream. Finish with a layer of cake slices, preserves-side facing inward. Press down lightly. • Freeze for at least 6 hours. • With mixer at high speed, beat the cream and confectioners' sugar in a medium bowl until stiff. • Turn the cake out onto a serving dish. Spread with the cream and decorate with raspberries and almonds.

1	large egg + 3 large egg yolks
³⁄₄	cup (150 g) sugar
¹⁄₂	cup (75 g) all-purpose (plain) flour
1	teaspoon vanilla extract (essence)
¹⁄₄	teaspoon salt
1²⁄₃	cups (400 ml) milk
1	tablespoon unflavored gelatin
¹⁄₄	cup (60 ml) water
1	Italian Sponge Cake (see page 594), cut into ¹⁄₂-inch (1-cm) thick slices
²⁄₃	cup (160 ml) raspberry liqueur
¹⁄₂	cup (150 g) raspberry preserves (jam)
1	cup (250 ml) heavy (double) cream
2	tablespoons confectioners' (icing) sugar
¹⁄₂	cup (75 g) fresh raspberries, to decorate
¹⁄₄	cup (30 g) slivered almonds, to decorate

Serves: 6–8
Preparation: 30 minutes
  + 6 hours to freeze
Level: 2

168

ZUCCOTTO WITH STRAWBERRIES & CREAM

Line a 6-cup (1.5-liter) domed pudding mold or a stainless steel domed bowl with plastic wrap (cling film). • Dip the cake in the rum until moist. Line the prepared mold with the cake slices. • Beat $1^1/2$ cups (375 ml) of the cream with the confectioners' sugar, and vanilla in a large bowl until stiff. • Gently fold in the strawberries. • Spoon the mixture into the mold, smoothing the top. Cover with a layer of cake. • Cover with a sheet of parchment paper and freeze for 12 hours, or overnight. • Invert and turn out onto a serving plate. • Beat the remaining cream in a medium bowl until stiff. Spread the cream over the top and serve.

$1/2$ **Italian Sponge Cake (see page 594), thinly sliced**

$1/3$ **cup (90 ml) rum**

2   **cups (500 ml) heavy (double) cream**

2   **tablespoons confectioners' (icing) sugar**

1   **teaspoon vanilla extract (essence)**

3   **cups (450 g) fresh strawberries, sliced**

Serves: 4–6
Preparation: 1 hour
   + 12 hours to freeze
Level: 2

STRAWBERRY ICE CREAM PIE

Crust: Preheat the oven to 350°F (180°C/gas 4).
• Place the cracker crumbs, butter, and brown sugar in a small bowl and stir to combine. Press into the base of a 9-inch (23 cm) springform pan. • Bake for 10–12 minutes, until lightly toasted. Remove from the oven and set aside to cool. • Topping: Beat the egg yolks and sugar in a medium bowl with an electric mixer until pale and creamy. • Place the cream, milk, vanilla bean and seeds in a large saucepan over medium heat and bring to a boil. • Gradually pour into the yolk mixture, stirring to combine. Return the mixture to the pan and simmer over low heat, stirring until thickened slightly. Do not allow the mixture to boil. Remove from the heat, transfer to a medium bowl and refrigerate until cooled, about 30 minutes. • Meanwhile, place the strawberries in a food processor and blend until puréed. • Cook in a small saucepan over medium-low heat until thick and syrupy, 5–10 minutes. Transfer to a small bowl and refrigerate until cooled, about 30 minutes. • Pour the cooled custard into an ice cream machine and churn according to manufacturer's instructions until almost frozen. Pour in half of the strawberry purée and finish churning. • Spread the base of the pie with half of the remaining strawberry purée. • Spoon the ice cream in over the top. • Cover with plastic wrap (cling film) and freeze overnight. • Drizzle the pie with the remaining strawberry purée and the melted chocolate. • Slice into portions using a hot knife.

Crust

1½ cups (185 g) graham cracker crumbs or digestive biscuit crumbs

3½ ounces (100 g) butter, melted

2 tablespoons light brown sugar

Topping

9 large egg yolks

½ cup (100 g) sugar

1¾ cups (450 ml) heavy (double) cream

1½ cups (375 ml) milk

1 vanilla bean, split lengthwise, seeds scraped

3 cups (450 g) strawberries

3½ ounces (100 g) white chocolate, melted, to decorate

Serves: 8–10
Preparation: 45 minutes to chill + 12 hours to freeze
Cooking: 10–12 minutes
Level: 3

CHOCOLATE SALAMI

174

Melt the chocolate with the condensed milk, butter, and liqueur in a double boiler over barely simmering water. Remove from the heat. • Transfer to a large bowl. Stir in the raisins, hazelnuts, walnuts, and candied fruit. • Set aside to cool slightly. Transfer to a sheet of parchment paper and shape into a log about 3 x 12 inches (8 x 36 cm). Wrap the log in aluminum foil and freeze for 2 hours. • Remove the foil and paper and slice thinly, as though you were serving salami.

12 ounces (350 g) dark chocolate, chopped

2/3 cup (150 ml) sweetened condensed milk

2 tablespoons butter

2 tablespoons orange liqueur

1/2 cup (80 g) raisins

1/3 cup (50 g) hazelnuts, chopped and toasted

1/3 cup (50 g) walnuts, coarsely chopped

2 tablespoons candied (glacé) fruit, coarsely chopped, such as apricots, pineapple, or mango

Serves: 8–12
Preparation: 15 minutes + 2 hours to freeze
Level: 1

■ ■ ■ *Children love the intense chocolate flavor of this dessert. If preparing it for a children's party, you may prefer to substitute the orange liqueur with 2 tablespoons of freshly squeezed orange juice mixed with 1 teaspoon of finely grated orange zest.*

FROZEN BANANA STICKS

Combine the chocolate chips and milk in a double boiler over barely simmering water and stir until melted and smooth. • Line a cookie sheet with parchment paper. • Place the toasted almonds on a large plate and set aside. • Peel the bananas and insert a bamboo skewer or wooden ice cream stick through the base going about one third of the way up. • Coat each banana in the melted chocolate and roll in the toasted almonds. Place the bananas on the prepared cookie sheet and place in the freezer for 2 hours. • Serve immediately.

176

3/4 cup (150 g) dark chocolate chips

1/3 cup (90 ml) milk

3/4 cup (120 g) flaked almonds, toasted

6 small sweet bananas, such as ladyfinger

Serves: 6
Preparation: 15 minutes
 + 2 hours to freeze
Level: 1

FRUIT
DESSERTS

FRESH FRUIT SOUP

Purée the strawberries in a blender then push them through a fine mesh sieve into a medium bowl. Discard the seeds. • Scrape out the seeds from the vanilla pod and stir them into the strawberry purée along with the 1 tablespoon of sugar and the lemon juice. • Combine the orange juice, wine, and honey in a saucepan over medium heat and stir until the honey dissolves. Stir in the strawberry purée and bring to a gentle simmer. • Mix the cornstarch and water in a small bowl until smooth. Pour into the soup. Stir until the soup thickens, then remove from the heat. Cool to room temperature. • Chill in the refrigerator for at least 2 hours. • About 15 minutes before you are ready to serve, prepare the garnish. Place the sliced strawberries on a large plate—large strawberries halved—and sprinkle with the remaining sugar. • Ladle the soup into 6–8 small bowls or cups. Divide the sliced strawberries among the bowls. Serve with a dollop of crème fraîche and top with mint leaves.

2 **pounds (1 kg) fresh strawberries + 1 cup (150 g) extra, sliced, to serve**

½ **vanilla pod, slit lengthwise**

2 **tablespoons sugar**

1 **tablespoon freshly squeezed lemon juice**

⅓ **cup (90 ml) freshly squeezed orange juice, strained**

⅓ **cup (90 ml) dry white wine**

⅓ **cup (90 ml) honey**

2 **tablespoons cornstarch (cornflour)**

3 **tablespoons cold water**

Mint leaves, to serve

Crème fraîche, to serve

Serves: 6–8
Preparation: 30 minutes
  + 2 hours to chill
Cooking: 10 minutes
Level: 1

■ ■ ■ *This "soup" is only good if made with fresh organic strawberries at the height of their spring / summer season. Don't even attempt to make it with frozen strawberries!*

SUMMER FRUIT SOUP

Combine the wine, port, Cointreau, orange zest and juice, sugar, cinnamon stick, vanilla bean, and mint sprigs in a large saucepan over medium-high heat and bring to a boil. Decrease the heat to medium-low and gently simmer for 10 minutes, skimming off any particles from the surface. • Remove from the heat, add the berries and cherries, and allow to cool for 15 minutes. Transfer the fruit soup to a large bowl and refrigerate until well chilled, about 2 hours. • Whisk the mascarpone, confectioners' sugar, and ground cinnamon until combined. Chill until ready to serve. • To serve, spoon or ladle the fruit soup into serving bowls, sprinkle with the extra chopped mint, and top with a dollop of sweetened mascarpone.

1½ cups (375 ml) dry red wine

1½ cups (375 ml) port

¼ cup (60 ml) Cointreau or other orange liqueur

Finely grated zest and juice of 1 orange

1 cup (200 g) sugar

1 cinnamon stick

1 vanilla bean, split lengthwise

3 sprigs fresh mint, sliced + extra, to decorate

2 cups (300 g) fresh blueberries

2 cups (300 g) fresh raspberries

2 cups (300 g) fresh blackberries

2 cups (300 g) fresh strawberries

2 cups (300 g) fresh cherries, pitted

¾ cup (180 g) mascarpone

1 tablespoon confectioners' (icing) sugar

½ teaspoon ground cinnamon

Serves: 6–8
Preparation: 15 minutes + 2 hours to chill
Cooking: 15 minutes
Level: 1

STRAWBERRY FLAMBÉ WITH VANILLA ICE CREAM

184

Place the orange juice, brown sugar, and zest in a medium saucepan over medium-high heat and bring to a boil. Decrease the heat to medium-low and simmer for 5 minutes. • Add the strawberries and cook for 1 minute. • Divide the strawberries among 6–8 serving bowls and drizzle some cooking syrup over the top. • Heat the brandy in a small saucepan over medium-low heat until warm. • Top the strawberries with 1–2 scoops of vanilla ice cream. Pour the brandy over the strawberries and carefully set alight. • Serve immediately.

2 **cups (500 ml) freshly squeezed orange juice, strained**

1 **cup (200 g) firmly packed light brown sugar**

1 **teaspoon finely grated orange zest**

2 **pounds (1 kg) strawberries, halved**

1 **cup (250 ml) brandy**

Vanilla Ice Cream, homemade (see page 124) or storebought, to serve

Serves: 6–8
Preparation: 15 minutes
Cooking: 10 minutes
Level: 1

EXOTIC FRUIT SALAD

Combine the mango, papaya, pineapple, banana, kiwifruits, peach, and blueberries in a large serving bowl. Add the kumquats. Scoop out the seeds and juice of the passion fruit with a teaspoon over a small bowl. Pass through a strainer, discard the seeds, and add to the bowl. • Mix the lime zest, lime juice, rum, and coconut in a small bowl then stir gently into the fruit salad. Leave to macerate for 30 minutes. • Meanwhile, make the cashew cream. Combine the cashews and juice concentrate in a blender and liquidize until smooth and thick, 3–4 minutes. Transfer the cream to a serving bowl. • Serve the fruit salad with a spoonful of cashew cream for each person.

1   **large mango, peeled, pitted, and cubed**

1   **papaya, peeled, seeded, and cubed**

1   **medium pineapple, peeled, cored, and cut into small pieces**

1   **banana, sliced**

2   **kiwifruits, peeled and cut into small pieces**

1   **large peach, peeled, pitted, and cubed**

2   **cup (300 g) fresh blueberries**

2   **kumquats, halved**

3   **passion fruit**

Finely grated zest of 1 lime

Freshly squeezed juice of 2 limes

2   **tablespoons white rum**

1   **tablespoon shredded (desiccated) coconut**

Cashew Cream

1½ **cups (250 g) cashew nuts**

1   **tablespoon apple juice concentrate**

Serves: 4–6
Preparation: 20 minutes + 30 minutes to macerate
Level: 1

CHAMPAGNE STRAWBERRIES

Place the strawberries in a medium glass bowl and drizzle with the orange-flavored liqueur. Pour 1 cup (250 ml) of champagne into the bowl. Cover and chill in the refrigerator for 2 hours. • Divide the strawberries and their juices evenly among 4–6 serving glasses. Pour the remaining champagne over the top and serve.

188

3   cups (450 g) strawberries, halved

¼   cup (60 ml) orange-flavored liqueur

2   cups (500 ml) chilled, very dry champagne

Serves: 4–6
Preparation: 10 minutes
    + 2 hours to chill
Level: 1

■ ■ ■ *These strawberries are perfect for elegant celebrations. Simple to prepare, they can be made ahead of time. They are especially suited to times when you have to serve large numbers of people; just multiply the ingredients to suit.*

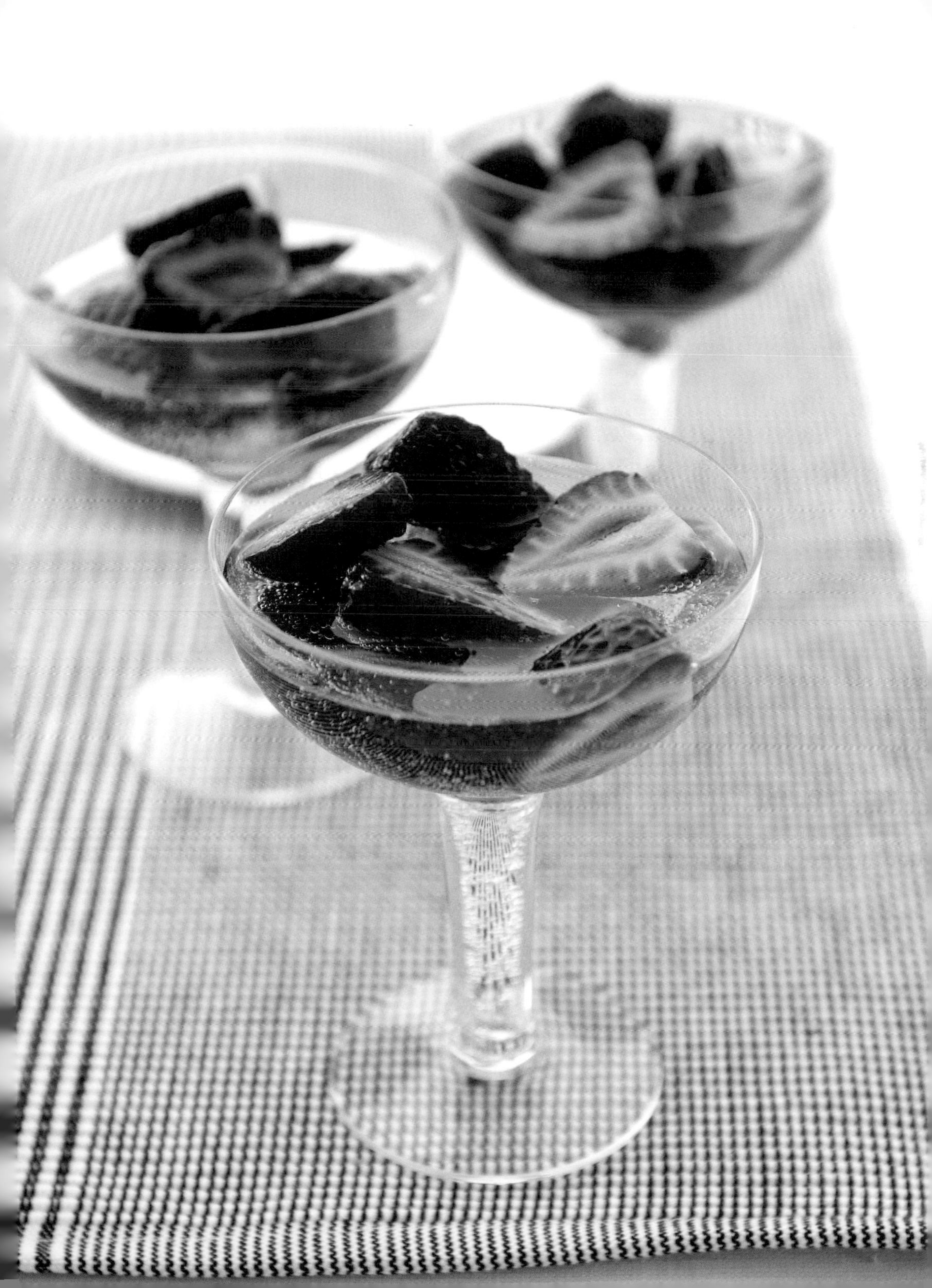

FRESH FRUIT SALAD WITH LEMON SYRUP

190

Put the lemon juice, water, and sugar in a small saucepan. Bring to a boil then simmer over low heat for 2 minutes. Let cool to room temperature.
• Place the bananas, pineapple, and strawberries in a large bowl. Cut the passion fruit in half and scoop the pulp and seeds into the bowl. Drizzle with the syrup and toss gently. • Chill in the refrigerator for 1–2 hours. Sprinkle with the coconut just before serving.

⅓ cup (90 ml) freshly squeezed lemon juice
⅓ cup (90 ml) water
2 tablespoons sugar
2 bananas, sliced
½ small pineapple, peeled and cut into chunks
2 cups (300 g) strawberries, sliced
4 passion fruit
3 tablespoons shredded (desiccated) coconut

Serves: 6
Preparation: 15 minutes
    + 1–2 hours to chill
Cooking: 2 minutes
Level: 1

FRESH FRUIT WITH CHOCOLATE FONDUE

192

Cut the larger pieces of fruit into bite-sized chunks. If using apple, pear, or banana, immerse the chunks in water and lemon juice for a few seconds to prevent the flesh from browning, then dry carefully. • Arrange the fruit in an attractive bowl or serving dish. • Melt the chocolate in a double-boiler over barely simmering water. Add the cream, butter, and sugar and mix thoroughly. Make sure that the sugar dissolves completely into the chocolate and is smooth. • Pour the chocolate mixture into a fondue pot and keep warm over the flame. Stir in the rum. • Place bowls filled with the almonds, hazelnuts, and coconut on the table, so that diners can dip their pieces of fruit into them, after having dipped them in the chocolate sauce.

2 **pounds (1 kg) mixed fresh seasonal fruit (strawberries, grapes, bananas, apples, apricots, peaches, figs, plums, pears, etc.)**

2 **cups (500 ml) water**

Freshly squeezed juice of 1 lemon

1 **pound (500 g) dark chocolate, chopped**

1 **cup (250 ml) light (single) cream**

¼ **cup (60 g) butter**

4 **tablespoons sugar**

3 **tablespoons dark rum**

⅓ **cup (50 g) almonds, toasted and chopped**

⅓ **cup (50 g) hazelnuts, toasted and chopped**

½ **cup (50 g) shredded (desiccated) coconut**

Serves: 10–12
Preparation: 15 minutes
Cooking: 15 minutes
Level: 1

■ ■ ■ *Fruit and chocolate go very well together. You can vary the types of fruit according to the season. For best results, always choose fresh, in-season fruit, preferably bought from a farmers' market which sells locally grown, organic produce.*

MELON SALAD WITH MINT & GINGER SYRUP

194

Heat the water, sugar, and ginger in a small saucepan over medium heat and bring to a boil. Decrease the temperature to medium-low and simmer for 5 minutes, or until the liquid has reduced to make a thin syrup. Remove from the heat, add the mint, and set aside to cool, about 30 minutes. • Slice the watermelon into 1/4-inch (5-mm) wedges. Slice the cantaloupe and honeydew melons into 1/4-inch (5-mm) strips. • Arrange the melons in a large serving bowl or individual serving plates and drizzle with the mint and ginger syrup.

1   cup (250 ml) water
1/2 cup (100 g) sugar
2   tablespoons candied (glacé) ginger, finely chopped
1/2 cup (25 g) finely chopped fresh mint
1/4 small watermelon
1   small cantaloupe (rock) melon, peeled, halved, and seeded
1   small honeydew melon, peeled, halved, and seeded

Serves: 6-8
Preparation: 15 minutes
    + 30 minutes to cool
Cooking: 5–10 minutes
Level: 1

BERRY FRUIT SALAD

196

Combine the wine, sugar, lemon zest, and clove in a small saucepan. Bring to a boil then simmer until the sugar is dissolved, 1–2 minutes. Remove from the heat and let cool a little. • Place the strawberries, raspberries, blackberries, and blackcurrants in a serving bowl. Pour the warm syrup over the top. Let cool to room temperature, about 1 hour. • Chill in the refrigerator for 1–2 hours. Remove the clove before serving.

1¼ cups (300 ml) dry white wine

¼ cup (50 g) sugar

1 teaspoon finely grated lemon zest

1 clove

2 cups (300 g) strawberries, sliced

2 cups (300 g) raspberries

1 cup (150 g) blackberries

1 cup (120 g) blackcurrants

Serves: 6
Preparation: 10 minutes + 2–3 hours to cool and chill
Cooking: 1–2 minutes
Level: 1

■ ■ ■ *Use any combination of fresh, in-season berries to make this salad.*

GOOSEBERRY FOOL

198

Place the gooseberries in a medium saucepan and add ⅓ cup (70 g) of sugar and the water. Simmer over low heat until the gooseberries burst their skins and are soft, 5–10 minutes. Leave to cool. • Transfer to a food processor and process until smooth. Taste the purée and add more sugar if needed. • Whip the cream until soft peaks form, then fold it into the custard. • Lightly fold in almost all the gooseberry purée (reserve a little to garnish) so that the fool is marbled. • Spoon the mixture into small serving glasses and chill in the refrigerator for 1–2 hours. • Garnish each portion with the reserved gooseberry purée just before serving.

14 **ounces (400 g) gooseberries, topped and tailed**

⅓ **cup (70 g) sugar, + more, as required**

1 **tablespoon water**

1 **cup (250 ml) heavy (double) cream**

1 **cup (250 ml) Vanilla Crème Anglaise (see page 586)**

Serves: 4–6
Preparation: 15 minutes
   + 1–2 hours to chill
Level: 1

■ ■ ■ *The name "fool" is thought to be derived from the French verb* fouler *(to mash) and has been used since the 17th century for desserts made with puréed fruit folded into cream.*

BLUEBERRY FOOL

Place the blueberries, sugar, and water in a medium saucepan over low heat. Simmer until softened, 5–10 minutes. Remove from the heat and set aside to cool, about 30 minutes. • Whisk the cream in a medium bowl with an electric mixer on high speed until soft peaks form. Add the yogurt and honey and stir to combine. • Place the blueberries in a food processor and blend until puréed. Stir three quarters of the purée into the yogurt mixture. • Pour the blueberry fool into serving glasses and top with the remaining blueberry purée. • Refrigerate until well chilled, 1–2 hours.

4 **cups (600 g) fresh blueberries**

2 **tablespoons sugar**

1 **tablespoon water**

1 **cup (250 ml) heavy (double) cream**

1 **cup (250 ml) plain yogurt**

¼ **cup (60 ml) honey**

Serves: 4–6
Preparation: 15 minutes
    + 30 minutes to cool
    + 1–2 hours to chill
Cooking: 5–10 minutes
Level: 1

■ ■ ■ *Use low-fat yogurt and half-and-half cream to prepare a reduced fat version of this healthy dessert.*

LIGHT RHUBARB FOOL

Preheat the oven to 350°F (180°C/gas 4). • Place the rhubarb in a baking pan, sprinkle with the sugar, and place the ginger in among the pieces. Bake, uncovered, for 15–20 minutes, until the rhubarb is tender but the pieces still retain their shape. • Drain the rhubarb, reserving the cooking juices. Transfer the rhubarb to a food processor with 1 tablespoon of the juice. Blend to a thick purée, adding a little more of the reserved juice if needed. Transfer to a bowl and chill in the refrigerator for 1–2 hours. • Empty the yogurt into a bowl, stir until smooth, then fold in half the purée until completely blended. Spoon the mixture into glass dishes. Thin the remaining purée with a little more of the juice and pour it over each serving. • Decorate with strips of ginger, if using, and a little fresh mint. Chill in the refrigerator until ready to serve.

1   **pound (500 g) rhubarb, trimmed and sliced 1 inch (2.5 cm) thick**

⅓   **cup (75 g) sugar**

1   **(³⁄₄-inch/2-cm) piece fresh root ginger, peeled and thinly sliced**

1   **(8-ounce/250-g) container plain yogurt**

    Strips of stem ginger preserved in syrup, to decorate (optional)

    Small mint sprigs or leaves, to decorate

Serves: 6–8
**Preparation: 30 minutes
    + 1–2 hours to chill**
Cooking: 15–20 minutes
Level: 2

RED RIPPLE FOOL

Combine the berries in a medium saucepan with the sugar. Bring to a gentle simmer. Remove from the heat when the fruit begins releasing its juices, about 5 minutes. • Strain through a sieve, reserving the juice. Chill the berries and juice separately in the refrigerator for 1–2 hours. • Stir in the vanilla sugar into the berries. • Whisk the cream with the vanilla in a bowl until soft peaks form. Fold into the berries, leaving a rippled effect. • Spoon into a glass bowl. • Drizzle with the reserved berry juice just before serving.

1	**pound (500 g) mixed berries**
3	**tablespoons sugar**
1	**tablespoon vanilla sugar**
1	**cup (250 ml) heavy (double) cream**
¼	**teaspoon vanilla extract (essence)**

Serves: 4
Prep: 10 minutes
    + 1–2 hours to chill
Cooking: 5 minutes
Level: 1

BAKED PLUMS WITH BLUEBERRIES & MASCARPONE

206

Preheat the oven to 400°F (200°C/gas 6). • Place the plums in a shallow baking dish, cut-side up. Sprinkle with the brown sugar, dot with the butter, and drizzle with the wine. Bake on the highest oven rack for 15 minutes. • Sprinkle with the blueberries and bake for 5 more minutes, until the plums are softened and have released their juices. Leave in the dish or divide among four individual serving bowls. • Pour 2–3 tablespoons of the cooking juices into a bowl, add the mascarpone and vanilla sugar, and beat lightly. • Serve the plums and cooking juices hot or at room temperature, topped with the sweetened mascarpone.

12 ripe plums or small nectarines, halved and pitted

2 tablespoons dark brown sugar

2 tablespoons butter

¼ cup (60 ml) dry red wine or black currant juice

1 cup (150 g) fresh blueberries

8 ounces (250 g) mascarpone

2 tablespoons confectioners' (icing) sugar

½ teaspoon vanilla extract (essence)

Serves: 4
Preparation: 10 minutes
Cooking: 20 minutes
Level: 1

SPICED FRUIT COMPOTE

Heat the water, wine, honey, cinnamon stick, star anise, orange zest, and orange juice in a large saucepan over medium-high heat until it reaches boiling point. • Decrease the heat to low and add the dried and fresh fruit to the spiced liquid. Simmer until the fruit is soft, 10–15 minutes. Remove from the heat and let cool to room temperature. • Whisk the crème fraîche or cream and confectioners' sugar in a small bowl until well combined and slightly thickened. (If using heavy cream, beat until soft peaks form). • To serve, place a large scoop of fruit compote into each serving bowl. Top with a dollop of sweetened crème fraîche or cream. Sprinkle with toasted almonds just before serving.

1¼ cups (300 ml) water
1½ cups (375 ml) red wine
¾ cup (180 ml) honey
1 cinnamon stick
1 whole star anise
1 teaspoon finely grated orange zest
¼ cup (60 ml) freshly squeezed orange juice
¾ cup (135 g) dried apricots
¾ cup (135 g) dried figs
¾ cup (135 g) prunes
4 tart apples, such as Granny Smiths, peeled, cored, and cut into wedges
4 pears, peeled, cored, and cut into wedges
⅓ cup (60 g) raisins
1 cup (250 ml) crème fraîche or heavy (double) cream
2 tablespoons confectioners' (icing) sugar
1 cup (150 g) flaked almonds, toasted

Serves: 8–10
Preparation: 15 minutes + 2 hours to cool
Cooking: 10–15 minutes
Level: 1

TURKISH STUFFED FIGS

Stuffed Figs: Steep the tea leaves in the boiling water for 2–3 minutes, allowing the flavor to infuse. Strain the tea into a medium bowl and add the figs. Set aside to plump for 6 hours. • Drain the figs, reserving the liquid for later use. • Combine the walnuts, almonds, and orange zest in a small bowl. Make a small incision in the bottom of each fig using a sharp knife and stuff with the nut mixture. Place the figs, stems facing upward, in an ovenproof dish. • Preheat the oven to 350°F (180°C/gas 4). • Syrup: Combine the reserved tea, rose water, honey, lemon zest, and bay leaves in a small saucepan over medium-high heat and bring to a boil. Decrease the heat to low and simmer for 10 minutes. Pour the hot syrup over the figs. Bake for 20 minutes. • Divide the figs evenly among four serving bowls and top with a dollop of yogurt.

Stuffed Figs

1	teaspoon tea leaves
1½	cups (375 ml) boiling water
8	ounces (250 g) dried figs
2	tablespoons coarsely chopped walnuts
2	tablespoons coarsely chopped almonds
1	teaspoon finely grated orange zest

Syrup

¼	cup (60 ml) rose water
3	tablespoons honey
1	teaspoon finely grated lemon zest
3	bay leaves
¾	cup (180 ml) plain Greek-style yogurt, to serve

Serves: 4
Preparation: 20 minutes
   + 6 hours to plump
Cooking: 35 minutes
Level: 2

APRICOTS EN PAPILLOTE

212

Preheat the oven to 400°F (200°C/gas 6).
• Combine the wine, brown sugar, honey, and cinnamon stick in a saucepan and simmer over low heat until syrupy, about 10 minutes. • Cut out six large pieces of baking parchment to make the packets. • Place two apricot halves in the center of each piece of paper. Pour a little of the syrup over the each one, then sprinkle with the crumbled amaretti cookies, pine nuts, and raisins. Fold the paper over the filling to form an envelope to seal.
• Bake for 15 minutes. • Serve hot, straight from the parchment packets at the table.

1   cup (250 ml) dry white wine

¼   cup (50 g) firmly packed dark brown sugar

2   tablespoons honey

1   (½-inch/2.5-cm) piece cinnamon stick

12   apricots, halved and pitted, with peel

10   amaretti cookies, crumbled

2   tablespoons pine nuts

2   tablespoons raisins

Serves: 6
Preparation: 15 minutes
Cooking: 25 minutes
Level: 1

■ ■ ■ *If liked, serve these hot little parcels with Vanilla or Malaga Ice Cream (see pages 124 and 134). They are also good with whipped cream or crème fraîche.*

GRILLED CARIBBEAN-STYLE FRUITS

Heat a grill pan or griddle on medium-high heat.
• Heat the butter, brown sugar, and rum in a small saucepan over medium-low heat until the sugar has dissolved. • Slice the mangoes lengthwise on either side of the pit to remove the cheeks, cut off the skin, and set aside. Peel the bananas, slice in half lengthwise, and set aside. • Brush the mango, banana, and pineapple with the rum sugar syrup and grill until golden brown, about 3 minutes on each side. • To serve, arrange the fruit on individual serving plates. Pour any remaining rum syrup over the fruit and sprinkle with coconut.

¼ cup (60 g) butter

⅓ cup (70 g) firmly packed dark brown sugar

⅓ cup (90 ml) white rum

2 ripe mangoes

4 small sweet bananas, such as ladyfinger

4 pineapple rings, fresh or canned

Shredded (dessicated) coconut or coconut curls, to garnish

Serves: 4
Preparation: 15 minutes
Cooking: 5–6 minutes
Level: 1

BAKED APPLES

Apples: Remove the core from each apple. Insert the apple corer two or three times, to make a wider hole. Score around the middle of each apple with a sharp knife, so the apples keep their shape. • Preheat the oven to 350°F (180°C/gas 4). Butter a shallow baking dish, small enough for the apples to fit in snugly and not topple over. • Filling: Combine all the filling ingredients in a medium bowl. • Divide the filling evenly among the apples, spooning it into each cavity and piling any excess on top. • To Bake: Stud each apple with 4 cloves, and place in the pan. Pour in the apple juice. Top each apple with 1/2 tablespoon of butter. Sprinkle with the raw sugar. • Bake, uncovered, for 20–30 minutes, basting the apples once or twice. • Combine the lemon juice and honey in a small saucepan and heat gently. Drizzle the apples with the warmed honey and return to the oven for 10 minutes, until puffed up and starting to split open. • Allow to cool for 10 minutes, spooning all the juices from the pan over the top. Serve warm.

■ ■ ■ *If liked, serve these apples with Vanilla Crème Anglaise (see page 586), ice cream (homemade or storebought), or crème fraîche).*

Apples

4   large tart apples (such as Cox, Granny Smith, Greening, or Braeburn)

Filling

2   tablespoons light brown sugar

2   tablespoons seedless raisins or currants

2   tablespoons golden raisins (sultanas)

1   tablespoon finely grated orange zest

2   tablespoons freshly squeezed orange juice

1   tablespoon orange marmalade

1/2   teaspoon ground ginger

1   teaspoon vanilla extract (essence)

To Bake

16   whole cloves, to stud

1/4   cup (60 ml) apple juice or apple brandy

2   tablespoons butter

1   tablespoon raw sugar

     Freshly squeezed juice of 1 lemon

2   tablespoons honey

Serves: 4
Preparation: 30 minutes
Cooking: 30–40 minutes
Level: 1

BAKED GINGER PEARS

Pears: Preheat the oven to 350°F (180°C/gas 4).
• Combine the ginger wine, pear or apple juice, and sugar in a small saucepan over medium heat and cook, stirring occasionally, until the sugar is dissolved. • Peel, halve, and core the pears, leaving the stems on where possible, and place cut-side down in a large baking pan. Pour the ginger liquid over the top. • Bake for 20 minutes. • Topping: Melt the butter and honey in a small saucepan over low heat. Combine the gingersnap cookies, almond meal, oats, cinnamon, nutmeg, and ginger in a medium bowl. Pour in the butter and honey and stir until combined. • Remove the pears from the oven and turn cut side up. Cover each pear with the topping. Return to the baking pan, filling-side up, and bake for 20 more minutes, or until fruit is tender and topping is crisp and golden. • To serve, place two pear halves on each serving plate with a spoon of crème fraîche to the side.

Pears

1	cup (250 ml) green ginger wine
½	cup (125 ml) pear or apple juice
½	cup (100 g) sugar
6	large, firm pears

Topping

⅓	cup (90 g) butter
¼	cup (60 ml) honey
7	gingersnap cookies (gingernuts), coarsely chopped
½	cup (50 g) almond meal
½	cup (50 g) quick-cooking oats
½	teaspoon ground cinnamon
¼	teaspoon ground nutmeg
½	teaspoon ground ginger
½	cup (125 g) crème fraîche or mascarpone

Serves: 6
Preparation: 10 minutes
Cooking: 40 minutes
Level: 1

MERINGUES

MERINGUES WITH RASPBERRY FILLING

Meringues: Preheat the oven to 250°F (130°C/gas ½). Line two baking sheets with parchment paper. Butter and flour the paper. • Mix the superfine sugar, confectioners' sugar, and cornstarch in a bowl. • Beat the egg whites with half the sugar mixture and salt in a large bowl with an electric mixer fitted with a wire whisk at medium speed until soft peaks form. Gradually beat in the remaining sugar mixture until stiff, glossy peaks form. • Spoon the mixture into a pastry bag with a ½-inch (1-cm) tip and pipe sixteen 3-inch (8-cm) spiral disks on the baking sheet. • Bake for 1 hour 30 minutes, until crisp. Turn the oven off and let cool with the door ajar, about 1 hour. • Filling: Heat the cornstarch and a little wine in a medium saucepan. Stir until smooth. Add the remaining wine and ½ cup (100 g) of sugar. Bring to a boil, stirring constantly. Add two cups (300 g) of raspberries and return to a gentle boil. Add the liqueur and simmer, stirring constantly, for 5 minutes. Remove from the heat and let cool. • Whip the cream with the remaining sugar in a large bowl. • Drizzle each of the meringues with a little chocolate. Pipe a border of raspberry cream onto half of the meringues. Spoon the raspberry sauce into the center of each one and then cover with the remaining meringues. Top with the remaining raspberries.

Meringues

1¼	cups (250 g) superfine (caster) sugar
2	cups (300 g) confectioners' (icing) sugar
2	tablespoons cornstarch (cornflour)
8	large egg whites
¼	teaspoon salt

Filling

2	tablespoons cornstarch (cornflour)
½	cup (125 ml) dry red wine
¾	cup (150 g) sugar
3	cups (450 g) raspberries, mashed with a fork
3	tablespoons raspberry liqueur
1½	cups (375 ml) heavy (double) cream
4	ounces (125 g) dark chocolate, melted

Serves: 8
Preparation: 45 minutes
  + 1 hour to cool
Cooking: 1 hour 30 minutes
Level: 2

ETON MESS

Meringues: Preheat the oven to 250°F (130°C/gas ½). Line two cookie sheets with parchment paper. • Beat the egg whites and salt in a large bowl with an electric mixer fitted with a whisk at medium speed until soft peaks form. • With the mixer at high speed, gradually add the superfine sugar and lemon juice, beating until stiff, glossy peaks form. • Drop rounded tablespoons of the mixture 1 inch (2.5 cm) apart on the prepared cookie sheets. • Bake for 50–60 minutes, until the meringues are crisp and dry to the touch, rotating the sheets halfway through for even baking. • Turn the oven off and leave the meringues for 30 minutes. Transfer to racks to cool. Don't worry if the meringues are still a bit soft inside. • Filling: Combine a little less than half the strawberries with the confectioners' sugar in a food processor and process until smooth.
• Whip the cream until it stands in soft peaks.
• To serve, break the meringues into pieces. Put the pieces in a large bowl, add the halved strawberries, and gently stir in the cream. Fold in 2–3 tablespoons of the strawberry purée. Pile the mixture into a glass bowl or individual dishes and top with the remaining purée. Serve immediately.

Meringues

2 large egg whites
⅛ teaspoon salt
½ cup (100 g) superfine (caster) sugar
¼ teaspoon freshly squeezed lemon juice

Filling

1 pound (500 g) strawberries, halved
1 tablespoon confectioners' (icing) sugar
1 cup (250 ml) light (single) cream

Serves: 4–6
Preparation: 20 minutes
  + 30 minutes to rest
Cooking: 50–60 minutes
Level: 1

■ ■ ■ *This strawberry and cream dessert is traditionally served at Eton College, the famous English school. No one knows if the broken meringues were originally the result of an accident, but they are certainly a great help to inexperienced meringue makers! With storebought meringues, you can whip up this dessert in no time.*

MERINGUES WITH BLUEBERRY CREAM

Meringues: Preheat oven to 300°F (150°C/gas 2). Line two baking sheets with parchment paper. Mark twelve 3-inch (8-cm) circles, as a guide for the meringues. Turn pencil-side down. • Beat the egg whites in a large bowl with an electric mixer fitted with a whisk until soft peaks form. • Gradually beat in the superfine sugar until the mixture is thick and glossy. • Spread the meringue within the pencil circles on the prepared baking sheets. • Bake for 40 minutes, until crisp. Turn the oven off. Let the meringues cool for about 1 hour with the door slightly ajar. • **Filling:** Combine the liqueur and half the blueberries in a large bowl. Mash a little using a fork. Add the remaining blueberries and cream and fold them in. • Place six meringues on individual serving plates. Spread with blueberry cream and top with the remaining meringues. • Serve at once.

4   **large egg whites**

1   **cup (250 g) superfine (caster) sugar**

2   **tablespoons frangelico (hazelnut liqueur)**

1½   **cups (375 g) fresh blueberries**

2   **cups (500 ml) heavy (double) cream, lightly whipped**

Serves: 6
Preparation: 25 minutes
  + 1 hour to cool
Cooking: 40 minutes
Level: 1

CHOCOLATE PAVLOVAS

228

Chocolate Pavlovas: Preheat the oven to 350°F (180°C/gas 4). • Line two large cookie sheets with parchment paper. • Beat the egg whites in a medium bowl with an electric mixer fitted with a whisk attachment on high speed until they begin to foam. Gradually add the superfine sugar, whisking constantly until stiff peaks form. • Combine the vinegar, vanilla, and cornstarch in a small bowl and add to egg whites, beating until thick and glossy. • Spread six 4-inch (10-cm) meringue disks onto the prepared sheets, smoothing with a spatula or palette knife. • Decrease the oven temperature to 250°F (130°C/gas $1/2$) and bake for 25 minutes. Turn the oven off and leave the meringues until they have cooled, at least 1 hour. • Topping: Beat the cream in a small bowl with an electric mixer fitted with a whisk until soft peaks form. • Spoon the cream onto the cooled meringues and spread with the back of a spoon. Pile the honeycomb on top. • Serve immediately.

Chocolate Pavlovas

4	large egg whites
1¼	cups (250 g) superfine (caster) sugar
1	teaspoon white vinegar
1	teaspoon vanilla extract (essence)
1	tablespoon cornstarch (cornflour)
1½	tablespoons unsweetened cocoa powder

Topping

1½	cups (375 ml) heavy (double) cream
2	chocolate-coated honeycomb bars, or other chocolate coated toffee candy bars, coarsely chopped

Serves: 6
Preparation: 20 minutes
+ 1 hour to cool
Cooking: 25 minutes
Level: 1

MERINGUE CAKES WITH CHOCOLATE MINT SAUCE

Meringue Cakes: Preheat the oven to 250°F (130°C/gas 1/2). • Line a baking sheet with parchment paper and mark eight 5-inch (13-cm) circles on the paper. • Cook 1 cup (200 g) of sugar and water in a saucepan over medium heat until the sugar has dissolved. Set aside to cool. • Beat the egg whites and salt in a large bowl with an electric mixer at medium speed until frothy. • With mixer at high speed, beat in the remaining sugar and sugar syrup until stiff, glossy peaks form. • Spoon the mixture into a pastry bag with a 1/2-inch (1-cm) tip and pipe the mixture into eight spiral disks on the paper. • Bake for about 2 hours, or until crisp. • Turn off the oven and let cool with the door ajar, about 1 hour. • Carefully remove the paper.

Chocolate Mint Sauce: Mix the egg yolks, sugar, vanilla, cornstarch, and milk in a saucepan. • Cook over low heat, stirring constantly, until the mixture thickens. Set aside to cool. • Stir the peppermint extract and food coloring into the sauce and spoon onto 4 dessert plates. • Place a meringue on each plate. Spread with chocolate ice cream. Top with a second meringue. • Dust with the cocoa.

Meringue Cakes

1 1/4 cups (250 g) superfine (caster) sugar
5 tablespoons water
6 large egg whites
1/8 teaspoon salt

Chocolate Mint Sauce

4 large egg yolks
1/3 cup (70 g) sugar
1 teaspoon vanilla extract (essence)
1 teaspoon cornstarch (cornflour)
1 cup (250 ml) milk
2 teaspoons peppermint extract
1 teaspoon green food coloring
1 cup (250 ml) chocolate ice cream, softened
Unsweetened cocoa powder, to dust

Serves: 4
Preparation: 30 minutes + 1 hour to cool
Cooking: 2 hours
Level: 2

MERINGUE BASKETS WITH STRAWBERRIES & MASCARPONE

Meringues: Preheat the oven to 250°F (130°C/gas ½). • Line a baking sheet with parchment paper. Butter and flour the paper. • Mix the sugar and confectioners' sugar in a medium bowl. • Beat the egg whites with half the sugar mixture and the salt in a large bowl with an electric mixer on high speed until stiff, glossy peaks form. Gradually beat in the remaining sugar mixture, 1 tablespoon at a time. • Spoon the mixture into a pastry bag with a ½-inch (1-cm) tip and pipe four 3-inch (8-cm) spiral disks on the baking sheet. Finish each circle with 3 rounds of meringue to form little baskets. • Bake for about 1 hour and 30 minutes, or until crisp. • Turn the oven off and let the meringues cool in the oven with the door ajar, about 1 hour. Carefully remove the paper. • Filling: Place the mascarpone and sugar in a small bowl and beat until smooth. Stir in the kirsch and lemon zest. • Divide most of the strawberries among the four meringue "baskets." Reserve a few to garnish. • Fold the cream into the mascarpone mixture and spoon over the strawberries. • Top with the reserved strawberries and serve.

Meringues

½ cup (100 g) sugar

⅔ cup (100 g) confectioners' (icing) sugar

3 large egg whites

¼ teaspoon salt

Filling

1 cup (250 g) mascarpone

¼ cup (50 g) sugar

2 tablespoons kirsch

1 tablespoon finely grated lemon zest

2 cups (300 g) strawberries, sliced

½ cup (125 ml) heavy (double) cream, whipped

Serves: 4
Preparation: 30 minutes + 1 hour to cool
Cooking: 1 hour 30 minutes
Level: 2

MERINGUES WITH ROSE CREAM

Meringues: Preheat the oven to 250°F (130°C/gas ½). • Line two baking sheets with parchment paper. • Combine the egg whites, confectioners' sugar, and salt in a large bowl. Beat with an electric mixer fitted with a whisk until soft peaks form. Gradually beat in the sugar, 1 tablespoon at a time, until stiff, glossy peaks form. Fold in the vanilla. • Spoon the meringue into a piping bag with a plain tip and pipe (or use a spoon) to place golf ball size blobs on the baking sheets, spacing about 1½ inches (4 cm) apart. • Bake until crisp and dry, about 1 hour. Turn off the oven and let cool completely with the door ajar, about 1 hour. • Filling: Beat the cream and confectioners' sugar in a medium bowl until stiff. Fold in the food coloring. • Spread half the meringues with cream and press together in pairs. Serve at once, garnishing the dish with fresh mint leaves, if liked.

Meringues

4   large egg whites

1   tablespoon confectioners' (icing) sugar

     Pinch of salt

1   cup (200 g) sugar

½   teaspoon vanilla extract (essence)

Filling

1   cup (250 ml) heavy (double) cream)

2   tablespoons confectioners' (icing) sugar

½   teaspoon red food coloring

     Candied flowers, to serve (optional)

Serves: 4-6
Preparation: 20 minutes + 1 hour to cool
Cooking: 1 hour
Level: 1

ALMOND DACQUOISE WITH APRICOT FILLING

Dacquoise: Preheat the oven to 300°F (150°C/gas 1). • Line two baking sheets with parchment paper and mark three 9-inch (23-cm) circles on them. Turn pencil-side down. • **Step 1:** Beat the egg whites and salt in a bowl with an electric mixer at medium speed until frothy. With the mixer at high speed, gradually add the sugar, beating until stiff, glossy peaks form. Use a spatula to fold in the almonds and cornstarch. **Step 2:** Spoon the meringue into a pastry bag fitted with a 1/2-inch (1-cm) plain tip. Pipe the meringue in a spiral to fill the circles. • Bake for 80–90 minutes, until crisp. Cool the disks for 10 minutes with the oven door ajar. Transfer to racks. Carefully remove the paper and let cool completely, about 50 minutes. • Filling: Beat the egg yolks and sugar in a large bowl with an electric mixer at high speed until pale and thick. • Bring the milk to a boil in a large saucepan over medium heat. Slowly beat the milk into the egg mixture. Return to the saucepan. Simmer over low heat, stirring constantly, until the mixture lightly coats a metal spoon. Gradually stir in the butter and almond extract. Transfer to a bowl. Press plastic wrap (cling film) directly on the surface, and refrigerate until chilled, at least 1 hour. • Reserve 3–4 apricot halves to decorate and coarsely chop the rest. • **Step 3:** Place a dacquoise on a plate and spread with one-third of the filling. Top with another dacquoise and spread with one-third of the filling. Place the remaining dacquoise on top. Spread with the remaining filling. Sprinkle with the almonds and top with the reserved apricots. Dust with confectioners' sugar.

Dacquoise

6 large egg whites
1/4 teaspoon salt
1 1/2 cups (300 g) granulated sugar
1 1/2 cups (225 g) finely ground almonds
1 tablespoon cornstarch (cornflour)

Filling

5 large egg yolks
1/2 cup (100 g) sugar
1/2 cup (125 ml) milk
1 cup (250 g) butter, softened and cut in cubes
1 teaspoon almond extract (essence)
1 (15-ounce/450-g) can apricot halves, drained
3/4 cup (100 g) flaked almonds
2 tablespoons confectioners' (icing) sugar

Serves: 6–8
Preparation: 30 minutes + 1 hour to cool and chill
Cooking: 1 hour 30 minutes
Level: 2

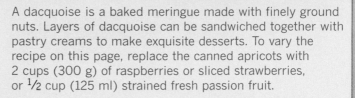

A dacquoise is a baked meringue made with finely ground nuts. Layers of dacquoise can be sandwiched together with pastry creams to make exquisite desserts. To vary the recipe on this page, replace the canned apricots with 2 cups (300 g) of raspberries or sliced strawberries, or $1/2$ cup (125 ml) strained fresh passion fruit.

1. BEAT the egg whites and salt in a bowl with an electric mixer until frothy. Gradually add the sugar, beating until stiff, glossy peaks form. Fold in the almonds and cornstarch.

2. SPOON the meringue into a pastry bag fitted with a $1/2$-inch (1-cm) plain tip. Pipe the meringue in a spiral to fill the circles. Bake for 80–90 minutes, until crisp.

3. SPREAD a dacquoise with one-third of the filling. Repeat with the remaining dacquoises and filling.

VACHERIN WITH RED CURRANT CHANTILLY

240

Vacherin: Preheat the oven to 250°F (130°C/gas ½).
• Line a baking sheet with parchment paper and mark two 9-inch (23-cm) circles on the paper.
• Beat the egg whites and brown sugar in a large bowl with an electric mixer at high speed until stiff, glossy peaks form. Add the vanilla. • Spoon the mixture into a pastry bag fitted with a ½-inch (1-cm) tip and pipe into two spiral disks, starting at the center of the circles and filling each one.
• Bake for about 1 hour, or until crisp. Turn off the oven and let cool with the door ajar, about 1 hour.
• Carefully remove the paper. • Filling: Beat the cream, confectioners' sugar, and vanilla in a large bowl until stiff. • Place two-thirds of the cream in a bowl and fold in the mashed red currants. • Place a meringue layer on a serving plate. Spread with the cream. Top with the remaining layer and spread with the remaining cream. • Top with the cream and decorate with the extra red currants.

Vacherin

5   large egg whites

1½   cups (300 g) firmly packed light brown sugar

1   teaspoon vanilla extract

1½   cups (375 ml) heavy (double) cream

2   tablespoons confectioners' (icing) sugar

Filling

2   cups (500 ml) heavy (double) cream

3   tablespoons confectioners' (icing) sugar

½   teaspoon vanilla extract (essence)

1   cup (150 g) fresh red currants, lightly mashed with a fork, + extra whole, to decorate

Serves: 6–8
Preparation: 30 minutes + 1 hour to cool
Cooking: 1 hour
Level: 2

COFFEE LIQUEUR VACHERIN

Vacherin: Preheat the oven to 250°F (130°C/gas ½).
• Line a baking sheet with parchment paper and mark two 9-inch (23-cm) circles on the paper.
• Beat the egg whites in a large bowl with an electric mixer at medium speed until frothy.
• With mixer at high speed, gradually beat in the sugar until stiff, glossy peaks form. Add the coffee liqueur. • Spoon the mixture into a pastry bag fitted with a ½-inch (1-cm) tip and pipe into two spiral disks, starting at the center of the circles and filling each one. • Bake for about 1 hour, or until crisp. Turn off the oven and leave the door ajar until the vacherins are completely cool, about 1 hour.
• Carefully remove the paper. • Coffee Cream: Beat the cream, confectioners' sugar, and the coffee liqueur in a large bowl with mixer at high speed until stiff. • Place a meringue layer on a serving plate. Spread with three-quarters of the cream. Top with the remaining meringue layer. Spoon the remaining cream into a pastry bag and decorate the top of the vacherin with 8–10 rosettes. Top each rosette with a coffee bean.

Vacherin

5	large egg whites
1½	cups (300 g) sugar
1	tablespoons coffee liqueur

Coffee Cream

1½	cups (375 ml) heavy (double) cream
2	tablespoons coffee liqueur
2	tablespoons confectioners' (icing) sugar
	Whole coffee beans, to decorate

Serves: 6–8
Preparation: 30 minutes + 1 hour to cool
Cooking: 1 hour
Level: 2

CARAMEL VACHERIN

244

Vacherin: Preheat the oven to 250°F (130°C/gas ½).
• Line a baking sheet with parchment paper and
mark two 9-inch (23-cm) circles on the paper.
• Beat the egg whites in a large bowl with an
electric mixer at medium speed until frothy.
• With mixer at high speed, gradually add both
sugars, beating until stiff, glossy peaks form.
• Add the vanilla. • Spoon the mixture into a pastry
bag fitted with a ½-inch (1-cm) tip and pipe the
mixture into two spiral disks, starting at the center
of the circles and filling each one. • Bake for about
1 hour, or until crisp. Turn off the oven and leave the
door ajar until the meringues are completely cool.
• Carefully remove the paper. • Filling: Beat the
cream and confectioners' sugar in a large bowl
with mixer at high speed until stiff. • Place a
meringue layer on a serving plate. Spread with
three-quarters of the cream. Top with the remaining
meringue layer and spread with the remaining
cream. • Caramel Sauce: Combine the butter,
cream, brown sugar, and vanilla in a small saucepan
over medium heat. Cook, stirring constantly, until
the sugar dissolves. Increase the heat to high and
boil for 2 minutes. • Remove from the heat and set
aside to cool and thicken. • Drizzle the caramel
sauce over the top.

Vacherin

5	large egg whites
¾	cup (150 g) sugar
¾	cup (150 g) firmly packed light brown sugar
1	teaspoon vanilla extract (essence)

Filling

1½	cups (375 ml) heavy (double) cream
2	tablespoons confectioners' (icing) sugar
1	quantity caramel sauce (or use caramel ice cream topping (plastic squeeze bottle)

Caramel Sauce

¼	cup (60 g) butter
¼	cup (60 ml) cream
½	cup (100 g) firmly packed brown sugar
½	teaspoon vanilla extract (essence)

Serves: 6–8
Preparation: 30 minutes
    + 1 hour to cool
Cooking: 1 hour
Level: 2

CHOCOLATE VACHERIN

Vacherin: Preheat the oven to 250°F (130°C/gas ¹/₂).
• Line a baking sheet with parchment paper and
mark two 9-inch (23-cm) circles on the paper.
• Beat the egg whites in a large bowl with an
electric mixer at medium speed until frothy.
• With mixer at high speed, gradually add the
sugar, beating until stiff, glossy peaks form. • Fold
in the cocoa and vanilla. • Spoon the mixture into
a pastry bag fitted with a ¹/₂-inch (1-cm) tip and
pipe the mixture into two spiral disks. • Bake for
about 1 hour, or until crisp. • Turn off the oven and
let cool. • Carefully remove the paper. • To Serve:
Place a meringue layer on a serving plate. Spread
with three-quarters of the Chantilly. Top with the
remaining meringue layer. • Top with the remaining
Chantilly. Sprinkle with the chocolate.

Vacherin

5   large egg whites

1½ cups (300 g) sugar

¹/₃ cup (50 g)
    unsweetened cocoa
    powder

1   teaspoon vanilla
    extract (essence)

To Serve

2   cups (500 ml)
    Chantilly Cream
    (see page 600)

2   ounces (60 g) dark
    chocolate, finely grated

Serves: 6-8
Preparation: 30 minutes
    + 1 hour to cool
Cooking: 1 hour
Level: 2

CHOCOLATE HAZELNUT MERINGUE LAYER CAKE

248

Meringue: Preheat the oven to 250°F (130°C/gas ½). • Line two baking sheets with parchment paper and mark four 9-inch (23-cm) circles on the paper. • Cook the sugar and water in a saucepan over medium heat until the sugar has dissolved. • Beat the egg whites and salt in a large bowl with an electric mixer at high speed until frothy. With mixer at high speed, add the hot sugar mixture and confectioners' sugar, beating until stiff, glossy peaks form. • Spoon the mixture into a pastry bag with a ½-inch (1-cm) tip and pipe into four spiral disks, starting at the center and filling the circles. • Bake for about 2 hours, or until crisp. • Turn off the oven and leave the meringues in the oven with the door slightly ajar until completely cool, about 1 hour. • Carefully remove the paper. • Filling: Beat the cream in a large bowl with an electric mixer at high speed until stiff. • Fold the chocolate cream into the beaten cream. • Place a meringue round on a serving plate and spread with one-third of the filling. Top with the another round of meringue and cover with one-third of the filling. Top with another round of meringue and spread with the remaining filling. Crumble the fourth meringue over the cake. • Serve immediately.

Meringue

1   cup (200 g) sugar
½   cup (125 ml) water
5   large egg whites
⅛   teaspoon salt
1⅔ cups (200 g) confectioners' (icing) sugar

Filling

2   cups (500 ml) heavy (double) cream
½   cup (125 g) chocolate hazelnut cream (Nutella), softened

Serves: 6–8
Preparation: 1 hour
    + 1 hour to cool
Cooking: 2 hours
Level: 2

PAVLOVA WITH FRESH FRUIT

Pavlova: Preheat the oven to 250°F (130°C/gas ¹/₂).
• Butter a baking sheet. Line with parchment paper.
Drizzle a little water over the paper. • Beat the egg
whites and salt in a large bowl with an electric
mixer at medium speed until frothy. • Gradually
beat in the sugar until stiff, glossy peaks form.
• Beat in the water, cornstarch, vanilla, and the
vinegar. • Spoon the meringue mixture in a circle on
the prepared sheet. Do not spread much; the
meringue will spread as it bakes. • Bake for about
50 minutes, or until crisp and pale gold. Turn the
oven off and leave in the oven with the door ajar
until cold, at least 1 hour. • Carefully remove the
paper. Transfer to a serving plate. • Topping: Beat
the cream, confectioners' sugar, and vanilla in a
medium bowl until stiff. • Spread the cream over
the meringue and decorate with the fruit.

■ ■ ■ *This is a classic dessert from Australia and New
Zealand. It was created in the early 1930s in honor of
the brilliant Russian ballet dancer Anna Pavlova, who
toured the region at that time.*

Pavlova

4	large egg whites
¹/₈	teaspoon salt
1¹/₄	cups (250 g) sugar
2	tablespoons water
1	tablespoon cornstarch (cornflour)
1	teaspoon vanilla extract (essence)
1	teaspoon white vinegar

Topping

1	cup (250 ml) heavy (double) cream
2	tablespoons confectioners' (icing) sugar
1	teaspoon vanilla extract (essence)
	Fresh fruit, to decorate

Serves: 6–8
Preparation: 20 minutes
  + 1 hour to cool
Cooking: 50 minutes
Level: 1

MERINGUE WITH CHOCOLATE & CANDIED CHESTNUTS

252

Meringue: Preheat the oven to 250°F (130°C/gas ¹/₂) • Cut out four 8-inch (20-cm) rounds of parchment paper and place on two baking sheets. • Mix the sugar and confectioners' sugar in a medium bowl. • Beat the egg whites with half the sugar mixture and the salt in a large bowl with an electric mixer at medium speed until stiff, glossy peaks form. Gradually beat in the remaining sugar mixture. • Spread a quarter of the meringue onto each parchment round. • Bake for about 1 hour 30 minutes, or until crisp and pale gold. • Turn the oven off and let cool with the door ajar for at least an hour. Carefully remove the paper. • Filling: Beat the cream and vanilla in a large bowl until stiff. • Fold in the chocolate chips and candied chestnuts. • Place one meringue round on a serving plate. Spread with one-third of the cream. Top with another meringue round and spread with one-third of the cream. Top with another round and spread with the remaining cream. • Crumble the remaining meringue round over the top.

Meringue

1	cup (200 g) sugar
²/₃	cup (100 g) confectioners' (icing) sugar
6	large egg whites
¹/₄	teaspoon salt

Filling

2	cups (500 ml) heavy (double) cream
¹/₂	teaspoon vanilla extract (essence)
¹/₂	cup (90 g) dark chocolate chips
6	candied chestnuts (marrons glacé), crumbled or coarsely chopped

Serves: 6-8
Preparation: 30 minutes
  1 hour to cool
Cooking: 1 hour 30 minutes
Level: 2

■ ■ ■ *The candied chestnuts, or marrons glacé, used to decorate this layer cake are available from specialty food stores. If preferred, substitute with coarsely grated dark chocolate.*

BAKED ALMOND MERINGUE CAKE

254

Filling: Crumble the almond paste into a medium saucepan. Add the water and milk. Simmer over low heat until the almond paste dissolves. Add the almond extract and gelatin and stir until dissolved. Remove from the heat and set aside to cool until it is just beginning to set around the edges, 15–20 minutes. • Beat the cream in a large bowl until stiff. Fold the almond mixture into the cream. • Line an 8-quart (2-liter) dome-shaped pudding mold with plastic wrap (cling film) and line with slices of cake. Brush with the rum mixture and fill with half the almond filling. Cover with a layer of cake and brush with rum mixture. Fill with the remaining almond filling and top with a layer of cake. Freeze for 12 hours. • Preheat the oven to 350°F (180°C/gas 4). • Meringue: Beat the egg whites, sugar, and salt in a large bowl with an electric mixer fitted with a whisk at high speed until stiff peaks form. • Unmold the cake onto an ovenproof plate, dome-side up. Spread the meringue over the cake and sprinkle with the almonds. • Bake for 5 minutes, or until the meringue is pale gold. Serve immediately.

Filling

8	ounces (250 g) almond paste (marzipan)
3/4	cup (180 ml) water
1/4	cup (60 ml) milk
1/2	teaspoon almond extract (essence)
2	tablespoons unflavored gelatin powder
1½	cups (375 ml) heavy (double) cream

1	Basic Sponge Cake (see page 592), thinly sliced
3	tablespoons rum mixed with 3 tablespoons water

Meringue

4	large egg whites
1/2	cup (100 g) sugar
1/8	teaspoon salt
2	tablespoons slivered almonds

Serves: 8-10
Preparation: 1 hour
+ 12 hours to freeze
Cooking: 5 minutes
Level: 3

RASPBERRY MERINGUE ROULADE

Roulade: Preheat the oven to 325°F (170°C/gas 3).
• Line a jelly-roll pan with parchment paper. Butter the paper. • Beat the egg whites in a large bowl with an electric mixer fitted with a whisk at high speed until soft peaks form. Gradually beat in half the superfine sugar. Beat in the remaining superfine sugar until stiff, glossy peaks form. Fold in the cornstarch and lemon juice. • Spread the meringue evenly in the prepared pan. Bake for 20 minutes, or until pale golden. Let cool for about 1 hour. • Place another sheet of parchment paper on a work surface and dust with confectioners' sugar and cocoa powder, reserving some for later. Invert the baked meringue and its paper onto the parchment. Carefully remove the paper (if it sticks, brush sparingly with water). • Filling: Beat the cream in a bowl until stands in soft peaks. Spread over the meringue with a palette knife. Sprinkle the raspberries and chocolate evenly over the cream. Use the paper to help you roll up the meringue from the short end. Lift one edge of the paper beneath the meringue and as it comes up, gently roll it over. Dust with the remaining sugar and cocoa. • Ease the roulade seam-side down onto a serving dish and refrigerate until ready to serve.

Roulade

6   large egg whites

1¼   cups (250 g) superfine (caster) sugar

1   tablespoon cornstarch (cornflour)

1   teaspoon freshly squeezed lemon juice, strained

2   tablespoons confectioners' (icing) sugar, for dusting

2   tablespoons unsweetened cocoa powder, to dust

Filling

1   cup (250 ml) heavy (double) cream

1½   cups (375 g) fresh raspberries

2–3 tablespoons coarsely grated dark chocolate

Serves: 6
Preparation: 40 minutes
    + 1 hour to cool
    + 5 hours to chill
Cooking: 30 minutes
Level: 3

■ ■ ■ *A meringue roulade makes a superb dessert, although it is not especially easy to make. However, practice makes perfect, and you can also recycle the meringue as Eton Mess (see page 224)!*

LAYER
CAKES
& ROLLS

BASIC GÉNOISE

Preheat the oven to 375°F (190°C/gas 5). • Butter one or two 9-inch (23-cm) springform pans. Line with parchment paper. • **Step 1:** Sift the flour and cornstarch into a medium bowl. **Step 2:** Beat the eggs and superfine sugar in a large heatproof bowl. Fit the bowl into a large wide saucepan of barely simmering water over low heat. (Bottom of bowl should not touch the water.) Beat constantly until the sugar has dissolved, the mixture is hot to the touch, and it registers 115°F (45°C) on an instant-read thermometer. Remove from the heat. • Beat the eggs with an electric mixer at high speed until cooled, tripled in volume, and very thick. **Step 3:** Use a large rubber spatula to gradually fold the dry ingredients into the batter. **Step 4:** Place 2 cups of batter in a small bowl and fold in the melted butter and vanilla. Fold the butter mixture into the batter. • Working quickly, spoon the batter into the prepared pan(s). • Bake for 20–30 minutes for two pans, and 30–40 minutes for one pan, or until golden brown, the cake shrinks from the pan sides, and a toothpick inserted into the center comes out clean. • Cool the cakes in the pans for 5 minutes. • Loosen and remove the pan sides. Invert the cake onto a rack. Loosen and remove the pan bottom. Carefully remove the paper. Turn the cake top-side up and let cool completely.

⅔ cup (100 g) **cake flour**

⅔ cup (100 g) **cornstarch (cornflour)**

6 **large eggs**

¾ cup (150 g) **superfine (caster) sugar**

⅓ cup (90 g) **butter, melted and cooled slightly**

1 teaspoon **vanilla extract (essence)**

Serves: 8–10
Preparation: 25 minutes
Cooking: 20–40 minutes
Level: 2

A Génoise is a classic French sponge cake. It is the basis of many cakes and desserts. It is said to have been made first in the 19th century by the Parisian pastry cook, Chiboust, who also invented the delicious Saint Honoré Gâteau. Two cakes may be sliced into two layers each. The larger cake may be sliced into three layers.

1. SIFT the flour and cornstarch into a medium bowl.

2. BEAT the eggs and sugar in a large bowl over barely simmering water. Remove from heat and beat until tripled in volume and very thick.

3. USE a large rubber spatula to gradually fold the dry ingredients into the batter.

4. PLACE 2 cups of batter in a small bowl and fold in the melted butter and vanilla. Fold into the batter. Spoon into the baking pans.

SUGAR PLUM DESSERT

Meringue: Preheat the oven to 250°F (130°C/gas ¹/₂). • Line a large baking sheet with parchment paper. • Beat the egg whites and lemon juice in a large bowl with an electric mixer at medium-high speed until soft peaks form. Gradually add the sugar, beating until stiff, glossy peaks form. • Place the meringue in a piping bag and pipe into fingers on the prepared baking sheet. • Bake for 1 hour, or until dry. • Remove from the oven and let cool completely, about 1 hour. • Filling: Poach the plums in the wine in a large saucepan over medium-low heat until softened, 10–15 minutes. • Remove from the heat and let cool. • Bring the milk to a boil in a medium saucepan. • Beat the egg yolks and sugar with an electric mixer on high speed until pale and creamy. • Beat in the cornstarch. • Stir in the hot milk by hand. • Return to the saucepan and cook over low heat until thick. Remove from heat and let cool slightly. • Add the butter and mix well. Set aside to cool. • Drain the plums, reserving the juice. Chop the plums and add to the custard. • Place a layer of cake on a serving dish and drizzle with the plum juice. Spread with half the custard and cover with half the meringue fingers. Top with the remaining custard. Crumble the remaining meringues over the top.

Meringue

6   large egg whites

    Freshly squeezed juice of ¹/₂ lemon

2¹/₂ cups (500 g) sugar

Filling

12   ounces (350 g) red plums, pitted

¹/₂   cup (125 ml) red wine

2   cups (500 ml) milk

3   large egg yolks

1   tablespoon cornstarch (cornflour)

¹/₂   cup (100 g) sugar

¹/₂   cup (125 g) butter

1   Basic Génoise (see page 260) or Basic Sponge Cake (see page 592), cut in half horizontally

Serves: 8–10
Preparation: 45 minutes + 1 hour to cool
Cooking: 1 hour 30 minutes
Level: 3

RED CURRANT & MERINGUE SPONGE

Sponge: Preheat the oven to 300°F (150°C/gas 2).
• Butter and flour two 8-inch (20-cm) springform pans. • Sift the flour, baking powder, and salt into a medium bowl. • Beat the eggs, egg yolks, sugar, and vanilla in a large bowl with an electric mixer at high speed until pale and creamy. • Use a large rubber spatula to fold in the dry ingredients.
• Spoon the batter into the prepared pans. • Bake for about 25 minutes, or until springy to the touch.
• Cool the cakes in the pans for 10 minutes. Loosen and remove the pan sides. • Transfer to racks and let cool completely. • Meringue: With mixer on medium-high speed beat the egg whites and sugar in a large bowl until soft peaks form. • Heat gently in a double boiler over barely simmering water to 160°F (71°C). Remove from the heat and beat until cool and thick. • Topping: Stir the jelly and rum in a bowl until well mixed. • Place a cake layer on a serving plate and spread with half the topping. Spread with one-third of the meringue. Spread the remaining topping over the remaining cake and place on top of the first cake. Spread the remaining meringue over the top and sides of the cake. Sprinkle with the almonds. Use a confectioners' blowtorch to brown the meringue. • Refrigerate for 2 hours before serving.

Sponge

²/₃ cup (100 g) all-purpose (plain) flour

½ teaspoon baking powder

¼ teaspoon salt

3 large eggs + 3 large egg yolks

½ cup (100 g) sugar

1 teaspoon vanilla extract (essence)

Meringue

8 large egg whites

1 cup (200 g) sugar

Topping

1½ cups (375 g) red currant jelly

1 tablespoon rum

½ cup (60 g) coarsely chopped almonds, to decorate

Serves: 8–10
Preparation: 45 minutes
+ 2 hours to chill
Cooking: 25 minutes
Level: 3

CREAM SPONGE WITH PASSION FRUIT FROSTING

Cream Sponge: Preheat the oven to 375°F (190°C/gas 5). • Butter two 8-inch (20-cm) round cake pans. Line with parchment paper. • Combine the cornstarch, flour, baking powder, and salt in a small bowl. • Beat the egg yolks and sugar in a large bowl with an electric mixer on high speed until pale and creamy. • Use a large rubber spatula to fold in the dry ingredients. • With mixer at high speed, beat the egg whites in a large clean bowl until stiff peaks form. Fold them into the batter. • Spoon half the batter into each of the prepared pans. • Bake for 20–25 minutes, or until a toothpick inserted into the center comes out clean. • Cool the cakes in the pans for 5 minutes. Turn out onto racks. Carefully remove the paper and let cool completely. • Passion Fruit Frosting: Beat the confectioners' sugar, passion fruit pulp, and butter in a medium bowl until smooth and well mixed. • Place one cake on a serving plate. Spread with the Chantilly Cream. Top with the remaining cake. Spread with the frosting.

Cream Sponge

3/4 cup (125 g) cornstarch (cornflour)

3 tablespoons all-purpose (plain) flour

1/2 teaspoon baking powder

1/4 teaspoon salt

4 large eggs, separated

3/4 cup (150 g) sugar

2 cups (500 ml) Chantilly Cream (see page 600)

Passion Fruit Frosting

1 1/2 cups (225 g) confectioners' (icing) sugar

6 tablespoons passion fruit pulp

1 tablespoon butter, melted

Serves: 8–10
Preparation: 30 minutes
Cooking: 20–25 minutes
Level: 2

CHOCOLATE SPONGE WITH CHANTILLY

Preheat the oven to 375°F (190°C/gas 5). • Butter two 8-inch (20-cm) round cake pans. Line with parchment paper. • Combine the flour, cocoa, baking powder, and salt in a medium bowl. • Beat the egg yolks and sugar in a large bowl with an electric mixer at high speed until pale and creamy. • With mixer at low speed, gradually beat in the dry ingredients, alternating with the milk. • With mixer at high speed, beat the egg whites in a large clean bowl until stiff peaks form. Use a spatula to fold them into the batter. • Spoon half the batter into each of the prepared pans. • Bake for about 30 minutes, or until springy to the touch and the cake shrinks from the pan sides. • Cool the cakes in the pans for 5 minutes. Turn out onto racks. Carefully remove the paper and let cool completely. • Place one cake on a serving plate and spread with the Chantilly Cream. Top with the remaining cake. Spread the top and sides with the frosting.

1	cup (150 g) all-purpose (plain) flour
4	tablespoons unsweetened cocoa powder
1	teaspoon baking powder
¼	teaspoon salt
4	large eggs, separated
¾	cup (150 g) sugar
¼	cup (60 ml) milk
2	cups (500 ml) Chantilly Cream (see page 600)
1	quantity Rich Chocolate Frosting (see page 598)

Serves: 6–8
Preparation: 25 minutes
Cooking: 25–30 minutes
Level: 2

MANDARIN CREAM SPONGE

272

Split the sponge cake in half horizontally. Place one layer on a serving plate. • Beat the cream, sugar, and vanilla in a medium bowl with an electric mixer at high speed until stiff. • Brush the cake with half the mandarin or orange juice. Spread with the sweetened cream. Top with the remaining cake layer and brush with the remaining juice. • Warm 1/2 cup (125 ml) of marmalade in a small saucepan over low heat. Brush the cake with the marmalade. Cover with plastic wrap (cling film) and refrigerate for 1 hour. • Decorate with the mandarin segments. Warm the remaining marmalade and brush over the fruit just before serving.

1 Italian Sponge Cake (see page 594)
1 cup (250 ml) heavy (double) cream
2 tablespoons sugar
1 teaspoon vanilla extract (essence)
1 cup (250 ml) freshly squeezed mandarin or orange juice, strained
1/2 cup (125 g) + 2 tablespoons orange marmalade
6-8 mandarins, broken into segments, to decorate

Serves: 8–10
Preparation: 40 minutes + 1 hour to chill
Level: 2

CHOCOLATE CHERRY CREAM GÂTEAU

274

<u>Chocolate Cake:</u> Preheat the oven to 350°F (180°C/gas 4). • Butter two 9-inch (23-cm) springform pans. • Combine the flour and baking powder in a large bowl. • Melt the chocolate and water in a double boiler over barely simmering water. • Beat the butter and brown sugar in a large bowl until creamy. • Add the eggs, one at a time, beating until just blended after each addition. • Gradually beat in the chocolate mixture, sour cream, and dry ingredients. • Spoon half the batter into each of the prepared pans. • Bake for 30–40 minutes, or until a toothpick inserted into the center comes out clean. • Cool on a cake rack for 5 minutes. Loosen the pan sides and invert the cakes onto the rack. Let cool completely. • Split the cakes in half horizontally. • <u>Cherry Cream Filling:</u> Mix the preserves and kirsch in a small bowl. • Beat the cream in a medium bowl with an electric mixer on high speed until stiff. • Place one cake layer on a serving plate. Spread with one-third of the preserves mixture and one-third of the whipped cream. Repeat with the remaining cake layers, finishing with a plain cake layer. Spread the frosting over the top and sides of the cake. Decorate with the cherries.

Chocolate Cake

1²/₃ cups (250 g) all-purpose (plain) flour

1½ teaspoons baking powder

5 ounces (150 g) dark chocolate, chopped

½ cup (125 ml) water

½ cup (125 g) butter

1¼ cups (250 g) firmly packed brown sugar

2 large eggs

½ cup (125 ml) sour cream

Cherry Cream Filling

1 cup (300 g) cherry preserves (jam)

3 tablespoons kirsch

2 cups (500 ml) heavy (double) cream

Candied cherries, to decorate

1 quantity Basic Chocolate Frosting (see page 596)

Serves: 8
Preparation: 30 minutes
Cooking: 30–40 minutes
Level: 2

COFFEE CREAM LAYERED GÂTEAU

Coffee Frosting: Melt the butter with the brown sugar in a medium saucepan over medium heat. Bring to a boil and stir until slightly thickened, 1–2 minutes. • Let cool slightly. • Beat in the coffee-flavored milk and confectioners' sugar until smooth. • Beat the cream in a large bowl with an electric mixer on high speed until stiff. • Place one layer of cake on a serving plate. Spread with one-third of the cream. Top with a layer of cake. Spread the cake with a quarter of the frosting. Cover with another layer of cake and spread with most of the remaining cream. Finish with the remaining cake layer. • Spread the top and sides of the cake with the remaining frosting. • Pipe the remaining cream in rosettes over the cake.

2 **Basic Génoises (see page 260), each baked in 1 pan and cut in half horizontally**

Coffee Frosting

3/4 **cup (125 g) butter**

1 **cup (150 g) brown sugar**

2 **teaspoons instant coffee granules dissolved in 3 tablespoons warm milk**

3 **cups (450 g) confectioners' (icing) sugar**

2 **cups (500 ml) Chantilly Cream (see page 600)**

Serves: 8–12
Preparation: 15 minutes
Cooking: 1–2 minutes
Level: 2

GOLDEN LAYER CAKE

Cake: Preheat the oven to 350°F (180°C/gas 4).
• Butter and flour three 9-inch (23-cm) round cake pans. • Combine the flour, baking soda, and salt in a large bowl. • Beat the butter, sugar, and vanilla in a large bowl until creamy. • Add the eggs, one at a time, beating until just blended after each addition. • Gradually beat in the dry ingredients, alternating with the sour cream. • Spoon one-third of the batter into each of the prepared pans. • Bake for 20–25 minutes, or until a toothpick inserted into the center comes out clean. • Cool the cakes in the pans for 15 minutes. Turn out onto racks to cool completely. • Golden Frosting: Melt the butter in a large saucepan over low heat. Add the brown sugar and milk and simmer for 5 minutes, stirring constantly. Remove from the heat and stir in the vanilla. • Beat in the confectioners' sugar until smooth. Set aside to cool. • Place one cake on a serving plate and spread with some frosting. Top with another cake and spread with frosting. Top with the remaining cake. Spread the top and sides of the cake with the remaining frosting.

Cake

2²⁄₃ cups (400 g) all-purpose (plain) flour

1 teaspoon baking soda (bicarbonate of soda)

¼ teaspoon salt

1 cup (250 g) butter

2 cups (400 g) sugar

2 teaspoons vanilla extract (essence)

6 large eggs

1 cup (250 ml) sour cream

Golden Frosting

½ cup (125 g) butter

1 cup (200 g) firmly packed brown sugar

¾ cup (200 ml) milk

2 teaspoons vanilla extract (essence)

3 cups (450 g) confectioners' (icing) sugar

Serves: 8–12
Preparation: 30 minutes
Cooking: 20–25 minutes
Level: 2

CHOCOLATE CAKE WITH RICOTTA FILLING

Chocolate Cake: Preheat the oven to 375°F (190°C/gas 5). • Butter two 9-inch (23-cm) round cake pans. • Stir the almonds, flour, cocoa, baking powder, and salt in a large bowl. • Beat the egg yolks, 1 cup (200 g) sugar, vanilla, and almond extract in a large bowl until pale and thick. • Gradually beat in the dry ingredients, alternating with the milk. • Beat the egg whites and remaining sugar in a large clean bowl with an electric mixer on high speed until stiff, glossy peaks form. • Fold them into the batter. • Spoon half the batter into each of the prepared pans. • Bake for 20–25 minutes, or until a toothpick inserted into the center comes out clean. • Cool in the pans for 10 minutes. Turn out onto racks and let cool completely. Ricotta Filling: Beat the cream in a medium bowl until stiff. • Process the ricotta, confectioners' sugar, and candied peel in a food processor until smooth. Transfer to a large bowl. • Fold the cream into the ricotta mixture. • Split the cakes in half horizontally. Place one layer on a serving plate. Spread with one-third of the filling. Repeat with two more layers. Place the remaining layer on top. • Spread the top and sides of the cake with the frosting. Top with the chocolate shavings.

Chocolate Cake

- 1½ cups (225 g) almonds, finely ground
- ⅔ cup (100 g) cake flour
- ⅔ cup (100 g) unsweetened cocoa powder
- 1½ teaspoons baking powder
- ¼ teaspoon salt
- 8 large eggs, separated
- 1½ cups (300 g) sugar
- 2 teaspoons vanilla extract (essence)
- ½ teaspoon almond extract
- ½ cup (125 ml) milk

Ricotta Filling

- 1 cup (250 ml) heavy (double) cream
- 2 cups (500 g) ricotta
- 1 cup (150 g) confectioners' (icing) sugar
- ½ cup (50 g) candied (glacé) orange peel
- 1 quantity Basic Chocolate Frosting (see page 596)

  Shavings of dark chocolate, to decorate

Serves: 8–10
Preparation: 50 minutes
Cooking: 20–25 minutes
Level: 2

JELLY ROLL DESSERT CAKE

Jelly Roll: Preheat the oven to 400°F (200°C/gas 6).
• Butter and flour a 10 x 15-inch (25 x 35-cm) jelly-roll pan. Line with parchment paper. • Combine the flour, baking powder, and salt in a medium bowl. • Beat the egg yolks, sugar, and vanilla in a large bowl with an electric mixer at high speed until pale and thick.
• With mixer at low speed, gradually beat in the dry ingredients, alternating with the milk. • With mixer at high speed, beat the egg whites and cream of tartar in a large bowl until stiff peaks form. • Gently fold them into the batter. • Spoon the batter into the prepared pan. • Bake for 15–20 minutes, or until lightly browned. • Dust a kitchen towel with confectioners' sugar. Turn the cake out onto the towel. Roll up the cake, using the towel as a guide. Leave, seam-side down, until cool. • Filling: Sprinkle the gelatin over $^1/_4$ cup (60 ml) of water in a saucepan. Let stand 1 minute. Stir over low heat until completely dissolved.
• Purée 2 cups (300 g) strawberries, $^1/_2$ cup (100 g) sugar, and the liqueur in a food processor. • Unroll the cake and spread with the strawberry mixture. Reroll the cake. • Stir the remaining water and sugar in a medium saucepan over medium heat until the sugar has dissolved. Stir in the gelatin mixture and orange juice. Set aside to cool. • Slice the remaining strawberries (reserving a few to decorate). • Cut the cake into 10 slices and line the base of a 9-inch (23-cm) springform pan, cutting to fit. • Drizzle the bananas with the lemon juice. Press against the pan sides. Fill with the fruit jelly mixture. • Refrigerate for 6 hours. • Decorate with the remaining berries.

Jelly Roll

1 cup (150 g) all-purpose (plain) flour

1½ teaspoons baking powder

¼ teaspoon salt

3 large eggs, separated

¾ cup (150 g) sugar

1 teaspoon vanilla extract (essence)

¼ cup (60 ml) milk

¼ teaspoon cream of tartar

Filling

1 tablespoon unflavored gelatin powder

3¼ cups (800 ml) cold water

3 cups (450 g) strawberries

1½ cups (300 g) sugar

¼ cup (60 ml) orange liqueur

¾ cup (200 ml) freshly squeezed orange juice

2 bananas, thinly sliced

2 tablespoons freshly squeezed lemon juice

Serves: 8–12
Preparation: 30 minutes + 6 hours to chill
Cooking: 15–20 minutes
Level: 3

GLUTEN-FREE RICH CHOCOLATE ROULADE

284

Chocolate Roulade: Preheat the oven to 350°F (180°C/gas 4). Butter a 10 x 15-inch (25 x 35-cm) jelly-roll pan. Line with parchment paper. • Melt the chocolate in a double boiler over barely simmering water. Let cool. • Beat the egg yolks and sugar in a large bowl with an electric mixer on high speed until pale and thick. Gradually beat in the chocolate. • Beat the egg whites and salt in a large bowl until stiff peaks form. Fold them into the chocolate mixture. • Spoon the batter into the prepared pan. • Bake for 20–25 minutes, or until springy to the touch. Cool the cake in the pan for 5 minutes. Chocolate Cream Frosting: Melt the chocolate, cream, and vanilla in a double boiler over barely simmering water. Sift in the confectioners' sugar and stir until combined. • Strain the frosting through a sieve to remove lumps and refrigerate until cooled and thickened, about 30 minutes. • Roll up the cake following the instructions on the next page. • Unroll the cake and spread with half the frosting. Reroll the cake and spread with the remaining frosting.

Chocolate Roulade

8   ounces (250 g) dark chocolate, coarsely chopped
8   large eggs, separated
1¼ cups (250 g) sugar
¼   teaspoon salt

Chocolate Cream Frosting

1   pound (500 g) bittersweet chocolate, coarsely chopped
1   cup (250 ml) heavy (double) cream
1   teaspoon vanilla extract (essence)
2   cups (300 g) confectioners' (icing) sugar

Serves: 8–12
Preparation: 30 minutes
    + 30 minutes to cool
Cooking: 25–30 minutes
Level: 3

■ ■ ■ *This delicious roll has no flour so is perfect for people with gluten intolerance. Be sure to use good-quality chocolate and vanilla extract from reliable manufacturers of gluten-free products. Keep the cake chilled in the refrigerator and take out about 30 minutes before serving.*

■ ROLLING A JELLY ROLL

Jelly rolls or roulades make superb desserts. Filled with preserves, frostings, or whipped or pastry creams, jelly rolls are rolled up and either dusted with confectioners' sugar or cocoa or spread with frosting. Rolling a jelly roll is not difficult but it does require a gentle touch, some patience, and a little practice.

1

2

3

285

1. LAY OUT a kitchen towel on a flat surface. Dust with 2–3 tablespoons of confectioners' (icing) sugar.

2. REMOVE the parchment paper from the hot cake and use a knife to cut away the crisp edges.

3. USE the cloth as a guide to roll up the cake. Stand seam-side down until cooled.

4

5

4. UNROLL the cake and spread with the filling. Reroll the cake and stand seam-side down.

5. SPREAD the roll with frosting or remaining filling, as required by the recipe.

CHOCOLATE HAZELNUT ROULADE

288

Preheat the oven to 350°F (180°C/gas 4). • Line a 10 x 15-inch (25 x 35-cm) jelly-roll pan with parchment paper. • Beat the egg yolks, confectioners' sugar, and vanilla in a large bowl until pale and creamy. • Fold in the flour and cornstarch. • Beat the egg whites and salt with an electric mixer at high speed until stiff. Gently fold them into the batter. • Spoon the batter into the prepared pan. • Bake for 15–20 minutes, or until risen and golden. • To roll the roulade, follow the instructions on page 285: Dust a clean kitchen towel with confectioners' sugar. Turn the cake out onto the towel, remove the paper, and trim the edges. Roll up the cake, using the towel as a guide. Leave, seam side down, until cool. • Unroll the sponge. Drizzle with the rum and cover with the chocolate spread. Roll up using the towel as a guide. Wrap the roulade in foil. Chill for 2 hours. • Unwrap and transfer to a serving dish. • Dust with the confectioners' sugar and sprinkle with the flakes of chocolate.

4	large eggs, separated
1	cup (150 g) confectioners' (icing) sugar + extra, to dust
1	teaspoon vanilla extract (essence)
⅓	cup (50 g) all-purpose (plain) flour
2	tablespoons cornstarch (cornflour)
¼	teaspoon salt
3	tablespoons rum
1	cup (250 g) chocolate hazelnut spread (Nutella), softened
4	tablespoons dark chocolate flakes

Serves: 6–10
Preparation: 30 minutes
   + 2 hours to chill
Cooking: 15–20 minutes
Level: 3

■ ■ ■ *This is a good basic recipe for a roll. If liked, substitute the hazelnut cream with 1 cup (300 g) of raspberry, cherry, strawberry, or apricot preserves (jam), or lemon curd. Dust with confectioners' sugar.*

SPICED JELLY ROLL
WITH APPLE FILLING

Spiced Jelly Roll: Preheat the oven to 375°F (190°C/gas 5). • Butter a 10 x 15-inch (25 x 35-cm) jelly-roll pan. Line with parchment paper. • Combine the flour, baking powder, cinnamon, and ginger in a medium bowl. • Beat the egg yolks and sugar in a large bowl with an electric mixer on high speed until pale and creamy. • With mixer at high speed, beat the egg whites and salt in a large clean bowl until stiff peaks form. Fold them into the egg yolk mixture. • Gradually fold the dry ingredients into the batter. • Spoon the batter into the prepared pan. • Bake for 15–20 minutes, or until springy to the touch. • To roll the roulade, follow the instructions on page 285: Dust a clean kitchen towel with confectioners' sugar. Turn the cake out onto the towel, remove the paper, and trim the edges. Roll up the cake, using the towel as a guide. Leave, seam-side down, until cool. • Filling: Bring the apples and water to a boil in a small saucepan over medium heat. Cover and simmer over low heat until tender, about 10 minutes. Stir in the sugar and lemon juice. Drain off some of the juice and set aside to cool. • Beat the cream in a large bowl until stiff. • Unroll the cake and spread with the cream. Spoon the apples over the cream. Reroll the cake. Dust with confectioners' sugar.

Spiced Jelly Roll

1	cup (150 g) cake flour
1	teaspoon baking powder
1	teaspoon ground cinnamon
1	teaspoon ground ginger
3	large eggs, separated
½	cup (100 g) sugar
¼	teaspoon salt

Filling

2	large tart green apples, peeled, cored, and coarsely chopped
¼	cup (60 ml) water
3	tablespoons sugar
1	tablespoon freshly squeezed lemon juice
1	cup (250 ml) heavy (double) cream
	Confectioners' (icing) sugar, to dust

Serves: 8–10
Preparation: 25 minutes
Cooking: 15–20 minutes
Level: 2

JELLY ROLL
WITH PEACH FILLING

<u>Filling:</u> Cook the peaches, sugar, and lemon zest in a large saucepan over medium-low heat, stirring often, until the peaches are tender, about 15 minutes. Set aside to cool. • <u>Jelly Roll:</u> Preheat the oven to 350°F (180°C/gas 4). • Butter a 10 x 15-inch (25 x 35-cm) jelly-roll pan. Line with parchment paper. • Beat the eggs, sugar, and salt in a large bowl with an electric mixer at high speed until pale and thick, about 20 minutes. • Use a large rubber spatula to fold the flour and vanilla into the beaten eggs. • Spoon the batter into the prepared pan. • Bake for 15–20 minutes, or until golden brown. • To roll the roulade, follow the instructions on page 285: Dust a clean kitchen towel with confectioners' sugar. Turn the cake out onto the towel, remove the paper, and trim the edges. Roll up the cake, using the towel as a guide. Leave, seam side down, until cool. • Unroll the cake and brush with the rum. Spread evenly with the peach filling. • Reroll the cake, wrap in plastic wrap (cling film), and refrigerate for 1 hour. • Dust with the confectioners' sugar. Cut into slices and top each one with a little chopped fresh peach.

Filling

1   pound (500 g) peaches, peeled, pitted, and chopped
1   cup (200 g) sugar
2   teaspoons finely grated lemon zest

Jelly Roll

2   large eggs
1/3   cup (70 g) sugar
1/4   teaspoon salt
1/2   cup (75 g) cake flour
1/2   teaspoon vanilla extract (essence)
3   tablespoons dark rum
1   large fresh peach, peeled and chopped
    Confectioners' (icing) sugar, to dust

Serves: 8–10
Preparation: 35 minutes + 1 hour to chill
Cooking: 30–40 minutes
Level: 2

CHOCOLATE JELLY ROLL WITH RASPBERRY FILLING

Chocolate Jelly Roll: Preheat the oven to 375°F (190°C/gas 5). • Butter a 10 x 15-inch (25 x 35-cm) jelly-roll pan. Line with parchment paper. • Melt the chocolate in a double boiler over barely simmering water. Let cool. • Sift the flour, baking powder, baking soda, and salt into a medium bowl. • Beat the eggs, sugar, and vanilla in a large bowl with an electric mixer at high speed until pale and thick. • Fold the dry ingredients into the egg mixture, alternating with the water and chocolate. • Spoon the batter into the prepared pan. • Bake for about 20 minutes, or until springy to the touch. • To roll the roulade, follow the instructions on page 285: Dust a clean kitchen towel with confectioners' sugar. Turn the cake out onto the towel, remove the paper, and trim the edges. Roll up the cake, using the towel as a guide. Leave, seam-side down, until cool.
Filling: Unroll the cake and spread with the Chantilly Cream. Sprinkle with the raspberries. • Reroll the cake. Dust with confectioners' sugar.

Chocolate Jelly Roll

3 ounces (90 g) dark chocolate, chopped

½ cup (75 g) all-purpose (plain) flour

½ teaspoon baking powder

½ teaspoon baking soda (bicarbonate of soda)

¼ teaspoon salt

4 large eggs

¾ cup (150 g) sugar

1 teaspoon vanilla extract (essence)

2 tablespoons cold water

Filling

2 cups (500 ml) Chantilly Cream (see page 600)

2 cups (300 g) fresh raspberries

   Confectioners' (icing) sugar, to dust

Serves: 6–10
Preparation: 25 minutes
Cooking: 20 minutes
Level: 2

COFFEE JELLY ROLL

Preheat the oven to 400°F (200°C/gas 6). • Butter a 10 x 15-inch (25 x 35-cm) jelly-roll pan. Line with parchment paper. • Combine the flour, baking powder, and salt in a large bowl. • Beat the eggs and 1 cup (200 g) of sugar in a large bowl with an electric mixer at high speed until pale and thick. • With mixer at low speed, gradually beat in the dry ingredients, alternating with the melted butter and coffee mixture. • Spoon the batter into the prepared pan. • Bake for 15–20 minutes, or until springy to the touch. • To roll the roulade, follow the instructions on page 285: Dust a clean kitchen towel with confectioners' sugar. Turn the cake out onto the towel, remove the paper, and trim the edges. Roll up the cake, using the towel as a guide. Leave, seam-side down, until cool. • Unroll the cake and spread evenly with the coffee-flavored Chantilly Cream. Reroll the cake. Dust with confectioners' sugar.

1	cup (150 g) all-purpose (plain) flour
1	teaspoon baking powder
¼	teaspoon salt
5	large eggs
1	cup (200 g) + 2 tablespoons sugar
⅓	cup (90 g) butter, melted
2	tablespoons freeze-dried coffee granules dissolved in 1 tablespoon boiling water
2	cups (500 ml) Chantilly Cream (see page 600), flavored with 2 tablespoons freeze-dried coffee granules
	Confectioners' (icing) sugar, to dust

Serves: 6–8
Preparation: 30 minutes
Cooking: 15–20 minutes
Level: 2

PISTACHIO JELLY ROLL WITH LEMON FILLING

Preheat the oven to 350°F (180°C/gas 4). • Butter a 10 x 15-inch (25 x 35-cm) jelly-roll pan. Line with parchment paper. • Process the pistachios and 2 tablespoons of sugar in a food processor until finely chopped. • Beat the egg yolks, remaining sugar, and vanilla in a medium bowl with an electric mixer at high speed until pale and thick. • With mixer at low speed, gradually beat in the flour and pistachio mixture. • With mixer at high speed, beat the egg whites and salt in a medium clean bowl until stiff peaks form. Fold them into the batter. • Spoon the batter into the prepared pan. • Bake for 12–15 minutes, or until springy to the touch. • To roll the roulade, follow the instructions on page 285: Dust a clean kitchen towel with confectioners' sugar. Turn the cake out onto the towel, remove the paper, and trim the edges. Roll up the cake, using the towel as a guide. Leave, seam side down, until cool. • Unroll the cake and drizzle with the rum. Spread with the lemon curd. • Reroll the cake, wrap in aluminum foil, and refrigerate for 1 hour. • Remove the foil and cut into slices. • Spread the Vanilla Crème Anglaise on 6–8 serving plates and arrange the slices on top. Sprinkle with the almonds and serve.

½	cup (60 g) shelled and peeled pistachios
½	cup (100 g) sugar
2	large eggs, separated
½	teaspoon vanilla extract (essence)
½	cup (75 g) all-purpose (plain) flour
¼	teaspoon salt
¾	cup (125 g) confectioners' (icing) sugar
2	tablespoons rum
1	cup (250 g) lemon curd
1	quantity Vanilla Crème Anglaise (see page 586)
4	tablespoons slivered almonds

Serves: 6–8
Preparation: 30 minutes + 1 hour to chill
Cooking: 15 minutes
Level: 2

PIES & TARTS

LEMON TART

Sweet Tart Pastry: Place the flour, confectioners' sugar, and butter in a food processor and pulse until the mixture resembles bread crumbs. • Add the yolk and 2 teaspoons of water, pulse, adding a little more water if necessary, until the dough comes together. • Remove from the processor and knead quickly until smooth. • Place in a small bowl, cover with plastic wrap (cling film) and refrigerate for 30 minutes. • Lightly grease a 10-inch (25-cm) tart pan with removeable base. • Roll the pastry out on a lightly floured work surface to 1/4 inch (5 mm) thick. • Line the prepared tart pan with the pastry and trim the edges (see facing page). Cover and refrigerate for 30 minutes. • Preheat the oven to 350°F (180°C/gas 4). • Cover the pastry case with parchment paper and fill with pie weights, dried beans, or rice. • Bake for 10–15 minutes until light brown and dry to the touch. Remove the paper and weights and set aside. • Decrease the oven temperature to 300°F (150°C/gas 2) and place a baking sheet in the oven. Filling: Break the eggs into a bowl, add the sugar, and beat for a few seconds—the mixture shouldn't be frothy. Pour in the lemon juice, zest, and cream, and whisk lightly until smooth. • Transfer the filling to a large pitcher (jug). Pour into the cooled pastry shell. • Bake for 35–40 minutes, until the filling is just set but still trembles a little in the center. • Leave to cool completely before removing from the pan.

Sweet Tart Pastry

1¼ cups (180 g) all-purpose (plain) flour

½ cup (75 g) confectioners' (icing) sugar

3½ ounces (100 g) cold unsalted butter, cubed

1 large egg yolk

2-3 teaspoons iced water

Filling

6 large eggs

1⅓ cups (250 g) superfine (caster) sugar

¾ cup (200 ml) freshly squeezed lemon juice

Finely grated zest of 3 lemons

¾ cup (200 ml) heavy (double) cream

Serves: 6–8
Preparation: 25 minutes
  + 1 hour to chill
Cooking: 50–60 minutes
Level: 2

◼ LINING A TART PAN AND BAKING THE TART SHELL

The pastry for tarts and pies is fragile and should be handled as little as possible. Here we show you how to get it into the pan without tearing or handling too much. Often the pastry needs to be baked "blind," or before the filling is added, and here we show you how to do that too.

1. ROLL the dough out just slightly larger than the pan. Roll it loosely around the rolling pin and drape it evenly over the prepared pan.

2. LIFT up the edges of the dough and press with your fingertips so that the dough adheres to the pan.

3. COVER the dough with a large piece of parchment paper and fill with dried beans or pie weights. Bake for 10–15 minutes.

4. REMOVE the paper and beans or weights. POUR the filling into the baked pie crust ready for the final baking (or chilling).

APPLE PIE

Shortcrust Pastry: Follow the step-by-step instructions on the facing page. Refrigerate for at least 30 minutes. • Preheat the oven to 425°F (220°C/gas 7) and put a baking sheet in at the same time. • Filling: Peel, core, and slice the apples. Mix them with the sugar, orange juice, flour, and cinnamon. • Divide the pastry into two disks, one slightly larger than the other. Lightly dust a work surface with flour and roll out the larger disk to fit into a 10-inch (25-cm) pie pan. Lift it into the pan by rolling it up on the floured rolling pin, then slowly unrolling it over the pan. Press the pastry into the corners and around the bottom and sides, allowing the extra pastry to overhang the edge of the pan. Spoon the filling into the pastry. • Roll out the smaller disk of pastry for the lid. Wet the pastry rim in the pan with water and place the pie lid on top. Press the lid firmly onto the rim and pinch the edges together to seal. Trim away any excess dough. • Make two slits in the top to let the steam out. Brush with milk and sprinkle with sugar. • Place the pie on the baking sheet and bake for 10 minutes. Decrease the heat to 375°F (190°C/gas 5) and bake for 30 minutes, or until the pastry is golden. • Serve warm or cold.

■ ■ ■ *The quantities for the shortcrust pastry given here make enough pastry for one double pie crust for a 9- or 10-inch (23- or 25-cm) pan.*

Shortcrust Pastry

- 2½ cups (375 g) all-purpose (plain) flour
- ½ teaspoon salt
- ⅔ cup (150 g) unsalted butter or ⅓ cup (90 g) butter and ⅓ cup (90 g) vegetable shortening

  About 7 tablespoons ice water, + extra, as needed

Filling

- 1½ pounds (750 g) tart cooking apples (6–8 medium-sized)
- ½ cup (100 g) sugar + 1 tablespoon, to sprinkle
- 1 tablespoon freshly squeezed orange or lemon juice
- 2 tablespoons all-purpose (plain) flour
- ½ teaspoon ground cinnamon
- 2 tablespoons milk, to glaze

Serves: 6–8
Preparation: 30 minutes + 30 minutes to chill
Cooking: 40 minutes
Level: 2

The pastry for pies and tarts should be prepared as quickly as possible, before the ingredients have time to warm. It is best to use a food processor, if you have one. The entire mixing job should not take longer than 1 minute.

1

2

1. PLACE the flour and salt in a food processor and pulse briefly to combine. Add the butter and pulse until the mixture resembles coarse crumbs, about 10 seconds. With the machine running, slowly add enough ice water to obtain a smooth dough.

2. IF MIXING BY HAND combine the flour and salt in a large bowl or on a clean work surface. Use a pastry blender to cut in the butter until the mixture resembles coarse crumbs. Slowly add enough ice water to obtain a smooth dough.

3

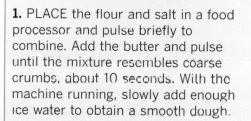

3. PRESS the dough together into a ball and flatten into a disk shape. Wrap in plastic wrap (cling film) and chill in the refrigerator for at least 30 minutes, or up to 2 days, before rolling.

CHOCOLATE AND RUM TART

Pastry: Lightly grease a 10-inch (25-cm) tart pan with removeable base. • Combine the flour and cocoa into a bowl. Place the flour mixture, sugar, and butter in a food processor and pulse until the mixture resembles bread crumbs. • Add the egg yolk and 2 teaspoons of water, pulse, adding a little more water if necessary, until the dough comes together. Remove from the processor and knead gently until smooth. • Place in a small bowl, cover with plastic wrap (cling film) and refrigerate for 30 minutes. • Roll the pastry out onto a lightly floured work surface to $1/4$ inch (5 mm) thick. • Line the prepared tart pan with pastry and trim the edges. Cover and refrigerate for 30 minutes. • Preheat the oven to 350°F (180°C/gas 4). • Cover the pastry with parchment paper and fill with pie weights or dried beans. Bake for 12 minutes. Remove paper and weights and bake for 5 minutes, or until golden. Filling: Place the chocolate and butter in a double boiler. Melt over barely simmering water, stirring occasionally until smooth. Add the rum and set aside to cool. • Beat the eggs, yolks, and sugar in a small bowl with an electric mixer on high speed until pale and creamy. • Gradually add the chocolate mixture, folding until just combined. • Pour into the pastry case and bake for 10 minutes, until the edges of the filling start to rise. Set aside to cool. • Combine the cocoa and confectioners' sugar in a small bowl. Dust over the tart. • Serve warm or chilled.

Pastry

1 cup (150 g) all-purpose (plain) flour

$1/4$ cup (30 g) unsweetened cocoa powder

$1/2$ cup (75 g) confectioners' (icing) sugar

$3^{1}/_{2}$ ounces (100 g) cold butter, cubed

1 large egg yolk

2-3 teaspoons iced water

Filling

12 ounces (350 g) dark chocolate, coarsely chopped

$3/4$ cup (180 g) butter, cubed

2 tablespoons dark rum

2 large eggs + 2 large egg yolks

2 tablespoons sugar

1 tablespoon unsweetened cocoa powder

1 tablespoon confectioners' (icing) sugar

Serves: 6–8
Preparation: 30 minutes + 1 hour to chill
Cooking: 35–40 minutes
Level: 2

GOLDEN MACADAMIA TART

Tart Base: Lightly grease a 10-inch (25-cm) tart pan with removeable base. • Prepare the pastry and refrigerate for 30 minutes. • Roll the pastry out on a lightly floured work surface to 1/4 inch (5 mm) thick. • Line the prepared tart pan with the pastry and trim the edges. Cover and refrigerate for 30 minutes. • Preheat the oven to 350°F (180°C/gas 4). • Cover the pastry case with parchment paper and fill with pie weights, dried beans, or rice. • Bake for 15 minutes until pale golden brown. • Remove the paper and weights and set aside. • Filling: Place the brown sugar, flour, cinnamon, eggs, corn syrup, butter, and brandy in a medium bowl and whisk until combined. Add the macadamia nuts and stir to combine. • Spoon the filling into the prepared pastry case and bake for 25–30 minutes, until set. • Serve warm or at room temperature.

1   recipe Sweet Tart Pastry (see page 302)

Filling

1/2   cup (100 g) firmly packed brown sugar

1   tablespoon all-purpose (plain) flour

1   teaspoon ground cinnamon

2   large eggs, lightly beaten

1/4   cup (60 ml) light corn (golden) syrup

1/4   cup (60 g) butter, melted

2   tablespoons brandy

1 1/2   cups (230 g) macadamia nuts, lightly toasted and coarsely chopped

Serves: 6–8
Preparation: 30 minutes
  + 1 hour to chill
Cooking: 40–45 minutes
Level: 2

PEAR AND ALMOND TART

314

Pastry: Lightly grease a 10-inch (25-cm) tart pan with removeable base. • Beat the butter and confectioners' sugar in a medium bowl with an electric mixer on medium-high speed until pale and creamy. • Beat the eggs in one at a time until fully combined. • Mix in the flour and enough water to bring the dough together. • Shape into a ball, cover in plastic wrap (cling film), and refrigerate for 1 hour. • Roll the pastry out on a lightly floured work surface to ¹/₄-inch (5 mm) thick. • Line the prepared tart pan with pastry and trim the edges. Cover and refrigerate for 30 minutes. • Preheat the oven to 350°F (180°C/gas 4). • Cover the pastry case with parchment paper and fill with baking weights, dried beans, or rice. • Bake for 15 minutes until pale golden brown. • Remove the paper and weights and set aside.
Filling: Beat the sugar, butter, and vanilla in a medium bowl with an electric mixer on high speed until pale and creamy. • Add the eggs one at a time, beating until just combined. • Stir in the almonds and flour. Cover and refrigerate until firm, about 20 minutes. • Spoon the filling into the prepared tart case. Slice the pear quarters in half and press decoratively around the tart. Scatter with flaked almonds. • Bake for 40–45 minutes, until set and golden brown. • Melt the honey in a small saucepan over low heat. Brush with the honey and serve warm or at room temperature.

Pastry

²/₃ cup (150 g) butter, cubed, softened

¹/₂ cup (75 g) confectioners' (icing) sugar

2 large egg yolks

1²/₃ cups (250 g) all-purpose (plain) flour

3-4 teaspoons iced water

Filling

1 cup (200 g) sugar

³/₄ cup (180 g) unsalted butter, softened

1 teaspoon vanilla extract (essence)

3 large eggs

2 cups (300 g) blanched almonds, ground finely in food processor

2 tablespoons all-purpose (plain) flour

4 small pears, peeled, cored, and quartered

3 tablespoons flaked almonds

3 tablespoons honey

Serves: 6–8
Preparation: 30 minutes
  + 1 hour to chill
Cooking: 55–60 minutes
Level: 2

RHUBARB AND SOUR CREAM TART

Tart Base: Lightly grease a 10-inch (25-cm) tart pan with removeable base. • Prepare the pastry and refrigerate for 30 minutes. • Roll the pastry out onto a lightly floured work surface to $1/4$ inch (5 mm) thick. • Line the prepared tart pan with the pastry and trim the edges. Cover and refrigerate for 30 minutes. • Preheat the oven to 350°F (180°C/gas 4). • Cover the pastry case with parchment paper and fill with pie weights, dried beans, or rice. • Bake for 15 minutes until pale golden brown. • Remove the paper and weights and set aside. • Filling: Place the rhubarb, $1/2$ cup (100 g) of sugar, the water, and vanilla bean in a medium saucepan over low heat and simmer until the rhubarb has softened, about 15 minutes. Discard the vanilla bean. • Beat the sour cream, eggs, and remaining sugar in a medium bowl. • Add the rhubarb and stir to combine. • Pour the filling into the prepared tart case. • Bake for 25 minutes, or until set. • Serve warm or at room temperature.

1   recipe Sweet Tart Pastry (see page 302)

Filling

$1^3/4$ pounds (800 g) trimmed rhubarb, cut into 2-inch (5 cm) lengths

$3/4$ cup (150 g) sugar

2   tablespoons water

1   vanilla bean, split lengthwise

$1^1/4$ cups (300 g) sour cream

2   large eggs, lightly beaten

Serves: 6–8
Preparation: 30 minutes
   + 1 hour to chill
Cooking: 40 minutes
Level: 2

FRESH FIG TART

Pastry: Lightly grease a 10-inch (25-cm) tart pan with removeable base. • Beat the butter, confectioners' sugar, and cinnamon with an electric mixer on medium-high speed until pale and creamy. • Beat the egg yolks in one at a time until fully combined. • Mix in the flour, orange zest, and enough water to bring the dough together. • Shape into a ball, cover in plastic wrap (cling film), and refrigerate for 1 hour. • Roll the pastry out on a lightly floured work surface to ¼ inch (5 mm) thick. • Line the prepared tart pan with the pastry and trim the edges. • Cover and refrigerate for 30 minutes. • Preheat the oven to 350°F (180°C/gas 4). • Cover the pastry case with parchment paper and fill with baking weights, dried beans, or rice. • Bake for 15 minutes until pale golden brown. • Remove the paper and weights and set aside. • Filling: Combine the flour and sugar in a medium bowl. Add the eggs and cream and whisk until smooth. • Pour the filling into the prepared tart case. Arrange the fig quarters decoratively around the tart. • Bake for 25–30 minutes, until the batter has set. • Melt the apricot preserves in a small saucepan over low heat. Brush the tart with the apricot glaze. • Serve warm or at room temperature.

Pastry

- ⅔ cup (150 g) butter, cubed, softened
- ½ cup (75 g) confectioners' (icing) sugar
- 1 teaspoon ground cinnamon
- 2 large egg yolks
- 1⅔ cups (250 g) all-purpose (plain) flour
- 1 teaspoon finely grated orange zest
- 3-4 teaspoons iced water

Filling

- ⅓ cup (50 g) all-purpose (plain) flour
- 3 tablespoons sugar
- 2 large eggs
- 1 cup (250 ml) heavy (double) cream
- 10 black figs, quartered
- 3 tablespoons apricot preserves (jam)

Serves: 6–8
Preparation: 30 minutes + 1 hour 30 minutes to chill
Cooking: 40–45 minutes
Level: 2

DATE, ORANGE AND HAZELNUT TART

Pastry: Lightly grease a 10-inch (25-cm) tart pan with removeable base. • Beat the butter and confectioners' sugar with an electric mixer on medium-high speed until pale and creamy. • Beat the egg yolks in one at a time until fully combined. • Mix in the flour and enough water to bring the dough together. • Shape into a ball, cover in plastic wrap (cling film), and refrigerate for 1 hour. • Roll the pastry out on a lightly floured surface to $1/4$ inch (5 mm) thick. • Line the prepared tart pan with the pastry and trim the edges. Cover and refrigerate for 30 minutes. • Preheat the oven to 350°F (180°C/gas 4). • Cover the pastry case with parchment paper and fill with baking weights, dried beans, or rice. • Bake for 15 minutes until pale golden brown. • Remove the paper and weights and set aside. Filling: Beat the sugar and butter in a medium bowl with an electric mixer on high speed until pale and creamy. • Add the eggs and orange flower water, beating until combined. • Stir in the hazelnuts, flour, and orange zest. Cover and refrigerate until firm, about 20 minutes. • Spoon the filling into the prepared tart case. Press the date halves decoratively around the tart. • Bake for 45 minutes, or until the filling is set and golden brown. • Melt the marmalade in a small saucepan over low heat. Brush the tart with marmalade glaze. • Serve warm or at room temperature.

Pastry

- ⅔ cup (150 g) butter, cubed, softened
- ½ cup (75 g) confectioners' (icing) sugar
- 2 large egg yolks
- 1⅔ cup (250 g) all-purpose (plain) flour
- 3-4 teaspoons iced water

Filling

- ¾ cup (180 g) butter, softened
- 1 cup (200 g) sugar
- 3 large eggs, beaten
- 2 tablespoons orange-flower water
- 2 cups (300 g) blanched hazelnuts, finely ground in food processor
- 2 tablespoons all-purpose (plain) flour
- 1 teaspoon finely grated orange zest
- 15 fresh dates, halved and pitted
- 3 tablespoons orange marmalade

Serves: 6–8
Preparation: 30 minutes + 1 hour 50 minutes to chill
Cooking: 1 hour
Level: 2

PLUM AND CINNAMON TART

Tart Base: Lightly grease a 10-inch (25-cm) tart pan with removeable base. • Prepare the pastry and refrigerate for 30 minutes. • Roll the pastry out on a lightly floured surface to ¼ inch (5 mm) thick. • Line the prepared tart pan with the pastry and trim the edges. Cover and refrigerate for 30 minutes. • Preheat the oven to 350 F (180 C/gas 4). • Cover the pastry case with parchment paper and fill with baking weights, dried beans, or rice. • Bake for 15 minutes until pale golden brown. • Remove the paper and weights and set aside. • Filling: Place the ricotta, sugar, preserves, and cinnamon in a medium bowl and stir to combine. • Arrange the plum halves, cut-side down in the prepared tart case. Sprinkle the ricotta mixture over the top, filling any gaps. • Bake for 30 minutes, or until plums are tender and the filling golden brown. • Serve warm or at room temperature.

1 recipe Sweet Tart Pastry (see page 302)

Filling

¾ cup (180 g) fresh ricotta, drained

3 tablespoons light brown sugar

2 tablespoons plum preserves (jam)

2 teaspoons ground cinnamon

1¼ pounds (600 g) plums, pitted and halved

Serves: 6–8
Preparation: 30 minutes + 1 hour to chill
Cooking: 45 minutes
Level: 2

STRAWBERRY MOUSSE TART

Pastry: Lightly grease a 10-inch (25-cm) tart pan with removeable base. • Beat the butter and sugar in a medium bowl with an electric mixer on medium-high speed until pale and creamy. • Add the egg yolks one at a time beating until fully combined. • Mix in the flour and enough water to bring the dough together. • Shape into a ball, cover in plastic wrap (cling film), and refrigerate for 1 hour. • Roll the pastry out on a lightly floured work surface to 1/4 inch (5 mm) thick. • Line the prepared tart pan with the pastry and trim the edges. Cover and refrigerate for 30 minutes. • Preheat the oven to 350°F (180°C/gas 4). • Cover the pastry case with parchment paper and fill with baking weights, dried beans, or rice. • Bake for 15 minutes. Remove the paper and weights and bake for 5 more minutes until golden brown. • **Filling:** Place half the strawberries in a food processor and blend until smooth. Strain through a fine mesh sieve into a small saucepan. • Place over medium heat and bring almost to a boil. Set aside. • Put the boiling water in a small cup, sprinkle with the gelatin, and stir until dissolved. • Beat the eggs, egg yolks, sugar, and vanilla in a medium bowl with an electric mixer until pale and creamy. • Gradually pour in the hot strawberry purée, beating until combined. • Return the mixture to the pan and stir over low heat until thickened slightly. Remove from the heat, add the gelatin, and stir to combine. • Pass the

Pastry

- 2/3 cup (150 g) unsalted butter, cubed, softened
- 1/2 cup (75 g) confectioners' (icing) sugar
- 2 large egg yolks
- 1 2/3 cup (250 g) all-purpose (plain) flour
- 3-4 teaspoons iced water

Filling

- 3 cups (450 g) strawberries
- 2 tablespoons boiling water
- 3 teaspoons unflavored powdered gelatin
- 2 large eggs + 2 large egg yolks
- 1/3 cup (70 g) sugar
- 1 teaspoon vanilla extract (essence)
- 1/2 cup (125 ml) heavy (double) cream

Confectioners' (icing) sugar, to dust

Serves: 6–8
Preparation: 45 minutes + 4 hours to chill
Cooking: 25 minutes
Level: 3

strawberry mixture through a fine mesh sieve into a medium bowl and refrigerate, stirring occasionally, until cooled, about 30 minutes. • Whip the cream in a small bowl with an electric mixer on high speed until soft peaks form. • Fold the cream into the cooled strawberry mixture and pour into the prepared tart case. • Slice the remaining strawberries and arrange decoratively around the top of the mousse. • Refrigerate until set, at least 2 hours. • Dust the tart with confectioners' sugar and serve.

■ ■ ■ *This attractive tart is perfect for special occasions. If preparing ahead of time for a party or celebration, don't fill until 2–3 hours before you plan to serve; if you fill it the day before the pastry will lose some of its crispness and become soggy.*

FRENCH APPLE TART

Tart Base: Lightly grease a 10-inch (25-cm) tart pan with removeable base. • Prepare the pastry and refrigerate for 30 minutes. • Roll the pastry out on a lightly floured surface to ¼ inch (5 mm) thick. Line the prepared tart pan with the pastry and trim the edges. Cover and refrigerate for 30 minutes. • Preheat the oven to 350°F (180°C/gas 4). • Cover the pastry case with parchment paper and fill with baking weights, dried beans, or rice. • Bake for 15 minutes until pale golden brown. • Remove the paper and weights and set aside. • Filling: Place the apples in a medium saucepan. Add the sugar, Calvados, butter, and cinnamon and simmer over medium-low heat, stirring occasionally, until softened, 10–15 minutes. • Mash the apples and cook until most of the liquid has evaporated. • Spoon the filling into the prepared base and set aside. • Topping: Thinly slice the apples into crescent shapes. Arrange over the filling in a circular pattern, starting from the center and working out to the edge of the tart. Brush with melted butter and sprinkle with sugar. • Bake for 20 minutes, until the apples are tender and golden. • Preheat the broiler (grill) to high heat. • Dust confectioners' sugar over the tart and cover the pastry edges with aluminum foil. Place the tart 4 inches (10 cm) from the heat source and broil until apples are golden brown, 1–2 minutes. Discard the foil. • Heat the apricot preserves and Calvados in a small saucepan until melted. • Brush with the apricot glaze. • Serve warm or at room temperature.

1 recipe Sweet Tart Pastry (see page 302)

Filling

1¾ pounds (800 g) tart cooking apples, such as Granny Smiths, peeled, cored, and diced

2 tablespoons sugar

1 tablespoon Calvados

1 tablespoon butter

½ teaspoon ground cinnamon

Topping

1 pound (500 g) tart cooking apples, such as Granny Smiths, , peeled and cored

1 tablespoon butter, melted

¼ cup (50 g) sugar

2 tablespoons confectioners' (icing) sugar

3 tablespoons apricot preserves (jam)

1 tablespoon Calvados

Serves: 6–8
Preparation: 30 minutes + 1 hour to chill
Cooking: 35-40 minutes
Level: 2

WALNUT AND MAPLE TART

Pastry: Lightly grease a 10-inch (25-cm) tart pan with removeable base. • Beat the butter and confectioners' sugar with an electric mixer on medium-high speed until pale and creamy. • Beat the egg yolks in one at a time until fully combined. • Mix in the flour and enough water to bring the dough together. • Shape into a ball, cover in plastic wrap (cling film), and refrigerate for 1 hour. • Roll the pastry out onto a lightly floured work surface to ¼ inch (5 mm) thick. • Line the prepared tart pan with the pastry and trim the edges. Cover and refrigerate for 30 minutes. • Preheat the oven to 350°F (180°C/gas 4). • Cover the pastry case with parchment paper and fill with baking weights, dried beans, or rice. • Bake for 15 minutes until pale golden brown. • Remove the paper and weights and set aside. • Filling: Beat the butter and sugar in a small bowl with an electric mixer until creamy. • Add the eggs, maple syrup, and vanilla, beating until combined. Stir in the walnuts and flour. • Brush the base of the prepared tart case with apricot preserves and spoon in the walnut filling. • Bake for 45–50 minutes, until the filling is set and golden brown. • Dust with confectioners' sugar. Slice into portions and serve at room temperature.

Pastry

⅔ cup (150 g) butter, cubed, softened

½ cup (75 g) confectioners' (icing) sugar

2 large egg yolks

1⅔ cups (250 g) all-purpose (plain) flour

3-4 teaspoons iced water

Filling

¾ cup (180 g) butter, softened

½ cup (100 g) firmly packed brown sugar

2 large eggs, lightly beaten

⅓ cup (80 ml) maple syrup

1 teaspoon vanilla extract (essence)

2 cups (250 g) walnut pieces, coarsely chopped

⅓ cup (50 g) all-purpose (plain) flour

3 tablespoons apricot preserves (jam)

Serves: 6–8
Preparation: 30 minutes + 1 hour 30 minutes to chill
Cooking: 60–65 minutes
Level: 2

PRUNE, ARMAGNAC AND MASCARPONE TART

Tart Base: Lightly grease a 10-inch (25-cm) tart pan with removeable base. • Prepare the pastry and refrigerate for 30 minutes. • Roll the pastry out on a lightly floured work surface to $1/4$ inch (5 mm) thick. • Line the prepared tart pan with the pastry and trim the edges. Cover and refrigerate for 30 minutes. • Preheat the oven to 350°F (180°C/gas 4). • Cover the pastry case with parchment paper and fill with baking weights, dried beans, or rice. • Bake for 15 minutes until pale golden brown. • Remove the paper and weights and set aside. • Filling: Beat the mascarpone, eggs, Armagnac, flour, and orange zest in a medium bowl with an electric mixer on medium speed until combined. • Stir in the prunes by hand. • Pour the filling into the prepared tart case. • Bake for 50–55 minutes, until set and golden brown. Set aside to cool. • Serve at room temperature with cream or crème fraîche.

1   recipe Sweet Tart Pastry (see page 302)

Filling

$1\frac{1}{3}$ cups (350 g) mascarpone

2   large eggs, lightly beaten

$\frac{1}{2}$ cup (100 g) sugar

2   tablespoons Armagnac

1   tablespoon all-purpose (plain) flour

1   teaspoon finely grated orange zest

8   ounces (250 g) pitted prunes

Whipped cream or crème fraîche, to serve

Serves: 6–8
Preparation: 30 minutes + 1 hour to chill
Cooking: 65–70 minutes
Level: 2

ORANGE RICOTTA TART

Tart Base: Lightly grease a 10-inch (25-cm) tart pan with removeable base. • Prepare the pastry and refrigerate for 30 minutes. • Roll the pastry out on a lightly floured work surface to ¼ inch (5 mm) thick. • Line the prepared tart pan with the pastry and trim the edges. Cover and refrigerate for 30 minutes. • Preheat the oven to 350°F (180°C/gas 4). • Cover the pastry case with parchment paper and fill with baking weights, dried beans, or rice. • Bake for 15 minutes until pale golden brown. • Remove the paper and weights and set aside. • Filling: Place the egg, egg yolk, ricotta, sugar, and orange zest and liqueur in a medium bowl and stir to combine. • Whip the cream in a small bowl with an electric mixer on high speed until soft peaks form. • Fold the cream into the ricotta mixture and spoon into the prepared tart case. • Bake for 20 minutes, or until golden. • Serve at room temperature with extra whipped cream, if desired.

1   recipe Sweet Tart Pastry (see page 302)

Filling

1   large egg + 1 large egg yolk

1   cup (250 g) ricotta, drained

½   cup (75 g) confectioners' (icing) sugar

2   teaspoons finely grated orange zest

1   tablespoon Grand Mariner or orange liqueur

½   cup (125 ml) heavy (double) cream, + extra, to serve (optional)

Serves: 6–8
Preparation: 30 minutes + 1 hour to chill
Cooking: 35 minutes
Level: 2

ALMOND CUSTARD TART

Pastry: Lightly grease a 10-inch (25-cm) tart pan with removeable base. • Beat the butter and confectioners' sugar with an electric mixer on medium-high speed until pale and creamy. • Beat the eggs in one at a time until fully combined. • Mix in the flour, ground almonds, and enough water to bring the dough together. • Shape into a ball, cover in plastic wrap (cling film), and refrigerate for 1 hour. • Roll the pastry out on a lightly floured surface to 1/4 inch (5 mm) thick. • Line the prepared tart pan with the pastry and trim the edges. Cover and refrigerate for 30 minutes. • Preheat the oven to 350°F (180°C/gas 4). • Cover the pastry case with parchment paper and fill with baking weights, dried beans, or rice. • Bake for 15 minutes until pale golden brown. • Remove the paper and weights and set aside. • Filling: Place the milk and vanilla bean in a medium saucepan over medium heat and bring to a boil. Set aside. • Beat the egg yolks and sugar in a medium bowl with an electric mixer on high speed until pale and creamy. • Stir in the flour and ground almonds. Gradually add the hot milk, stirring until combined. Return the pan to the heat and cook, stirring constantly on low heat, until thick, 2–3 minutes. Discard the vanilla bean. • Brush the base of the tart case with cherry preserves and spread the custard over the top. Scatter with almonds. • Bake for 20 minutes, or until golden brown. • Dust with confectioners' sugar. Serve warm or at room temperature.

Pastry

2/3 **cup (150 g) butter, cubed, softened**

1/2 **cup (75 g) confectioners' (icing) sugar**

2 **large egg yolks**

1 1/3 **cup (200 g) all-purpose (plain) flour**

1/2 **cup (50 g) finely ground almonds**

3-4 **teaspoons iced water**

Filling

2 **cups (500 ml) milk**

1 **vanilla bean, split lengthwise**

4 **large egg yolks**

1/2 **cup (100 g) sugar**

1/3 **cup (50 g) all-purpose (plain) flour**

1/3 **cup (30 g) ground almonds**

1/3 **cup (50 g) black cherry preserves (jam)**

1/3 **cup (50 g) flaked almonds**

Confectioners' (icing) sugar, to dust

Serves: 6–8
Preparation: 30 minutes + 1 hour 30 minutes to chill
Cooking: 35 minutes
Level: 2

IMPOSSIBLY EASY PEACH AND COCONUT PIE

338

Preheat the oven to 350°F (180°C/gas 4). • Lightly grease a 9-inch (23-cm) pie pan. • Place the sugar, coconut, flour, and cinnamon in a medium bowl and stir to combine. • Whisk the milk, coconut milk, eggs, butter, and lime zest in a medium bowl. • Add the dry ingredients and chopped peaches and stir to combine. • Spoon the batter into the prepared pie pan and scatter with the almonds. • Bake for 40–45 minutes, until set and golden. • Serve warm with whipped cream or crème fraîche.

1	cup (200 g) sugar
1	cup (125 g) shredded (desiccated) coconut
½	cup (75 g) all-purpose (plain) flour
2	teaspoons ground cinnamon
1	cup (250 ml) milk
1	cup (250 ml) coconut milk
4	large eggs, lightly beaten
½	cup (125 g) butter, melted
2	teaspoons finely grated lime zest
1	(14-ounce/400-g) can peach halves, drained and coarsely chopped
¼	cup (40 g) flaked almonds
	Whipped cream or crème fraîche, to serve

Serves: 6–8
Preparation: 15 minutes
Cooking: 40–45 minutes
Level: 1

CHOCOLATE MERINGUE PIE

Pastry: Lightly grease a 10-inch (25-cm) tart pan with removeable base. • Combine the flour and cocoa. Place the flour mixture, confectioners' sugar, and butter in a food processor and pulse until the mixture resembles bread crumbs. • Add the egg yolk and 2 teaspoons of water and pulse, adding a little more water if necessary, until the dough comes together. • Knead gently until smooth. Place in a small bowl, cover with plastic wrap (cling film), and refrigerate for 30 minutes. • Roll the pastry out on a lightly floured work surface to ¼ inch (5 mm) thick. • Line the prepared tart pan with the pastry and trim the edges. Cover and refrigerate for 30 minutes. • Preheat the oven to 350°F (180°C/gas 4). • Cover the pastry case with parchment paper and fill with baking weights, dried beans, or rice. • Bake for 15 minutes until pale golden brown. • Remove the paper and weights and set aside. • Filling: Place the chocolate, cream, and vanilla in a double boiler over barely simmering water and stir until smooth. Set aside to cool. • Beat the butter and ⅓ cup (70 g) of sugar in a small bowl with an electric mixer on high speed until pale and creamy. • Add the egg yolks and chocolate mixture, beating to combine. • Fold in the ground almonds. • Spread over the tart case and bake for 10 minutes. • Meanwhile, to make the meringue, whisk the egg whites in a medium bowl with an electric mixer until foamy. Gradually add the remaining sugar, whisking until smooth, glossy peaks form. • Spoon the meringue over the filling and bake for 15 minutes, or until golden. • Serve warm or at room temperature.

Pastry

- 1 cup (150 g) all-purpose (plain) flour
- ¼ cup (30 g) unsweetened cocoa powder
- ½ cup (75 g) confectioners' (icing) sugar
- 3½ ounces (100 g) cold butter, cubed
- 1 large egg yolk
- 2-3 teaspoons iced water

Filling

- 5 ounces (150 g) dark chocolate, chopped
- ¼ cup (60 ml) heavy (double) cream
- 1 teaspoon vanilla extract (essence)
- ¼ cup (60 g) unsalted butter, softened
- 1 cup (200 g) sugar
- 3 large eggs, separated + 1 large egg yolk
- 1 cup (100 g) ground almonds

Serves: 6–8
Preparation: 45 minutes
  + 1 hour to chill
Cooking: 40 minutes
Level: 2

RASPBERRY & COCONUT PIE

Pastry: Lightly grease a 10-inch (25-cm) tart pan with removeable base. • Place the flour, confectioners' sugar, and butter in a food processor and pulse until the mixture resembles bread crumbs. • Add the egg yolks and half the water and pulse, adding a little more water if necessary, until the dough comes together. • Knead gently until smooth. • Place in a small bowl, cover with plastic wrap (cling film), and refrigerate for 30 minutes. • Divide the pastry in half and roll out two rounds on a lightly floured work surface to ¼ inch (5 mm) thick. • Line the prepared tart pan with one of the rounds and trim the edges. • Place the remaining round on a plate. Cover and refrigerate both for 30 minutes. • Preheat the oven to 350°F (180°C/gas 4). • Cover the pastry case with parchment paper and fill with baking weights, dried beans, or rice.• Bake for 15 minutes until pale golden brown. • Remove the paper and weights and set aside. • Filling: Combine ¾ cup (90 g) of the coconut, butter, sugar, crème fraîche, 1 egg yolk, and vanilla in a medium bowl. Add the raspberries and stir to combine. • Spoon the filling into the prepared tart case. Lay the remaining pastry on top, pinching the edges to secure. Cut a few slits in the top with a small knife for the steam to escape. • Combine the egg yolk and milk in a small bowl and brush over the pastry. Sprinkle with the remaining coconut. • Bake for 20 minutes, or until golden brown. • Dust with confectioners' sugar. Serve warm or at room temperature.

Pastry

- 2½ cups (375 g) all-purpose (plain) flour
- 1 cup (150 g) confectioners' (icing) sugar
- 7 ounces (200 g) cold unsalted butter, cubed
- 2 large egg yolks
- 1-2 tablespoons iced water

Filling

- 1 cup (125 g) shredded (desiccated) coconut
- ⅓ cup (90 g) butter, melted
- ⅓ cup (70 g) sugar
- 3 tablespoons crème fraîche
- 2 large egg yolks
- 1 teaspoon vanilla extract (essence)
- 4 cups (600 g) fresh raspberries
- 1 tablespoon milk
  Confectioners' (icing) sugar, to dust

Serves: 6–8
Preparation: 30 minutes
  + 1 hour to chill
Cooking: 35 minutes
Level: 2

PLUM PIE

Pastry: Lightly grease a 9-inch (23-cm) pie pan.
• Mix the flour, cinnamon, salt, and butter in a food processor until it resembles fine crumbs. Add the confectioners' sugar and blend. • Combine the water and egg yolk in a small bowl and gradually add to the flour mixture until it comes together as a dough. • Transfer to a lightly floured work surface and shape into two disks. Cover with plastic wrap (cling film) and refrigerate for 1 hour. • Roll the pastry disks out on a lightly floured work surface to ¼ inch (5 mm) thick. • Line the prepared pan with one of the disks, leaving any excess pastry hanging over the edge. Place the other disk of pastry on a plate and refrigerate both for 30 minutes. • Preheat the oven to 400°F (200°C/gas 6). • Filling: Combine the plums, brown sugar, flour, cinnamon, and nutmeg in a medium bowl and toss to coat. • Spoon the filling into the prepared pie pan and dot with butter. Lay the remaining pastry on top, pinching the edges to seal. Trim off any excess pastry. • Beat the egg yolk and milk in a small bowl and brush over the pastry. Cut a few slits in the pastry using a small knife to allow steam to escape during baking.
• Bake for 40–45 minutes, or until the pastry is golden brown and the filling is cooked. • Serve warm or at room temperature.

Pastry

2⅔ cup (400 g) all-purpose (plain) flour

1 teaspoon ground cinnamon

Pinch of salt

¾ cup (180 g) butter, cubed

2 tablespoons confectioners' (icing) sugar

¼ cup (60 ml) iced water + extra, as required

1 large egg yolk

Filling

1¾ pounds (800 g) plums, pitted and sliced

⅓ cup (70 g) firmly packed brown sugar

2 tablespoons all-purpose (plain) flour

1 teaspoon ground cinnamon

¼ teaspoon ground nutmeg

1 tablespoon butter

1 large egg yolk

1 tablespoon milk

Serves: 6–8
Preparation: 30 minutes + 1 hour 30 minutes to chill
Cooking: 40–45 minutes
Level: 2

KEY LIME PIE

Tart Base: Lightly grease a deep 8½-inch (21-cm) pie pan with removeable base. • Prepare the pastry and refrigerate for 30 minutes. • Roll the pastry out on a lightly floured surface to ¼ inch (5 mm) thick. • Line the prepared pie pan with pastry and trim the edges. Cover and refrigerate for 30 minutes. • Preheat the oven to 350°F (180°C/gas 4). • Cover the pastry case with parchment paper and fill with baking weights, dried beans, or rice. • Bake for 12 minutes. Remove the paper and weights and cook for 5 more minutes until golden brown. • Filling: Put the lime juice in a small saucepan and sprinkle with the gelatin. Set aside to soak for 5 minutes. • Beat the egg yolks in a medium bowl with an electric mixer on high speed until pale and thick. • Stir the lime juice and gelatin mixture over low heat until the gelatin is dissolved. • Add the condensed milk, lime juice mixture, and 1 teaspoon of the lime zest to the egg yolks, beating to combine. • Pour the filling into the prepared pie case. Refrigerate until set, about 3 hours. • Whip the cream in a small bowl with an electric mixer until soft peaks form. • Spoon the cream over the filling and sprinkle with the remaining lime zest. Slice and serve.

1   recipe Sweet Tart
    Pastry (see page 302)

Filling

½   cup (125 ml) freshly
    squeezed lime juice

2   teaspoons unflavored
    gelatin powder

3   large egg yolks

1   (14-ounce/400-g) can
    sweetened condensed
    milk

3   teaspoons finely grated
    lime zest

1¼ cups (300 ml) heavy
    (double) cream

Serves: 6–8
Preparation: 30 minutes
    + 4 hours to chill
Cooking: 5 minutes
Level: 2

CHOCOLATE PECAN TART

Tart Base: Lightly grease a 10-inch (25-cm) tart pan with removeable base. • Prepare the pastry and refrigerate for 30 minutes. • Roll the pastry out on a lightly floured surface to ¼ inch (5 mm) thick. • Line the prepared tart pan with pastry and trim the edges. Cover and refrigerate for 30 minutes. • Preheat the oven to 350°F (180°C/gas 4). • Cover the pastry case with parchment paper and fill with baking weights, dried beans, or rice. • Bake for 15 minutes until pale golden brown. • Remove the paper and weights and set aside. • Filling: Place the chocolate in a double boiler over barely simmering water and stirring occasionally until melted and smooth. • Beat the butter, brown sugar, and corn syrup in a medium bowl with an electric mixer on medium speed until smooth. • Add the egg, vanilla, and chocolate, beating until incorporated. • Stir in the pecans by hand. • Pour the filling into the prepared tart case. • Bake for 30–35 minutes, until set. • Serve warm with whipped cream or ice cream, if desired.

1   recipe Sweet Tart Pastry (see page 302)

Filling

4   ounces (120 g) dark chocolate, coarsely chopped

¼   cup (60 g) butter, softened

⅔   cup (140 g) firmly packed brown sugar

⅔   cup (150 ml) light corn (golden) syrup

3   large eggs, lightly beaten

1   teaspoon vanilla extract (essence)

2   cups (250 g) pecans, coarsely chopped

Whipped cream or ice cream, to serve

Serves: 6–8
Preparation: 30 minutes
    + 1 hour to chill
Cooking: 45–50 minutes
Level: 2

POLENTA AND LEMON LIME TART

Pastry: Beat the butter and sugar in a medium bowl with an electric mixer on high speed until pale and creamy. • Beat in the egg yolks one at a time. • Combine the flour, cornmeal, and salt in a bowl and stir into the egg mixture. • Shape the dough into a ball, cover in plastic wrap (cling film), and refrigerate for 1 hour. • Preheat the oven to 325°F (170°C/gas 3). • Lightly grease a 9½-inch (24-cm) tart pan with a removeable bottom. • Roll out the pastry on a lightly floured surface to ⅛ inch (3 mm) thick. • Line the prepared pan with the pastry. Press the pastry into the corners and around the bottom and sides and trim away the excess. Refrigerate for 30 minutes. • Line the tart shell with parchment paper and fill with pie weights, dried beans, or rice. • Bake for 15 minutes, until pale golden brown. Remove the paper and weights. • Increase the oven temperature to 375°F (190°C/gas 5). • Filling: Beat the eggs and sugar with an electric mixer on high speed until stiff. • Stir in the flour, citrus zests, and citrus juices with a wooden spoon. • Pour in the melted butter and ground almonds and stir until well combined. • Pour into the prepared tart shell. • Bake for 30 minutes, or until set. • Beat the cream in a small bowl with an electric mixer on high speed until it begins to thicken. Add the confectioners' sugar and continue beating until soft peaks form. Stir in the almonds. • Serve warm with a dollop of the whipped cream.

Pastry

½ cup (125 g) butter

½ cup (100 g) sugar

2 large egg yolks

1 cup (150 g) all-purpose (plain) flour

6 tablespoons cornmeal

Pinch of salt

Filling

3 large eggs

⅔ cup (140 g) sugar

6 tablespoons all-purpose (plain) flour

Finely grated zest and juice of 3 lemons

Finely grated zest and juice of 3 limes

½ cup (125 g) butter, melted

1 cup (100 g) ground almonds, toasted

1 cup (250 ml) heavy (double) cream

2 tablespoons confectioners' (icing) sugar

½ cup (80 g) flaked almonds, toasted

Serves: 6–8
Prep: 30 minutes + 1 hour 30 minutes to chill
Cooking: 30 minutes
Level: 2

CALVADOS APPLE TART

Tart Base: Lightly grease a 10-inch (25-cm) tart pan with removeable base. • Prepare the pastry and refrigerate for 30 minutes. • Preheat the oven to 325°F (170°C/gas 3). • Roll out the pastry on a lightly floured surface to ⅛ inch (3 mm) thick. • Lift it into the pan by rolling it up on the floured rolling pin, then slowly unroll it over the pan. Press the pastry into the corners and around the bottom and sides and trim away the excess. Refrigerate for 30 minutes. • Line the tart shell with parchment paper and fill with pie weights, dried beans, or rice. • Bake for 15 minutes, until pale golden brown. • Remove the paper and weights. • Calvados Apple Filling: Combine the Calvados, Demerara sugar, vanilla bean and seeds, and cinnamon in a large saucepan over medium-low heat and cook until the sugar has dissolved. • Add the apples and simmer, stirring often, until the apples are well coated and have softened a little, 5–10 minutes. Stir in the pecans. • Arrange the apple quarters decoratively in the pastry shell. Remove the vanilla bean from the syrup and pour over the apples. • Bake for 30–40 minutes, until the apples are cooked through and caramelized. • Serve at room temperature with a dollop of cinnamon or vanilla ice cream on the side.

1   recipe Sweet Tart Pastry (see page 302)

Calvados Apple Filling

¼   cup (60 ml) Calvados or similar apple liqueur

4   tablespoons Demerara sugar

½   vanilla bean, split lengthwise and seeds scraped

½   teaspoon ground cinnamon

6   Granny Smith apples, peeled, cored, and quartered

¾   cup (90 g) pecans

Cinnamon or vanilla ice cream, to serve

Serves: 6–8
Preparation: 30 minutes
  + 1 hour to chill
Cooking: 45–50 minutes
Level: 2

RASPBERRY CUSTARD TART

Tart Base: Lightly grease a 10-inch (25-cm) tart pan with removeable base. • Prepare the pastry and refrigerate for 30 minutes. • Preheat the oven to 325°F (170°C/gas 3). • Roll out the pastry on a lightly floured surface to ⅛ inch (3 mm) thick. Lift it into the pan by rolling it up on the floured rolling pin, then slowly unroll it over the pan. Press the pastry into the corners and around the bottom and sides and trim away the excess. Refrigerate for 30 minutes. • Line the tart shell with parchment paper and fill with pie weights or dried beans. • Bake for 55 minutes, until pale golden brown. • Remove the paper and weights. • Increase the oven temperature to 450°F (230°C/gas 8). • Filling: Combine the milk and cinnamon stick in a small saucepan over medium heat and bring to a boil. Decrease the heat to low, cover, and simmer for 15 minutes. • Strain the milk through a fine mesh sieve into a pitcher (jug). • Whisk the egg yolks, sugar, and cornstarch in a medium bowl until combined. • Gradually pour in the milk, stirring with a wooden spoon until incorporated. Pour the custard into a small saucepan and simmer over medium-low heat, stirring continuously, until thickened. Remove from the heat, stir in the butter, and set aside to cool a little. • Pour the custard into the prepared tart shell and sprinkle with the raspberries. Bake for 15 minutes. • Serve warm.

1 recipe Sweet Tart Pastry (see page 302)

Filling
2 cups (500 ml) milk
2-inch (5-cm) piece cinnamon stick
2 large egg yolks
¼ cup (50 g) sugar
2 tablespoons cornstarch (cornflour)
2 teaspoons butter
1½ cups (375 g) raspberries

Serves: 6–8
Preparation: 30 minutes
+ 1 hour to chill
Cooking: 30 minutes
Level: 2

BLACKBERRY AND HAZELNUT STREUSEL PIE

Tart Base: Lightly grease a 9-inch (23 cm) pie pan.
• Prepare the pastry and refrigerate for 30 minutes.
• Roll the pastry out onto a lightly floured surface to
$1/4$ inch (5 mm) thick. Line the prepared pie pan
with pastry and trim the edges. Cover and
refrigerate for 30 minutes. • Preheat the oven to
350°F (180°C/gas 4). • Cover the pastry case with
parchment paper and fill with baking weights, dried
beans, or rice. • Bake for 15 minutes. Remove the
paper and weights and set aside. • Filling: Place the
blackberries, sugar, hazelnuts, and orange zest in a
medium bowl and toss to combine. Spoon the filling
into the prepared pie pan. • Topping: Place the flour,
sugar, and cinnamon in a small bowl. Rub in the
butter using your finger tips until mixture resembles
fine bread crumbs. Add the coarsely chopped
hazelnuts and stir to combine. Scatter the topping
over the filling. • Bake for 30–35 minutes, until the
topping is crisp and golden. • Serve warm with
cream or ice-cream, if desired.

1   recipe Sweet Tart
    Pastry (see page 302)

Filling

1¾ pounds (800 g)
    blackberries
¼   cup (50 g) sugar
2   tablespoons ground
    hazelnuts
1   teaspoon finely grated
    orange zest

Topping

½   cup (75 g) all-purpose
    (plain) flour
¼   cup (50 g) firmly
    packed brown sugar
1   teaspoon ground
    cinnamon
¼   cup (60 g) butter,
    cubed
½   cup (80 g) hazelnuts,
    coarsely chopped

    Whipped cream or ice
    cream, to serve
    (optional)

Serves: 6–8
Preparation: 30 minutes
    + 1 hour to chill
Cooking: 30–35 minutes
Level: 2

APPLE & BLUEBERRY PIE

Pastry: Lightly grease a 9-inch (23-cm) pie pan.
• Process the flour, salt, and butter in a food processor until the mixture resembles fine crumbs.
• Add the confectioners' sugar and blend.
• Combine the water and egg yolk in a small bowl and gradually add to the flour mixture until it comes together as a dough. • Transfer to a lightly floured work surface and shape into two disks. Cover with plastic wrap (cling film), and refrigerate for 1 hour. • Roll the pastry disks out on a lightly floured work surface to ¼ inch (5 mm) thick. • Line the prepared pan with one of the disks, leaving any excess pastry hanging over the edge. Place the other disk on a plate and refrigerate both for 30 minutes. • Preheat the oven to 400°F (200°C/gas 6). • Filling: Peel, core, and slice the apples into a medium bowl. • Add the blueberries, sugar, flour, cinnamon, and lemon zest and toss to coat. Spoon the filling into the prepared pie pan and dot with butter. Lay the remaining pastry round on top, pinching the edges to seal. Trim off any excess pastry. • Create leaves and blueberries out of the remaining pastry to decorate the top. • Beat the egg yolk and milk in a small bowl and brush over the pastry. Cut a few slits in the pastry using a small knife to allow steam to escape during baking.
• Bake for 40–45 minutes, or until the pastry is golden brown and the filling is cooked.
• Serve warm.

Pastry

2⅔ cup (400 g) all-purpose (plain) flour
   Pinch of salt
¾ cup (180 g) butter, cubed
2 tablespoons confectioners' (icing) sugar
¼ cup (60 ml) iced water + extra, as required
1 large egg yolk

Filling

1½ pounds (750 g) tart apples, such as Granny Smiths
1 cup (250 g) fresh or frozen blueberries
⅓ cup (70 g) sugar
2 tablespoons all-purpose (plain) flour
1 teaspoon ground cinnamon
2 teaspoons finely grated lemon zest
1 tablespoon butter
1 large egg yolk
1 tablespoon milk

Serves: 6–8
Preparation: 30 minutes + 1 hour 30 minutes to chill
Cooking: 40–45 minutes
Level: 2

RHUBARB LATTICE PIE

Pastry: Lightly grease a 9-inch (23 cm) pie pan.
• Process the flour, cinnamon, salt, and butter in a food processor until the mixture resembles fine crumbs. • Add the confectioners' sugar and blend.
• Combine the water and egg yolk in a small bowl and gradually add to the flour mixture until it comes together as a dough. • Transfer to a lightly floured work surface and shape into two disks. Cover the disks with plastic wrap (cling film), and refrigerate for 1 hour. • Roll one of the pastry disks out on a lightly floured work surface to $^1/_4$ inch (5 mm) thick. Line the prepared pie pan, leaving any excess pastry hanging over the edge. Roll the remaining disk out to $^1/_8$ inch (3 mm) thick. Cut into $^1/_4$-inch (5-mm) thick lengths and lay on a plate. Refrigerate the pastry case and the strips for 30 minutes. • Preheat the oven to 400 F (200 C/gas 6). • Filling: Combine the rhubarb, sugar, flour, and vanilla in a medium bowl and toss to coat. • Spoon the filling into the prepared pie pan and dot with butter. Arrange the pastry strips over the top to form a lattice pattern, pinching the edges to seal. • Beat the egg yolk and milk in a small bowl and brush over the pastry.
• Bake for 40–45 minutes, or until the pastry is golden brown and the filling is cooked.
• Serve warm.

Pastry

2$^2/_3$ cups (400 g) all-purpose (plain) flour

1 teaspoon ground cinnamon

Pinch of salt

$^3/_4$ cup (180 g) butter, cubed

2 tablespoons confectioners' (icing) sugar

$^1/_4$ cup (60 ml) iced water + extra, as required

1 large egg yolk

Filling

1$^3/_4$ pounds (800 g) rhubarb, cut into 2-inch (5 cm) lengths

$^1/_3$ cup (70 g) firmly packed brown sugar

2 tablespoons all-purpose (plain) flour

1 teaspoon vanilla bean paste

1 tablespoon butter

1 large egg yolk

1 tablespoon milk

Serves: 6–8
Preparation: 30 minutes + 1 hour 30 minutes to chill
Cooking: 40–45 minutes
Level: 2

FREE FORM APRICOT PIE

362

Pastry: Lightly grease a large cookie sheet.
• Mix the flour, cinnamon, salt, and butter in a
food processor until the mixture resembles fine
crumbs. • Add the confectioners' sugar and blend.
• Combine the water and egg yolk in a small bowl
and gradually add to the flour mixture until it comes
together as a dough. • Cover with plastic wrap
(cling film), and refrigerate for 1 hour. • Preheat the
oven to 400°F (200°C/gas 6). • Roll the pastry out
on a lightly floured surface to 1/4 inch (5 mm) thick
to make a 14-inch (35-cm) round. Place on the
prepared cookie sheet. • Filling: Combine the
apricots, sugar, ground almonds, and marmalade in
a medium bowl and mix well. • Spoon the filling
into the center of the pastry round. Draw the pastry
up roughly around the filling, so that it is enclosed
but not completely covered. • Beat the egg yolk and
milk in a small bowl and brush over the pastry.
Sprinkle with the almonds and raw sugar. • Bake
for 35–40 minutes, until the pastry is golden
brown and the filling is cooked. • Serve warm
or at room temperature.

Pastry

2²/₃ cups (400 g) all-
purpose (plain) flour

1 teaspoon ground
cinnamon

Pinch of salt

3/4 cup (180 g) butter,
cubed

2 tablespoons
confectioners' (icing)
sugar

1/4 cup (60 ml) iced water
+ extra, as required

1 large egg yolk

Filling

1¼ pounds (600 g)
apricots, pitted and
sliced

1/4 cup (50 g) sugar

2 tablespoons ground
almonds

2 tablespoons orange
marmalade

1 large egg yolk

1 tablespoon milk

2 tablespoons almonds
slivers

1 tablespoon raw sugar

Serves: 6–8
Preparation: 30 minutes
+ 1 hour to chill
Cooking: 35–40 minutes
Level: 2

CHERRY PIE

Pastry: Lightly grease a 9-inch (23-cm) pie pan.
• Process the flour, salt, and butter in a food processor until the mixture resembles fine crumbs.
• Add the confectioners' sugar and blend. •
Combine the water and egg yolk in a small bowl and gradually add to the flour mixture until it comes together as a dough. • Transfer to a lightly floured work surface and shape into two disks. Cover with plastic wrap (cling film), and refrigerate for 1 hour. •
Roll the pastry disks out on a lightly floured work surface to ¼ inch (5 mm) thick. • Line the prepared pan with one of the disks, leaving any excess pastry hanging over the edge. Place the other disk on a plate and refrigerate both for 30 minutes. • Preheat the oven to 400°F (200°C/gas 6). • Filling: Place the cherries, sugar, and almond in a medium saucepan. Put the cornstarch in a small bowl and gradually add the reserved juice, stirring to combine. • Pour the juice into the cherry mixture and simmer over medium-low heat, stirring constantly, until the mixture begins to thicken.
• Spoon the filling into the prepared pie pan and dot with butter. • Lay the remaining pastry round on top, pinching the edges to seal. Trim off any excess pastry. • Beat the egg yolk and milk in a small bowl and brush over the pastry. Cut a few slits in the pastry using a small knife to allow steam to escape during baking. • Bake for 40–45 minutes, until the pastry is golden brown. • Serve warm.

Pastry

2⅔ cup (400 g) all-purpose (plain) flour

1 teaspoon ground cinnamon

Pinch of salt

¾ cup (180 g) butter, cubed

2 tablespoons confectioners' (icing) sugar

¼ cup (60 ml) iced water + extra, as required

1 large egg yolk

Filling

2 (14-ounce/400-g) cans unsweetened tart cherries, drained, 1 cup (250 ml) juice reserved

⅓ cup (75 g) sugar

½ teaspoon almond extract (essence)

1 tablespoon cornstarch (cornflour)

1 tablespoon butter

1 large egg yolk

1 tablespoon milk

Serves: 6–8
Preparation: 30 minutes + 1 hour 30 minutes to chill
Cooking: 40–45 minutes
Level: 2

TIPSY PRUNE TART

Combine the prunes, tea, and lemon zest in a saucepan and slowly bring to a boil. Remove from the heat and let cool for 15 minutes. Drain. • Place the pitted prunes in a bowl, stir in the Armagnac, and leave to macerate for about 2 hours. • Preheat the oven to 375°F (190°C/gas 5). • Butter a 10-inch (25-cm) oval gratin dish with butter. • Pour the melted butter into a medium bowl and add the almonds, flour, and confectioners' sugar. Stir in 2 tablespoons of the Armagnac from the soaked prunes and the almond extract and mix well.
• Whisk the egg whites in another bowl until they form stiff peaks. Gradually fold them into the butter and almond mixture with a large metal spoon. Do not worry if the mixture looks lumpy at this stage—it will be fine once baked. • Spoon into the dish and smooth the top. Arrange the prunes on top in a circle, lightly pressing them down into the mixture. (Reserve any Armagnac liquid for later.) • Bake for 15 minutes. Decrease the oven temperature to 325°F (170°C/gas 3) and bake for another 10–15 minutes, until risen and golden. • Stir the reserved Armagnac liquid into the crème fraîche. • Serve the tart warm, straight from the dish with the crème fraîche or mascarpone mixture.

8   ounces (250 g) prunes, pitted

3/4   cup (200 ml) weak Earl Grey tea

3   strips of lemon zest

1/4   cup (60 ml) Armagnac

7   tablespoons (100 g) unsalted butter, melted

1⅓   cups (130 g) ground almonds

3   tablespoons all-purpose (plain) flour

3/4   cup (125 g) confectioners' (icing) sugar

1/2   teaspoon almond extract (essence)

2   large egg whites

1   cup (250 g) crème fraîche or mascarpone, to serve

Serves: 6
Preparation: 15 minutes
   + 15 minutes to cool
   + 2 hours to macerate
Cooking: 25–30 minutes
Level: 2

CRISPS, PUDDINGS & SOUFFLÉS

BLACKBERRY CLAFOUTIS

Preheat the oven to 350°F (180°C/gas 4). • Lightly brush a 6-cup (1.5-liter) ovenproof dish with 1 tablespoon of butter and set aside. • Combine the flour and eggs in a medium bowl. Add the sugar, milk, and remaining 2 tablespoons melted butter, stirring with a wooden spoon to form a smooth batter. • Pour into the prepared dish. Sprinkle the blackberries on top. • Bake for 30–35 minutes, or until a skewer comes out clean when inserted into the center. • Remove from the oven and dust with confectioners' sugar. • Serve hot, with a dollop of whipped cream on the side.

3   tablespoons butter, melted

2/3   cup (100 g) all-purpose (plain) flour

2   large eggs, lightly beaten

1/2   cup (100 g) superfine (caster) sugar

1   cup (250 ml) milk

3   cups (500 g) fresh blackberries

Confectioners' (icing) sugar, to dust

3/4   cup (180 ml) heavy (double) cream, whipped, to serve

Serves: 6
Preparation: 10 minutes
Cooking: 30–35 minutes
Level: 1

GLUTEN-FREE PLUM CLAFOUTIS

372

Combine the amaranth flour, 5 tablespoons of sugar, salt, and almonds in a large bowl. Mix well. • Beat the eggs and cream in a medium bowl with an electric mixer fitted with a whisk until pale and creamy. • Add to the dry ingredients, whisking until smooth. Stir in 2 tablespoons of the melted butter and the rum. • Preheat the oven to 375°F (190°C/gas 5). • Brush a 9-inch (23-cm) gratin dish or shallow baking pan with the remaining 1 tablespoon of melted butter. • Put the plums in the baking dish. Beat the batter until smooth and pour over the plums. • Bake for 25–35 minutes, or until puffed up and golden brown. It should be set, but still slightly gooey. • Sprinkle with the extra sugar and serve hot with plenty of fresh cream.

⅓ cup (50 g) amaranth flour

5 tablespoons sugar + 2 tablespoons extra, to sprinkle

Pinch of salt

½ cup (50 g) ground almonds

3 large eggs

1 cup (250 ml) light (single) cream or milk

3 tablespoons butter, melted

1 tablespoon rum

1¼ pounds (600 g) small fresh plums, pitted and halved

Fresh cream, to serve

Serves: 4–6
Preparation: 20 minutes
Cooking: 25–30 minutes
Level: 1

■ ■ ■ *Amaranth flour is milled from the seeds of the amaranth plant. It does not contain gluten so is perfect for gluten-free baking. You can buy it in many natural and food stores and from online suppliers.*

BOYSENBERRY CLAFOUTIS

374

Preheat the oven to 350°F (180°C/gas 4). • Lightly grease an 8-inch (20 cm) shallow ovenproof dish. • Place the cream, milk, and vanilla bean in a small saucepan over medium heat and bring almost to a boil. Set aside. • Beat the eggs and sugar in a medium bowl with an electric mixer on high speed until pale and creamy. • Stir in the almonds and flour. • Discard the vanilla bean, then gradually pour the cream mixture into the batter, stirring to combine. • Scatter the boysenberries over the base of the prepared dish. Pour the batter over the top. • Bake for 30–35 minutes, until set and golden. Remove from the oven and let stand for 10 minutes. • Dust with confectioners' sugar. • Serve warm with cream or crème fraiche, if desired.

²⁄₃ cup (150 ml) double (heavy) cream

½ cup (125 ml) milk

1 vanilla bean, split lengthwise

4 large eggs

½ cup (100 g) sugar

⅓ cup (50 g) ground almonds

¼ cup (30 g) all-purpose (plain) flour

1 pound (500 g) boysenberries

Confectioners' (icing) sugar, to dust

Whipped cream or crème fraîche, to serve (optional)

Serves: 4
Preparation: 15 minutes
+ 10 minutes to stand
Cooking: 30–35 minutes
Level: 1

AUSTRIAN APPLE DELIGHT

Cook the apples with the sugar in a heavy-bottomed pan over medium-low heat until softened, about 10 minutes. Do not add any water. Mash coarsely with a fork and leave to cool. • Preheat the oven to 375°F (190°C/gas 5). • Butter an 8-inch (20-cm) pie pan or small gratin dish. • While the apples are cooking, melt the butter in a large frying pan over low heat. When the butter has turned golden brown, add the brown sugar and stir over medium-low heat until the sugar has dissolved, 2–3 minutes. • Add the bread crumbs to the sugar mixture and increase the heat to medium-high. Fry the crumbs until they are toffee-coated, about 5 minutes. • Spread a layer of the bread crumbs over the bottom of the prepared pan, followed by a layer of apple mash and top with the remaining bread crumbs. • Bake for 20 minutes, or until the mixture is bubbling and golden brown. • Let cool to warm, then sprinkle with the grated chocolate, if using. Serve hot with plain yogurt or cream.

1½ **pounds (750 g) Golden Delicious or Gala apples, peeled, cored, and cut into ¼-inch (5-mm) dice**

¼ **cup (50 g) sugar**

¼ **cup (60 g) butter**

¼ **cup (50 g) firmly packed dark brown sugar**

2½ **cups (150 g) fresh white bread crumbs**

2 **tablespoons grated dark chocolate, for sprinkling (optional)**

Plain yogurt or fresh cream, to serve

Serves: 4
Preparation: 25 minutes
Cooking: 30 minutes
Level: 1

PEACH & CHERRY CRISP

378

Filling: Preheat the oven to 350°F (180°C/gas 4).
• Slice the peaches and place in a 6-cup (1.5-liter) ovenproof dish. Add the cherries, sugar, and orange zest and stir to combine. • Topping: Place the flour and cinnamon in a medium bowl. Stir in the sugar then rub in the butter using your finger tips until it resembles bread crumbs. • Stir in the coconut and almonds. • Scatter the topping over the filling in the dish. • Bake for 30–35 minutes, or until golden brown. • Remove from the oven and let stand for 10 minutes. • Serve warm with cream, ice cream, or crème anglaise, if desired.

■ ■ ■ *Crisps are known as crumbles in the United Kingdom, Australia, and New Zealand.*

Filling

2 pounds (1 kg) peaches, peeled, pitted, and halved

1 pound (500 g) cherries, pitted

2 tablespoons sugar

1 teaspoon finely grated orange zest

Topping

1 cup (150 g) all-purpose (plain) flour

1 teaspoon ground cinnamon

⅓ cup (70 g) firmly packed brown sugar

½ cup (125 g) butter, diced

¼ cup (30 g) shredded (desiccated) coconut

¼ cup (40 g) flaked almonds

Ice cream or Vanilla Crème Anglaise (see page 586), to serve (optional)

Serves: 6
Preparation: 30 minutes
+ 10 minutes to stand
Cooking: 30–35 minutes
Level: 1

RHUBARB CRISP

Filling: Preheat the oven to 350°F (180°C/gas 4). Butter a 9-inch (23-cm) pie pan or ovenproof dish. • Melt the butter in a large frying pan over medium heat. When the butter is bubbling, add the rhubarb, sugar, orange zest, orange juice, and vanilla. Stir in the cornstarch. • Simmer over medium heat until the rhubarb is softened but still holds its shape, about 5 minutes. Spoon the rhubarb and its juices into the prepared dish. • Topping: Mix the flour and ginger in a medium bowl. Rub the butter into the flour mixture using your finger tips until the mixture resembles coarse bread crumbs. Stir in the brown sugar and almonds. • Spoon the topping over the rhubarb in the dish. Spread it out so it covers all the fruit, then sprinkle with the water. • Bake for 30–40 minutes, until the topping is golden brown and the juices are bubbling. • Serve hot.

Filling

1	tablespoon butter
1½	pounds (750 g) rhubarb stalks, cut into short lengths
3	tablespoons sugar
	Finely grated zest of 1 orange
1	tablespoon freshly squeezed orange juice
1	tablespoon vanilla extract (essence)
1½	teaspoons cornstarch (cornflour)

Topping

1	cup (150 g) all-purpose (plain) flour
½	teaspoon ground ginger
⅔	cup (150 g) butter, chilled and diced
½	cup (100 g) firmly packed light brown sugar
1	cup (100 g) ground almonds
2	teaspoons water, to sprinkle

Serves: 4
Preparation: 20 minutes
Cooking: 35–45 minutes
Level: 1

ROSE WATER QUINCE WITH PISTACHIO CRISPS

Filling: Preheat the oven to 350°F (180°C/gas 4). • Combine the water, sugar, rose water, vanilla bean, cloves, and lemon zest and juice in a large saucepan over medium-low heat. Simmer until the sugar dissolves, about 10 minutes. • Cut the quinces in half lengthwise, scrape out the hard core with a spoon, and chop coarsely. Place in four 1-cup (250-ml) ramekins. • Pour the cooking liquid over the quinces and cover with aluminum foil. • Bake for 1 hour. • Pistachio Topping: Combine the butter, brown sugar, flour, cinnamon, and pistachios in a medium bowl and mix with your fingertips until the crumbs begin to cling together. Top the quinces with the crumble mixture. • Bake for 30–45 more minutes, until the quinces are tender and crumble is golden. • Serve warm with the yogurt to the side.

Filling

4	cups (1 liter) water
2	cups (400 g) sugar
¼	cup (60 ml) rose water
1	vanilla bean, split lengthwise
5	cloves
1	lemon, zest removed in strips and juiced
4	quinces, peeled

Pistachio Topping

½	cup (125 g) butter, softened
¼	cup (50 g) firmly packed brown sugar
½	cup (75 g) all-purpose (plain) flour
1	teaspoon ground cinnamon
1	cup (150 g) pistachios, ground
¾	cup (180 ml) plain yogurt

Serves: 4
Preparation: 20 minutes
Cooking: 1 hour 40–55 minutes
Level: 2

APPLE & DATE CRISP

384

Filling: Preheat the oven to 350°F (180°C/gas 4).
• Place the apples in a 6-cup (1.5-liter) ovenproof
dish. Add the dates, sugar, lemon juice, and
cinnamon and stir to combine. • Topping: Place the
flour and cinnamon in a medium bowl. Add the
sugar then rub in the butter using your finger tips
until the mixture resembles fine bread crumbs. Stir
in the oats and walnuts. • Scatter over the filling in
the dish. • Bake for 30–35 minutes, or until golden
brown. • Remove from the oven and let stand for
10 minutes. • Serve warm with cream, ice cream,
or crème anglaise, if desired.

Filling

2   pounds (1 kg) tart
    apples, such as
    Granny Smiths, peeled,
    cored, and sliced

¾   cup (135 g) dried
    dates, pitted and
    coarsely chopped

2   tablespoons sugar

2   tablespoons freshly
    squeezed lemon juice

1   teaspoon ground
    cinnamon

Topping

⅔   cup (100 g) all-
    purpose (plain) flour

1   teaspoon ground
    cinnamon

½   cup (125 g) butter,
    diced

⅓   cup (70 g) firmly
    packed brown sugar

⅓   cup (50 g) rolled oats

¼   cup (30 g) walnuts,
    coarsely chopped

    Whipped cream, ice
    cream, or Vanilla
    Crème Anglaise (see
    page 586), to serve
    (optional)

Serves: 4–6
Preparation: 20 minutes
    + 10 minutes to stand
Cooking: 30–35 minutes
Level: 1

PEACH COBBLER

386

Filling: Preheat the oven to 350°F (180°C/gas 4).
• Place the peaches, golden raisins, cinnamon, and orange zest in a 6-cup (1.5-liter) ovenproof dish and stir to combine. • Topping: Combine the flour and baking powder in a medium bowl. Add the sugar and rub in the butter using your finger tips until it resembles fine bread crumbs. Stir in the coconut.
• Combine the milk and lemon juice in a small cup and add to the dry mixture. Stir with a spoon to create a sticky batter. • Drop dollops of the batter over the fruit filling. • Bake for 45–50 minutes, until golden brown. Remove from the oven and let stand for 10 minutes. • Serve warm with cream, ice cream, or crème anglaise, if desired.

Filling

1 (28-ounce/800-g) can peach halves

⅓ cup (60 g) golden raisins (sultanas)

2 tablespoons brown sugar

1 teaspoon ground cinnamon

1 teaspoon finely grated orange zest

Topping

1½ cups (225 g) all-purpose (plain) flour

1½ teaspoons baking powder

⅓ cup (70 g) sugar

⅓ cup (50 g) shredded (desiccated) coconut

½ cup (125 g) butter, diced

½ cup (125 ml) milk

2 teaspoons freshly squeezed lemon juice

Whipped cream, ice cream or Vanilla Crème Anglaise (see page 586), to serve (optional)

Serves: 6
Preparation: 15 minutes
+ 10 minutes to stand
Cooking: 45–50 minutes
Level: 1

QUINCE & BLACKBERRY COBBLER

388

Filling: Put the water, sugar, vanilla bean, and lemon zest in a medium saucepan over medium-high heat and bring to a boil. Add the quinces, decrease the heat to low, cover, and simmer until quinces are tender, about 20 minutes. • Preheat the oven to 350°F (180°C/gas 4). • Drain the syrup off the quinces and reserve. Place the quinces in an 8-cup (2-liter) baking dish. Add the blackberries and ¹/₂ cup (125 ml) of quince juice and stir to combine. • Topping: Combine the flour, baking powder, sugar, and cinnamon in a medium bowl. Rub in the butter using your finger tips until the mixture resembles coarse bread crumbs. Stir in the walnuts.
• Combine the milk and lemon juice in a small cup and add to the dry mixture. Stir with a spoon to create a sticky batter. • Drop dollops of the batter over the fruit filling in the baking dish. • Bake for 40 minutes, until golden brown. • Remove from the oven and let stand for 10 minutes. • Serve warm with ice cream or crème anglaise, if desired.

Filling

2	cups (500 ml) water
³/₄	cup (150 g) sugar
1	vanilla bean, split lengthwise
1	teaspoon finely grated lemon zest
2	pounds (1 kg), quinces, peeled, cored, and chopped
2	cups (300 g) blackberries

Topping

1½	cups (225 g) all-purpose (plain) flour
1½	teaspoons baking powder
¹/₃	cup (70 g) sugar
1½	teaspoons cinnamon
¹/₂	cup (125 g) butter
¹/₃	cup (50 g) walnuts, finely chopped
¹/₂	cup (125 ml) milk
2	teaspoons freshly squeezed lemon juice
	Ice cream or Vanilla Crème Anglaise (see page 586), to serve (optional)

Serves: 6–8
Preparation: 30 minutes
    + 10 minutes to stand
Cooking: 1 hour
Level: 2

APPLE & PLUM COBBLER

Filling: Preheat the oven to 350°F (180°C/gas 4).
• Peel, core, and slice the apples. Place in a
6-cup (1.5-liter) baking dish. Add the plums, sugar,
lemon juice, and cinnamon and stir to combine.
Topping: Combine the flour and baking powder
in a medium bowl. Stir in the sugar then rub in
the butter using your finger tips until the mixture
resembles coarse bread crumbs. • Combine the
milk and lemon juice in a small cup then add to the
dry mixture. Stir with a spoon to create a sticky
batter. • Drop dollops of batter over the fruit filling
in the baking dish. Scatter the almonds over the
top. • Bake for 45–50 minutes, or until golden
brown. Remove from the oven and let stand for
10 minutes. • Serve warm with cream, ice cream,
or crème anglaise, if desired.

Filling

2   pounds (1 kg) tart
    apples, such as Granny
    Smiths

1   (14-ounce/400-g) can
    plums, pitted

¼   cup (50 g) sugar

2   tablespoons freshly
    squeezed lemon juice

1   teaspoon ground
    cinnamon

Topping

1½ cups (225 g) all-
    purpose (plain) flour

1½ teaspoons baking
    powder

⅓   cup (70 g) sugar

½   cup (125 g) butter

½   cup (125 ml) milk

2   teaspoons freshly
    squeezed lemon juice

⅓   cup (75 g) flaked
    almonds

    Whipped cream, ice
    cream or Vanilla Crème
    Anglaise (see page
    586), to serve
    (optional)

Serves: 6–8
Preparation: 20 minutes
    + 10 minutes to stand
Cooking: 45–50 minutes
Level: 1

SPICED APRICOT COBBLER

Filling: Preheat the oven to 350°F (180°C/gas 4).
• Place the apricots, sugar, lemon juice, and orange zest in a 6-cup (1.5 liter) ovenproof dish. Add the spices and stir to combine. • Topping: Combine the flour, baking powder, cinnamon, and cardamom in a medium bowl. • Stir in the sugar then rub in the butter using your finger tips until the mixture resembles coarse bread crumbs. • Combine the milk and lemon juice in a small cup and add to the dry mixture. Stir with a spoon to create a sticky batter. • Drop dollops of batter over the fruit filling in the baking dish. • Bake for 45–50 minutes, until golden brown. • Remove from the oven and let stand for 10 minutes. • Serve warm with ice cream or crème anglaise, if desired.

Filling

2   pounds (1 kg) apricots, pitted and halved

¼   cup (50 g) sugar

2   tablespoons freshly squeezed lemon juice

2   teaspoons finely grated orange zest

1   teaspoon cinnamon

½   teaspoon ground cardamom

¼   teaspoon ground cloves

Topping

1½   cups (225 g) all-purpose (plain) flour

1½   teaspoons baking powder

1½   teaspoons cinnamon

½   teaspoon ground cardamom

⅓   cup (70 g) sugar

½   cup (125 g) butter

½   cup (125 ml) milk

2   teaspoons lemon juice

Ice cream or Vanilla Crème Anglaise (see page 586), to serve (optional)

Serves: 6
Preparation: 30 minutes
    + 10 minutes to stand
Cooking: 45–50 minutes
Level: 1

ORANGE & GINGER PUDDING

394

Preheat the oven to 350°F (180°C/gas 4). • Lightly grease a 4–6 cup (1-1.5-liter) ovenproof pudding basin. • Beat the butter, sugar, candied ginger, and orange zest together in a medium bowl with an electric mixer on high speed until pale and creamy. • Add the egg yolks one at a time, beating to combine. • Stir in the flour, baking powder, and ground ginger. Add the orange juice and milk and stir to combine. • Beat the egg whites in a medium bowl with an electric mixer on medium-high speed until soft peaks form. Stir half of the egg whites into the batter and then gently fold in the remaining whites. • Pour the batter into the prepared pudding basin and place in a deep roasting pan. Add enough boiling water to the pan to come a third of the way up the sides of the basin. • Bake for 45–50 minutes, until the pudding is set and golden brown. Remove from the oven and let stand for 10 minutes. Dust with confectioners' sugar. • Serve warm with ice cream or crème anglaise, if desired.

¼ cup (60 g) butter, softened

¾ cup (150 g) sugar

1 tablespoon candied (glacé) ginger, finely chopped

1 teaspoon finely grated orange zest

3 large eggs, separated

½ cup (75 g) all-purpose (plain) flour

½ teaspoon baking powder

½ teaspoon ground ginger

¾ cup (180 ml) freshly squeezed orange juice

1½ cups (375 ml) milk

Confectioners' sugar, to dust

Ice cream or Vanilla Crème Anglaise (see page 586), to serve (optional)

Serves: 4–6
Preparation: 20 minutes
  + 10 minutes to stand
Cooking: 45–50 minutes
Level: 1

EVE'S PUDDING

Filling: Preheat the oven to 350°F (180°C/gas 4).
• Place a baking sheet in the oven. Generously
butter a 5-cup (1.2-liter) baking dish or 8-inch
(20-cm) pie dish. • Pack the apple slices in the dish
and sprinkle them with brown sugar, lemon zest,
lemon juice, and water. • Topping: Beat the butter
and sugar in a medium bowl with an electric mixer
at high speed until light and creamy. Beat in the
vanilla and lemon extracts. • Add the eggs, a little
at a time, beating in a spoonful of flour after each
addition. • Fold in the remaining flour with a rubber
spatula, along with as much of the milk as required
to make a soft, cake-like batter. • Spoon the batter
over the apples and spread evenly. Make sure the
mixture touches the sides of the dish all around.
• Place the dish on the baking sheet and bake for
40–45 minutes, until the fruit is cooked and the
top is well risen, golden brown, and springy to the
touch. • Dust with confectioners' sugar and serve
hot with cream or crème anglaise.

Filling

1½ pounds (750 g) apples,
    peeled, cored, and thinly
    sliced

⅓   cup (75 g) firmly packed
    light brown sugar

2   teaspoons finely grated
    lemon zest

1   tablespoon freshly
    squeezed lemon juice

1   tablespoon water

Topping

¾   cup (180 g) butter,
    softened

¾   cup (150 g) sugar

¾   teaspoon vanilla extract
    (essence)

⅓   teaspoon lemon extract
    (essence)

3   large eggs, beaten

1⅓ cups (200 g) all-
    purpose (plain) flour

2–3 tablespoons milk

2   tablespoons
    confectioners' (icing)
    sugar, to dust

    Heavy (double) cream or
    Vanilla Crème Anglaise
    (see page 586), to serve

Serves: 4–6
Preparation: 15 minutes
Cooking: 50 minutes
Level: 1

QUEEN OF PUDDINGS

Preheat the oven to 325°F (170°C/gas 3). Butter a 5-cup (1.2-liter) round baking dish. • <u>Pudding:</u> Warm the milk over low heat and add the butter and lemon zest. Remove from the heat. • Lightly whisk the egg yolks with the vanilla sugar and stir into the milk. Mix in the bread crumbs and pour into the pie dish. Let stand for 15 minutes. • Bake for 25–30 minutes, or until lightly set. Remove from the oven and let cool for 5 minutes. • Increase the oven temperature to 350°F (180°C/gas 4). • Warm the preserves in a small pan and spread over the top of the pudding. • <u>Meringue:</u> Beat the egg whites until soft peaks form. Add half the sugar and continue beating until stiff, glossy peaks form. Fold in the rest of the sugar. • Pile the meringue on top of the pudding. • Return the pudding to the oven and bake for 15 more minutes, or until the meringue topping is light golden brown. • Serve warm.

Pudding

1½	cups (375 ml) milk
2	tablespoons butter
2	teaspoons finely grated lemon zest
3	large egg yolks
2	tablespoons vanilla sugar or superfine (caster) sugar
1½	cups (85 g) fresh white bread crumbs
2	tablespoons raspberry preserves (jam)

Meringue

3	large egg whites
⅓	cup (75 g) superfine (caster) sugar

Serves: 4
Preparation: 30 minutes
+ 20 minutes to rest and cool
Cooking: 40–45 minutes
Level: 2

BREAD & BUTTER PUDDING

400

Preheat the oven to 350°F (180°C/gas 4). • Butter a small baking dish measuring about 8 inches (20 cm) square and 2 inches (5 cm) deep. • Spread the butter generously on the bread. Cut each slice into quarters. Layer the pieces of bread, alternating with the raisins, apricots, and lemon zest. Finish with a layer of bread, buttered side up. • Beat the eggs with the superfine sugar and 1/4 cup (60 ml) of the milk in a medium bowl. • Slowly heat the remaining 1³/4 cups milk until hot but not boiling. Gradually pour into the egg mixture. Add the vanilla and stir well. • Pour over the bread in the dish and let stand for 15 minutes, to allow the bread soak up the custard. Sprinkle with Demerara sugar. • Place the baking dish in a roasting pan. Add enough hot water to the roasting pan to come halfway up the sides of the dish. • Bake for 35–40 minutes, until the custard is set and the top is golden and crisp. • Let rest for 10 minutes before serving.

1/4 cup (60 g) butter, softened

6 slices white day-old bread, cut 1/2-inch (1-cm) thick

2/3 cup (120 g) golden raisins (sultanas) or dark raisins

1/3 cup (60 g) ready-to-eat dried apricots, cut into small pieces

Finely grated zest of 1 lemon

3 large eggs

1/4 cup (35 g) superfine (caster) sugar

2 cups (500 ml) milk (or half milk and half cream)

1 teaspoon vanilla extract (essence)

1 tablespoon Demerara sugar, to sprinkle

Serves: 4
Preparation: 25 minutes
    + 25 minutes to stand
Cooking: 35–40 minutes
Level: 1

PAIN AU CHOCOLATE PUDDING

402

Preheat the oven to 350°F (180°C/gas 4). • Butter a 4-cup (1-liter) shallow ovenproof dish. • Slice the pains au chocolat across the chocolate filling about $1/2$-inch (1-cm) thick. • Arrange the slices in the dish overlapping them to fit. Sprinkle with the chocolate chips and dried cherries or cranberries. • Combine the milk and cream in a small saucepan and warm over medium heat. Bring near to boiling point. • Whisk the eggs and sugar in a medium bowl. Slowly add the hot milk mixture and melted butter, whisking continuously until smooth. • Add the vanilla and pour over the pain au chocolat in the dish. Let soak for 10 minutes. • Bake for 30–35 minutes, or until the pudding is set and the top is golden. • Serve hot or warm.

3   day-old pains au chocolat or chocolate croissants

$1/2$ cup (90 g) dark chocolate chips

$1/2$ cup (90 g) dried cherries or cranberries

$1^{1}/_4$ cups (300 ml) milk

$1^{1}/_4$ cups (300 ml) light (single) cream

3   large eggs, beaten

5   tablespoons superfine (caster) sugar

$1/4$ cup (60 g) butter, melted

$1/2$ teaspoon vanilla extract (essence)

Serves: 4
Preparation: 15 minutes + 10 minutes to soak
Cooking: 30–35 minutes
Level: 2

CHOCOLATE VOLCANO

Filling: Combine the chocolate, butter, cream, and sugar in a medium saucepan over very low heat. Stir until the chocolate is melted and the mixture is smooth. Pour into a bowl of the same diameter as your pudding basin, cover, and place in the freezer until firm, about 30 minutes. • Pudding: Butter a 6-quart (1.5-liter) pudding basin or deep ceramic bowl and dust with flour. • Melt the chocolate in a double boiler over barely simmering water. Let cool for a few minutes. • Beat the butter and brown sugar in a large bowl with an electric mixer on high speed until pale and creamy. • With the mixer on medium speed, beat in the egg yolks, one at a time. • Stir in the flour, cornstarch, and baking powder. • Beat the egg whites in a clean bowl with an electric mixer on high speed until soft peaks start to form. • Fold the melted chocolate and 2 tablespoons of the egg whites into the pudding mixture to loosen it. Fold in the remaining egg whites. • Fill the pudding basin with one-third of the pudding mixture. Take the filling out of the freezer and plop it into the basin. Cover with the remaining pudding mixture and level the top. • Butter the basin lid and put it on. (If your basin does not have a lid, or if you are using a bowl, make a double foil square, about 9 inches (23 cm) square, and butter one side. Place the foil over the basin, buttered side downward. Fold in the edges to seal.) • Place the

Filling

5 ounces (150 g) dark chocolate (70% cacao solids), coarsely chopped

1 tablespoon butter

¼ cup (60 ml) heavy (double) cream

2 tablespoons superfine (caster) sugar

Pudding

8 ounces (250 g) dark chocolate, coarsely chopped

⅓ cup (90 g) unsalted butter, softened

½ cup (100 g) firmly packed light brown sugar

6 large eggs, separated

⅔ cup (100 g) all-purpose (plain) flour

3 tablespoons cornstarch (cornflour)

1½ teaspoons baking powder

Serves: 6
Preparation: 30 minutes
  + 30 minutes to freeze
  + 15 minutes to stand
Cooking: 1 hour 10 minutes
Level: 2

pudding basin in a large saucepan. Fill the saucepan with enough cold water to reach halfway up the side of the pudding basin. Cover the pan with a lid and bring to a boil. • Simmer over very low heat until the pudding is firm and risen, about 1 hour. Be careful not to let the pan boil dry and add more water as necessary. • Alternatively, cook the pudding in a steamer. • Carefully remove the basin from the saucepan and let stand for 5 minutes. Remove the lid or foil, loosen the edges with a knife, and turn the pudding out onto a serving plate. • Let rest for 10 minutes before cutting into the chocolate volcano.

RUSSIAN RASPBERRY PUDDING

408

Preheat the oven to 300°F (150°C/gas 2). • Pour the raspberries into a shallow 9-inch (23-cm) gratin dish and sprinkle with 2 tablespoons of the sugar. • Bake on the middle rack of the oven for 5–8 minutes, or until the raspberries are hot. Remove from the oven. • Beat the sour cream with the eggs in a medium bowl with an electric mixer fitted with a whisk until combined. Beat in the flour and remaining sugar. • Pour over the raspberries in the dish. • Bake on the top rack of the oven for 40–45 minutes, until the topping is golden brown. Sprinkle with the confectioners' sugar. • Serve hot or at room temperature.

3	cups (450 g) raspberries
½	cup (100 g) superfine (caster)
¾	cup (200 ml) sour cream
2	large eggs
1	tablespoon all-purpose (plain) flour or potato flour
1	tablespoon confectioners' (icing) sugar

Serves: 4
Preparation: 15 minutes
Cooking: 45–50 minutes
Level: 1

OLD-FASHIONED RICE PUDDING WITH CHERRY SAUCE

410

Rice Pudding: Preheat the oven to 300°F (150°C/ gas 2). Butter a 6-cup (1.5-liter) deep ovenproof dish. • Rinse the rice in cold water and drain well. Combine the rice, 2$\frac{1}{2}$ cups (600 ml) milk, cream, brown sugar, salt, and lemon zest in the dish. Stir well and sprinkle half the nutmeg over the top. Dot the top with 1$\frac{1}{2}$ tablespoons of butter. • Bake for 50 minutes on a low oven rack. • Remove the pudding from the oven and stir in the remaining 1$\frac{1}{2}$ tablespoons of butter. • Return to the oven for another 50–60 minutes. • Remove, stir again, and add a few more tablespoons of milk if the rice looks dry. Sprinkle a little more nutmeg over the top and return the dish to the oven. • Bake for another 30–40 minutes. The rice should have absorbed the liquid and be softly creamy, with a lovely golden crust on top. • Let cool for about 20 minutes.

Cherry Sauce: Put the cherries in a saucepan with the juice and half the sugar. Bring to a simmer over low heat. Simmer for 5–7 minutes, until the cherries are just soft. Add more sugar to taste. • Serve the rice pudding with the cherry sauce spooned over the top.

Rice Pudding

$\frac{1}{2}$ cup (100 g) short-grain pudding or arborio rice

2$\frac{1}{2}$ cups (600 ml) milk, + extra, as needed

2 cups (500 ml) heavy (double) cream

$\frac{1}{4}$ cup (50 g) firmly packed light brown sugar

Pinch of salt

2 strips lemon zest

Large pinch freshly grated nutmeg

3 tablespoons salted butter

Cherry Sauce

12 ounces (350 g) fresh morello cherries, pitted

$\frac{1}{4}$ cup (50 g) firmly packed light brown sugar + extra, to taste

3 tablespoons freshly squeezed orange juice or cranberry juice

Serves: 4–6
Preparation: 10 minutes
    + 20 minutes to cool
Cooking: 2 hours 15
    minutes
Level: 1

MOCHA PUDDING

412

Preheat the oven to 350°F (180°C/gas 4). Lightly grease a 8-cup (2-liter) baking dish. • Combine the flour, baking powder, and cocoa in a medium bowl. • Stir in the sugar, melted butter, egg, and milk until smooth and well combined. • Stir in the chocolate. • Pour the batter into the prepared dish. Pour the hot espresso over the top of the pudding. • Bake for 40 minutes, or until the pudding has risen and is springy to the touch. • Spoon the pudding into six serving bowls, dust with confectioners' sugar, and place a scoop of ice cream to the side.

1½ cups (225 g) all-purpose (plain) flour

1½ teaspoons baking powder

⅓ cup (50 g) unsweetened cocoa powder

1 cup (200 g) sugar

¼ cup (60 g) salted butter, melted

1 large egg, lightly beaten

¾ cup (180 ml) milk

3 ounces (90 g) bittersweet or dark chocolate (70 % cacao), coarsely chopped

2 cups (500 ml) hot espresso coffee

Confectioners' (icing) sugar, for dusting

Vanilla ice cream, to serve

Serves: 6
Preparation: 15 minutes
Cooking: 40 minutes
Level: 1

WARM CRANBERRY & PECAN RISOTTO

Melt the butter in a medium wide-bottomed saucepan over medium-low heat. Add the rice and vanilla bean and cook, stirring with a wooden spoon, for 3 minutes. • Pour in half the milk and $1/4$ cup (50 g) of the sugar and cook, stirring constantly, until the milk has been absorbed. • Add the cranberries, pecans, and remaining milk as required and continue to cook until the rice is tender. • Combine the orange juice, zest, and remaining $1/4$ cup (50 g) sugar in a small saucepan over medium heat and cook until it has reduced to a syrup consistency, about 5 minutes. • Divide the risotto among four serving bowls, top with ricotta, and drizzle with the orange syrup.

414

$1/4$	cup (60 g) butter
$3/4$	cup (150 g) arborio rice
1	vanilla bean, split lengthwise
	About 3 cups (750 ml) milk
$1/2$	cup (100 g) sugar
$1/2$	cup (90 g) dried cranberries
$1/2$	cup (60 g) pecans, toasted
	Finely grated zest and juice of 4 oranges
$3/4$	cup (180 g) ricotta, drained

Serves: 4
Preparation: 15 minutes
Cooking: 25 minutes
Level: 1

PINEAPPLE & COCONUT PUDDING

416

Preheat the oven to 350°F (180°C/gas 4). • Lightly grease a 6 cup (1.5 liter) ovenproof pudding basin. • Combine the flour, baking powder, and baking soda in a medium bowl. Stir in the sugar and coconut. • Combine the eggs, 1/3 cup (90 ml) of coconut milk, and butter in a small bowl. Add the egg mixture and pineapple to the dry ingredients and stir to combine. Pour into the prepared pudding basin. • Bake for 40–45 minutes, until golden and a skewer comes out clean. • Remove from the oven and let stand for 10 minutes. • Meanwhile, place the reserved pineapple juice, remaining coconut milk, and brown sugar in a small saucepan over medium heat. Gently simmer until thickened slightly to make a sauce, 5–10 minutes. • Serve warm with the pineapple sauce and cream or ice-cream, if desired.

1⅓ cups (200 g) all-purpose (plain) flour

1 teaspoon baking powder

½ teaspoon baking soda (bicarbonate of soda)

½ cup (100 g) superfine (caster) sugar

¼ cup (30 g) shredded (desiccated) coconut

2 large eggs, lightly beaten

⅔ cup (180 ml) coconut milk

¼ cup (60 g) butter, melted

1 (14-ounce/400-g) can crushed pineapple, drained, juice reserved

¼ cup (50 g) firmly packed brown sugar

Whipped cream or ice cream, to serve (optional)

Serves: 6–8
Preparation: 25 minutes
  + 10 minutes to stand
Cooking: 40–45 minutes
Level: 1

STEAMED CHOCOLATE & BANANA PUDDING

Lightly grease a 4–6 cup (1–1.5-liter) ovenproof pudding basin. • Beat the butter and sugar in a medium bow with an electric mixer on high speed until creamy. • Add the eggs one at a time, beating until just combined after each addition. • Combine the flour, cocoa, and baking powder in a small bowl. Add the dry ingredients and milk to the egg mixture, stirring to combine. • Mix in the almonds, banana, and chocolate. • Pour the mixture into the prepared pudding basin. Loosely cover with parchment paper or foil, leaving room for the pudding to rise. Secure with kitchen string. • Place the pudding in a large saucepan and add enough boiling water to the pan to come halfway up the sides of the basin. Cover with a tight fitting lid. Steam the pudding over medium-low heat, refilling the water as required, until a skewer comes out clean, 1^1/2–2 hours. • Remove from the steamer and let stand for 10 minutes. • Serve warm with cream, ice-cream or crème anglaise, if desired.

½   cup (125 g) butter, softened

½   cup (100 g) firmly packed dark brown sugar

2   large eggs

¾   cup (125 g) all-purpose (plain) flour

¼   cup (30 g) unsweetened cocoa powder

1½   teaspoons baking powder

¼   cup (60 ml) milk

²⁄₃   cup (60 g) ground almonds

2   large ripe bananas, mashed

3½   ounces (100 g) dark chocolate, coarsely chopped

Whipped cream, ice cream, or Vanilla Crème Anglaise (see page 586), to serve (optional)

Serves: 6
Preparation: 20 minutes + 10 minutes to stand
Cooking: 1 hour 30 minutes–2 hours
Level: 2

STICKY CHOCOLATE & DATE PUDDING

420

Pudding: Preheat the oven to 350°F (180°C/gas 4). • Lightly grease an 8-inch (20 cm) cake pan and line the base with parchment paper. • Place the dates, water, and baking soda in a medium bowl and let stand for 15 minutes. • Beat the butter and sugar in a medium bowl with an electric mixer on high speed until creamy. • Add the eggs one at a time, beating until just combined after each addition. Beat in the vanilla. • With mixer on low speed, add the flour and cocoa powder. • Stir the date mixture and chocolate in by hand. • Spoon the batter into the prepared pan. • Bake for 40–45 minutes, until a skewer comes out clean. • Remove from the oven and let stand for 10 minutes.
• Sauce: Melt the sugar, cream, and chocolate in a small saucepan over low heat, stirring until smooth.
• Serve the pudding warm with chocolate sauce spooned over the top.

Pudding

1⅓ cups (240 g) dried dates, pitted & coarsely chopped

1¼ cups (300 ml) boiling water

1 teaspoon baking soda (bicarbonate of soda)

⅓ cup (90 g) butter, softened

¾ cup (150 g) firmly packed brown sugar

2 large eggs

1 teaspoon vanilla extract (essence)

1 cup (150 g) self-rising flour

2 tablespoons unsweetened cocoa powder

3½ ounces (100 g) dark chocolate, coarsely chopped

Sauce

½ cup (100 g) firmly packed brown sugar

1 cup (250 ml) cream

3½ ounces (100 g) dark chocolate, chopped

Serves: 6–8
Preparation: 30 minutes + 25 minutes to stand
Cooking: 40–45 minutes
Level: 1

FIG BREAD & BUTTER PUDDING

422

Preheat the oven to 350°F (180°C/gas 4).
• Lightly grease a deep 8-inch (20-cm) ovenproof dish. • Place the cream, milk, and vanilla bean in a small saucepan over medium heat and bring almost to a boil. Set aside. • Beat the eggs and sugar in a medium bowl with an electric mixer on high speed until pale and creamy. • Gradually pour in the cream mixture, stirring to combine. Discard the vanilla bean. • Butter the slices of panettone and spread with marmalade. Layer into the prepared dish and scatter with figs. Pour the custard mixture over the top, pushing the panettone down so that it soaks the custard up. Sprinkle with the raw sugar. • Bake for 40–45 minutes, until risen, set, and golden. Remove from the oven and let stand for 10 minutes. • Serve warm with cream or ice-cream, if desired.

1	cup (250 ml) half-and-half (single) cream
1	cup (250 ml) milk
1	vanilla bean, split lengthwise
3	large eggs
½	cup (100 g) sugar
12	ounces (350 g) panettone, sliced
½	cup (125 g) butter, softened
⅓	cup (100 g) orange marmalade
1¼	cups (225 g) dried figs, sliced
1	tablespoon raw sugar
	Whipped cream or ice cream, to serve (optional)

Serves: 6
Preparation: 20 minutes
    + 10 minutes to stand
Cooking: 40–50 minutes
Level: 1

■ ■ ■ *Panettone is a sweet, light raisin and candied fruit cake that Italians eat at Christmas time. It is widely available in many parts of the world in December. If making this pudding at other times of the year, substitute with the same quantity of sweet raisin bread.*

CHOCOLATE SOUFFLÉS WITH CHERRIES

424

Brush the insides of eight 5-ounce (150-ml) ramekins or soufflé dishes with a generous coating of melted butter. Pour in the chocolate and rotate until the sides and bottom are evenly coated with a thick covering of grated chocolate. Shake out any excess and reserve for sprinkling on the baked soufflé. Place the dishes in a baking dish and set aside. • <u>Soufflés:</u> Heat the milk until almost boiling in a small heavy-bottomed saucepan. Gradually add the chocolate, stirring over low heat until melted. • Melt the butter in a medium saucepan, remove from the heat, and stir in the flour. Return to low heat and cook without browning, stirring constantly for 1 minute. • Remove from the heat and whisk in the chocolate milk. Bring to simmering over low heat, stirring constantly, for 2–3 minutes, until smooth and thickened. Stir in the coffee and vanilla extracts. Remove from the heat and let cool slightly. • Stir half the sugar and the almonds into the chocolate mixture. • Whisk in the egg yolks one at a time. (The soufflés can be prepared ahead of time up to this point.) • Preheat the oven to 375°F (190°C/gas 5). Place a spoonful of cherries in each prepared soufflé dish. • Beat the egg whites and salt in a large bowl with an electric mixer fitted with a whisk at high speed until soft peaks form. Gradually add the remaining sugar and whisk until stiff and glossy. • Fold 1 large spoonful of egg whites

| 3 | tablespoons butter, melted |
| 6 | tablespoons finely grated dark chocolate |

Soufflés

1	cup (250 ml) milk
8	ounces (250 g) dark chocolate, coarsely chopped
¼	cup (60 g) unsalted butter
3	tablespoons all-purpose (plain) flour
1	tablespoon coffee extract (essence) or coffee liqueur
2	teaspoons vanilla extract (essence)
⅓	cup (60 g) sugar
2	tablespoons almonds, toasted and ground
6	large eggs, separated
½	cup (125 g) canned or bottled maraschino or morello cherries, drained and pitted
	Pinch of salt
2	tablespoons confectioners' (icing) sugar, to dust

Serves: 8
Preparation: 40 minutes
Cooking: 12–15 minutes
Level: 2

into the chocolate mixture to lighten it, and then gently fold the chocolate mixture into the remaining egg whites. • Set the soufflé dishes on a baking sheet and fill to just below the rim ($\frac{1}{2}$ inch/1 cm from the top) with the mixture. Level off the tops with the back of a spoon. • Bake for 12–15 minutes on a high oven rack, until the soufflés have risen, the tops are dry and almost crisp, and the edges lightly set. • Dust with confectioners' sugar and sprinkle with the reserved grated chocolate. Serve immediately.

■ ■ ■ *From the French, the word soufflé means "puffed up," and is a culinary term for a light frothy dish. Soufflés are renown for being difficult to make, but this is not always so. The flavored base can be made in advance and stored in the refrigerator. Bring the mixture to room temperature before adding the beaten eggs. Just before baking, fold in the stiffly beaten egg whites. As the hot air expands inside the tiny air bubbles, the soufflés will rise. They should be towering successes when you bring them to the table and will sink gracefully as they cool.*

CHOCOLATE SOUFFLÉS

Preheat the oven to 375°F (190°C/gas 5). • Grease four ³/₄-cup (180-ml) soufflé dishes or ramekins with the melted butter. Sprinkle with the superfine sugar to coat, tapping out any excess. Place the dishes in a baking dish and set aside. • Soufflés: Combine the chocolate, cognac, and 3 tablespoons of the superfine sugar in a heatproof bowl. Place over a saucepan of just simmering water and heat until melted, stirring to combine. Remove from the heat and stir in the egg yolks. • Beat the egg whites with an electric mixer on high speed until foamy. • Add the remaining 3 tablespoons of superfine sugar and beat until stiff peaks form. • Stir one-third of the egg whites into the chocolate mixture; gently fold in the remaining whites. • Pour the soufflé mixture into the prepared ramekins. Tap them on a work surface to knock out any air bubbles and smooth the top with the back of a knife or a spatula. Clean around the rim of the ramekins by running your fingers around the edges. Place on a baking sheet. • Bake for 10–15 minutes, or until well risen. • Dust with confectioners' sugar and serve immediately.

2	tablespoons butter, melted
3	tablespoons superfine (caster) sugar

Soufflés

5	ounces (150 g) dark chocolate
1½	tablespoons (25 ml) cognac
6	tablespoons superfine (caster) sugar
4	large egg yolks, lightly beaten
6	large egg whites
	Confectioners' (icing) sugar, to dust

Serves: 4
Preparation: 15 minutes
Cooking: 15–20 minutes
Level: 2

RASPBERRY SOUFFLÉS

Preheat the oven to 350°F (180°C/gas 4). • Use a pastry brush to brush the butter onto the insides of four 1¼-cup (300-ml) ovenproof ramekins. • Sprinkle with the superfine sugar to coat well, then shake out any excess. Place the dishes in a baking dish and set aside. • Soufflés: Melt the butter in a small saucepan over medium-low heat. Add the flour and, stirring constantly, cook for 1 minute. Remove from the heat and gradually add the milk, stirring with a wooden spoon. • Return to the heat and simmer for 5 more minutes, stirring constantly, until the sauce thickens and begins to boil. Decrease the heat to low and simmer gently, stirring constantly, for 2 minutes. • Transfer the mixture to a medium bowl and stir in the superfine sugar and the mashed raspberries. • Beat the egg whites with an electric mixer on high speed until stiff. • Stir a large spoonful of egg white into the raspberry mixture. Gently fold in the remaining egg whites until just incorporated. • Spoon the mixture into the prepared ramekins, leveling the top with the back of a spoon. • Bake for 15–20 minutes, or until well risen and just firm to the touch. • Dust with confectioners' sugar and serve immediately.

3   tablespoons butter, melted
4   tablespoons superfine (caster) sugar

Soufflés

3   tablespoons butter
½   cup (100 g) superfine (caster) sugar
2   tablespoons all-purpose (plain) flour
¾   cup (180 ml) milk
2   cups (300 g) fresh raspberries, mashed with a fork
6   large egg whites
    Confectioners' (icing) sugar, to dust

Serves: 4
Preparation: 15 minutes
Cooking: 25–30 minutes
Level: 2

SALZBURGER NOCKERL

432

Preheat the oven to 400°F (200°C/gas 6). • Scrape the seeds from the vanilla pod into a small bowl and mix with the sugar. • Beat the egg whites in a large bowl with an electric mixer on high speed until soft peaks form. Gradually beat in the sugar until very stiff. • Lightly beat the egg yolks. Fold into the egg white mixture with a large metal spoon. Fold in the lemon and orange zests. • Dust with the flour and fold in gently, taking care to keep as much air in the mix as possible. • Melt the butter in a shallow 9-inch (23-cm) square baking pan or gratin dish. Stir in the cream. • Spoon the egg mixture into the dish. • Bake for 10–15 minutes, until golden and risen. • Dust with confectioners' sugar and serve immediately.

¼	vanilla pod, slit lengthways
⅓	cup (90 g) sugar
5	large eggs, separated
	Finely grated zest of 1 lemon
	Finely grated zest of 1 orange
1	heaped tablespoon all-purpose (plain) flour
2	tablespoons butter
¼	cup (60 ml) heavy (double) cream
2	tablespoons confectioners' (icing) sugar, to dust

Serves: 4
Preparation: 20 minutes
Cooking: 10–15 minutes
Level: 2

■ ■ ■ *This sweet dumpling soufflé comes from Mozart's hometown of Salzburg in Austria.*

ORANGE & LEMON SOUFFLÉS

434

Brush half the melted butter inside four 1-cup (250-ml) soufflé dishes. Chill for 5 minutes. Brush with the remaining melted butter. • Mix the almonds with the sugar. Spoon into the dishes and rotate until the sides and bottom are evenly coated. Shake out any excess. • Soufflés: Melt the butter in a medium saucepan. Remove from the heat and stir in the flour. Return to low heat and simmer gently, stirring constantly, without browning for 1 minute. • Remove from the heat, beat in the warm milk, and return to the heat. Simmer for 1–2 minutes over medium heat, stirring constantly, until thickened and bubbles appear on the surface. Remove from the heat and let cool slightly. • Whisk in the egg yolks one at a time. • Combine the lemon and orange zests, orange juice, 2 tablespoons of the superfine sugar, and the Cointreau in a small bowl. Stir into the milk and egg mixture. • Preheat the oven to 375°F (190°C/gas 5). • Place a baking sheet in the oven. • Beat the egg whites and salt in a large bowl with an electric mixer on high speed until soft peaks form. Add the remaining 1 tablespoon superfine sugar and beat until stiff and glossy. • Stir a generous spoonful of the whites into the citrus mixture then fold in the rest, working quickly. • Spoon into the individual dishes to ½ inch (1 cm) from the top • Bake for 15–18 minutes, until golden and risen above the rim, but still slightly soft in the center. • Dust with confectioners' sugar and serve immediately.

3   tablespoons butter, melted

4   tablespoons finely ground almonds

1   tablespoon superfine (caster) sugar

Souffles

2   tablespoons butter

2   tablespoons all-purpose (plain) flour

²/₃   cup (150 ml) milk, heated

3   large egg yolks

1   teaspoon finely grated lemon zest

    Zest and freshly squeezed juice of 1 orange, about ⅓ cup (75 ml)

3   tablespoons superfine (caster) sugar

1   tablespoon Cointreau or Grand Marnier

4   large egg whites

    Pinch of salt

    Confectioners' (icing) sugar, to dust

Serves: 4
Preparation: 35 minutes
Cooking: 15–18 minutes
Level: 2

BLACKBERRY SOUFFLÉS

Preheat the oven to 375°F (190°C/gas 5). • Grease six ³/₄-cup (180-ml) soufflé dishes or ramekins with melted butter. Sprinkle with superfine sugar to coat, tapping out any excess. Place the dishes in a baking dish and set aside. • Soufflés: Beat the egg yolks and 2 tablespoons of sugar in a small bowl with an electric mixer on high speed until pale and creamy. • Sift in the cornstarch and flour, beating to combine. • Place the milk, 2 tablespoons of sugar, and vanilla bean in a small saucepan over medium heat and bring almost to a boil.• Gradually strain the milk into the egg mixture, stirring to combine. Discard the vanilla bean. • Return the mixture to the pan and bring to a simmer over medium heat, stirring continuously until thickened, 3–4 minutes. Transfer to a bowl, cover with plastic wrap (cling film), and set aside. • Place the blackberries and 2 tablespoons of sugar in a food processor and blend until smooth. Strain through a fine mesh sieve into a medium bowl. • Add the egg mixture and beat to combine. • Beat the egg whites in a medium bowl with an electric mixer on high speed until foamy. Gradually add the remaining 2 tablespoons of sugar, beating until smooth, glossy peaks form. • Fold half of the whites into the blackberry mixture. Gently fold in the remaining egg whites. • Spoon into the prepared dishes and gently tap on the bench. Run your thumb around the inside rim of the dishes to help prevent them from sticking. • Bake for 15–17 minutes, until well risen. Dust with confectioners' sugar and serve immediately.

3	tablespoons butter, melted
4	tablespoons superfine (caster) sugar

Soufflés

3	large egg yolks
½	cup (100 g) superfine (caster) sugar
1	tablespoon cornstarch (cornflour)
²/₃	tablespoon all-purpose (plain) flour
1	cup (250 ml) milk
1	vanilla bean, split lengthwise
3	cups (450 g) blackberries
2	large egg whites
	Confectioners' (icing) sugar, to dust

Serves: 6
Preparation: 20 minutes
Cooking: 20–25 minutes
Level: 2

MANGO SOUFFLÉS

438

Preheat the oven to 375°F (190°C/gas 5). • Grease six ¾-cup (180-ml) soufflé dishes or ramekins with melted butter. Sprinkle with superfine sugar to coat, tapping out any excess. Place dishes in a baking dish and set aside. • <u>Soufflés:</u> Beat the egg yolks and 2 tablespoons of sugar in a small bowl with an electric mixer on high speed until pale and creamy. • Sift in the cornstarch and flour, beating to combine. • Place the milk and 2 tablespoons of sugar in a small saucepan over medium heat and bring almost to a boil. • Gradually strain the milk into the egg mixture, stirring to combine. Return the mixture to the pan and bring to a simmer over medium heat, stirring continuously until thickened, 3–4 minutes. Transfer to a bowl, cover with plastic wrap (cling film), and set aside. • Place the mango and 2 tablespoons of sugar in a food processor and blend until smooth. Transfer to a medium bowl. Add the lime zest and egg mixture and beat to combine. • Beat the egg whites in a medium bowl with an electric mixer on high speed until foamy. Gradually add the remaining 2 tablespoons of sugar, beating until smooth, glossy peaks form. • Fold half of the egg whites into the mango mixture. Gently fold in the remaining egg whites. • Spoon into the prepared dishes and gently tap on the bench. Level the tops using the back or a knife or spoon. Run your thumb around the inside rim of the dishes to help prevent them from sticking. • Bake for 15–17 minutes, until well risen and golden. • Dust with confectioners' sugar and serve immediately.

3 tablespoons butter, melted

4 tablespoons superfine (caster) sugar

Soufflés

3 large egg yolks

½ cup (100 g) superfine (caster) sugar

1 tablespoon cornstarch (cornflour)

⅔ tablespoon all-purpose (plain) flour

1 cup (250 ml) milk

1 pound (500 g) mango, coarsely chopped

2 teaspoons finely grated lime zest

2 large egg whites

Confectioners' (icing) sugar, to dust

Serves: 6
Preparation: 20 minutes
Cooking: 20–25 minutes
Level: 2

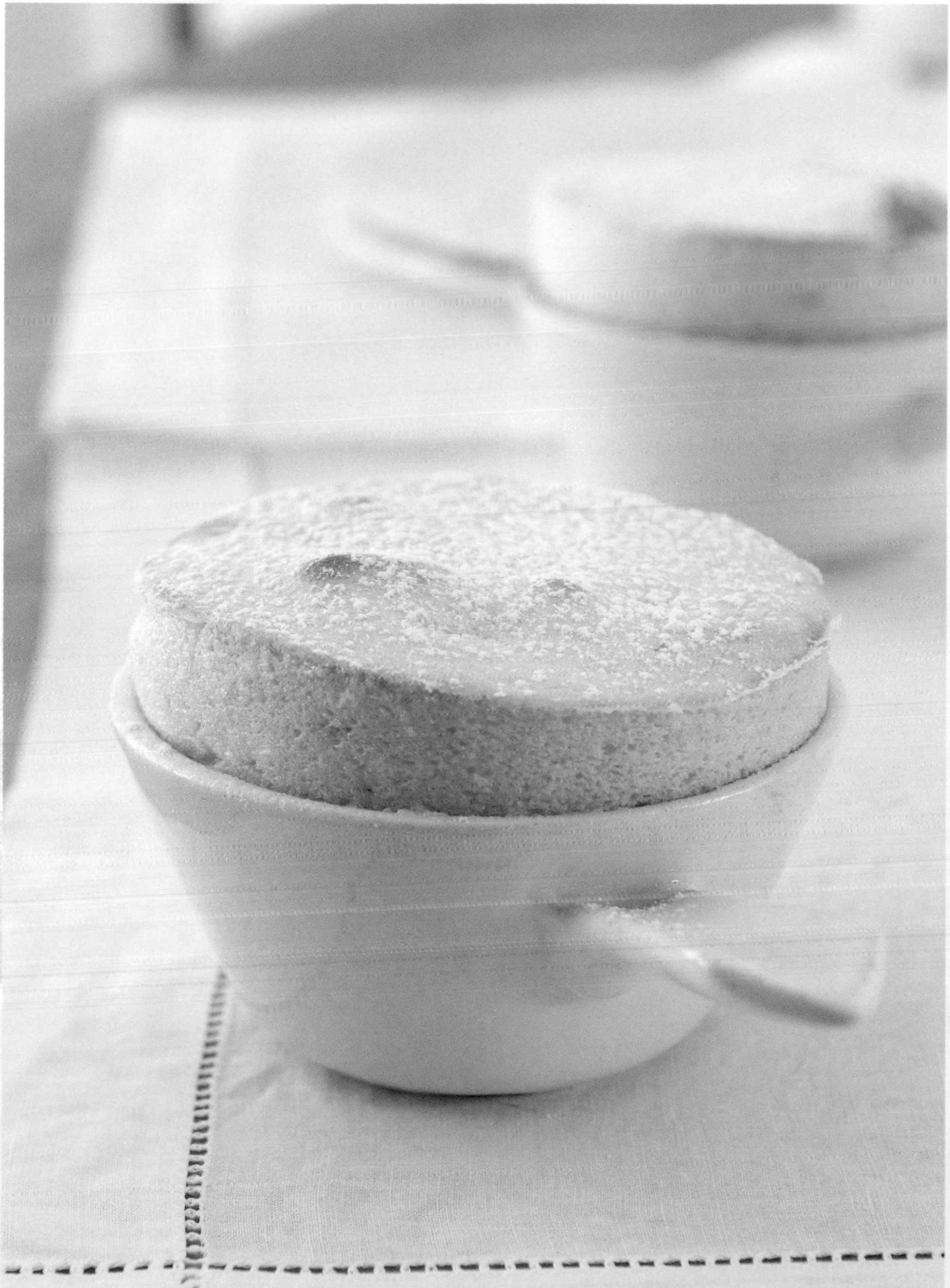

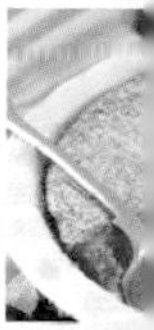

CHOCOLATE CHERRY SOUFFLÉS

Preheat the oven to 375°F (190°C/gas 5). • Grease six ¾ cup (180 ml) soufflé dishes or ramekins with the melted butter. Sprinkle with the superfine sugar to coat, tapping out any excess. Place the dishes on a baking dish and set aside. • <u>Soufflés:</u> Beat the egg yolks and 2 tablespoons of sugar in a small bowl with an electric mixer on high speed until pale and creamy. • Sift in the cornstarch and flour, beating to combine. • Place the milk and 2 tablespoons of sugar in a small saucepan over medium heat and bring almost to a boil. • Gradually strain the milk into the egg mixture, stirring to combine. Return the mixture to the pan and bring to a simmer over medium heat, stirring continuously until thickened, 3–4 minutes. • Transfer to a bowl, cover with plastic wrap (cling film), and set aside. • Heat the chocolate in a double boiler over barely simmering water until melted. • Place the cherries, 2 tablespoons of sugar, and the liqueur in a food processor and blend until smooth. Transfer to a medium bowl. Add the egg mixture and chocolate, whisking to combine. • Beat the egg whites in a medium bowl with an electric mixer until foamy. Gradually add the remaining 2 tablespoons of sugar, beating until stiff, glossy peaks form. • Fold half of the egg whites into the cherry mixture. Gently fold in the remaining egg whites. • Spoon into the prepared dishes. Level the tops using the back or a knife or spoon. Run your thumb around the inside rim of the dishes to help prevent them from sticking. • Bake for 15–17 minutes, until well risen and golden. Dust with confectioners' sugar and serve immediately.

3 tablespoons butter, melted

4 tablespoons superfine (caster) sugar

Soufflés

3 large egg yolks

½ cup (100 g) superfine (caster) sugar

1 tablespoon cornstarch (cornflour)

⅔ tablespoon all-purpose (plain) flour

1 cup (250 ml) milk

3½ ounces (100 g) dark chocolate, coarsely chopped

1 (14-ounce/400-g) can pitted cherries, in syrup, drained

1 tablespoon cherry liqueur

2 large egg whites

Confectioners' (icing) sugar, to dust

Serves: 6
Preparation: 20 minutes
Cooking: 25–30 minutes
Level: 2

CRÊPES, WAFFLES & FRITTERS

CRÊPES WITH CHERRY-ORANGE SAUCE

444

Basic Crepes: Mix the flour and salt in a medium bowl. Beat in the eggs one at a time. Gradually add the milk, beating until smooth. Set the batter aside to rest for 1 hour. • **Step 1:** Melt 1 teaspoon of butter in a crêpe pan or small frying pan over medium heat. Pour in 2–3 tablespoons of batter and swirl the pan to form a thin even layer. • **Step 2:** Cook the crêpe until golden brown, about 2 minutes. • **Step 3:** Use a metal spatula to help turn the crêpe and cook the other side until golden brown, about 2 minutes. Remove from the pan and stack on a plate. Add another teaspoon of batter and cook the next crêpe in the same way. Repeat until all the batter is used. Keep the cooked crêpes in a stack in a warm oven. • Filling: Combine the cherries, water, and sugar in a medium saucepan over medium heat. Bring to a boil. Lower the heat and simmer until the sauce has thickened to make a syrup, about 10 minutes. Remove from the heat and let cool. Stir in the Grand Marnier. • **Step 4:** Fold the crêpes in half and spread with cherry sauce. Fold in half again to form triangles. • Dust with confectioners' sugar and serve warm.

Basic Crêpes

1	cup (150 g) all-purpose (plain) flour
	Pinch of salt
4	large eggs
2	cups (250 ml) milk
⅓	cup (90 g) butter

Filling

14	ounces (400 g) cherries, pitted
1	cup (250 ml) water
½	cup (100 g) sugar
¼	cup (60 ml) Grand Marnier
3	tablespoons confectioners' (icing) sugar, to dust

Serves: 6
**Preparation: 15 minutes
    + 1 hour to rest**
Cooking: 30 minutes
Level: 1

■ ■ ■ *This recipe for basic crêpes makes 12 thin dessert crêpes using a 9-inch (23-cm) pan. Allow two crêpes per person when serving.*

Prepare the batter at least 1 hour before cooking the crêpes. Cover and place in the refrigerator for up to 24 hours. Crêpes are best served as soon as they are made but they can be layered between greaseproof paper and chilled in the refrigerator for 2–3 days. Reheat before serving.

1. MELT 1 teaspoon of butter in a crêpe pan over medium heat. Pour in 2–3 tablespoons of batter. Swirl the pan to form a thin even layer.

2. COOK the crêpe until golden brown, about 2 minutes. Use a metal spatula to turn the crêpe.

3. COOK the other side until golden brown, about 2 minutes. Transfer to a plate. Add another teaspoon of butter and cook the next crêpe.

4. FOLD the crêpes in half and spread with filling. Fold in half again to make a triangle. Dust with confectioners' sugar and serve.

CRÊPES WITH MARMALADE & STRAWBERRIES

Prepare the crêpe batter and use it to make 12 crêpes. Stack on a plate and set aside in a warm oven. • <u>Filling:</u> Stir the marmalade and Grand Marnier in a heavy-bottomed saucepan over medium heat until warmed. Set aside to cool. Stir in the strawberries. • Place 2 crêpes on each of 6 individual serving dishes. Spoon 1–2 tablespoons of filling onto one half of each crêpe and fold over.
• Sprinkle each dish with 1 tablespoon of sugar.
• Sprinkle with the extra strawberries and serve.

1   **recipe Basic Crêpes (see page 444)**

Filling

1   **cup (300 g) orange marmalade**

⅓   **cup (90 ml) Grand Marnier**

2   **cups (300 g) strawberries, sliced**

6   **tablespoons sugar**

Serves: 6
Preparation: 20 minutes + time to prepare the crêpes
Cooking: 30 minutes
Level: 1

■ ■ ■ *If liked, replace the Grand Marnier with cassis and use raspberries or cranberries instead of strawberries.*

RASPBERRY & RICOTTA CRÊPE PARCELS

Prepare the crêpe batter and use it to make 12 crêpes. Stack on a plate and set aside in a warm oven. • <u>Filling:</u> Beat the ricotta and sugar in a medium bowl until creamy. • Add the candied lemon peel, chocolate, cinnamon, rum, and orange juice and mix well. • Spoon 1 tablespoon of the filling onto the center of each crêpe. Fold up the corners to make small parcels and tie with the orange peel. • <u>Sauce:</u> Heat the sugar and orange juice in a heavy-bottomed saucepan over medium heat until the sugar has dissolved. • Place the raspberries in a small bowl and mash with a fork until smooth. • Add the raspberries to the sugar and orange mixture. Simmer over low heat until slightly reduced and thickened, about 5 minutes. • Press through a sieve to remove the seeds. • Serve the crêpes hot with the raspberry sauce on the side.

■ ■ ■ *The filling, sauce, and crêpe batter can all be prepared ahead of time and kept in the refrigerator. When ready to serve, cook the crêpes, fill, and serve hot with the sauce on the side ready to be spooned over the top.*

1   **recipe Basic Crêpes (see page 444)**

Filling

1   **cup (250 g) very fresh ricotta cheese, drained**

¼   **cup (50 g) sugar**

2   **ounces (60 g) candied lemon peel, coarsely chopped**

2   **ounces (60 g) dark chocolate, coarsely chopped**

1   **teaspoon ground cinnamon**

1   **teaspoon rum**

2   **tablespoons freshly squeezed orange juice**

Sauce

½   **cup (100 g) sugar**

2   **tablespoons freshly squeezed orange juice**

3   **cups (450 g) fresh raspberries**

Peel of 1 large orange, cut in one long thin strip, then cut in pieces 6 inches (15 cm) long

Serves: 6
Preparation: 20 minutes + time to prepare the crêpes
Cooking: 10 minutes
Level: 2

CRÊPES WITH BANANA & LEMON FILLING

Prepare the crêpe batter and use it to make 12 crêpes. Stack on a plate and set aside in a warm oven. • Beat the cream and 2 tablespoons sugar together until thickened. • Carefully stir in the banana and lemon juice. • Spread each crêpe with 3-4 tablespoons of filling and roll up. Sprinkle with the remaining sugar. • Serve immediately.

1 recipe Basic Crêpes
   (see page 444)

Filling

1 cup (250 ml) heavy
   (double) cream

6 tablespoons sugar

3 large bananas, mashed

2 tablespoons freshly
   squeezed lemon juice

Serves: 6
Preparation: 15 minutes
   + time to prepare the
   crêpes
Level: 1

CRÊPES SUZETTE

Prepare the crêpe batter, mixing in 1 tablespoon of Grand Marnier, and use it to make 12 crêpes. Stack on a plate and set aside in a warm oven. • Rub the sugar lumps with the orange and lemon and set aside for 15 minutes so that the sugar is perfumed with the zest of the fruit. • Combine the butter with the sugar lumps, orange juice, and orange and lemon zest in a large heavy-bottomed saucepan. Place over low heat and stir until the sugar is melted. Simmer for 5 minutes, then stir in 4 tablespoons of Grand Marnier. • Dip the crêpes into the mixture one by one, then fold each one in quarters and arrange on a warm, heatproof serving plate. • Sprinkle with the sugar and drizzle with the remaining 4 tablespoons of Grand Marnier. Carefully light the alcohol. Serve while still burning.

1	recipe Basic Crêpes (see page 444)

Filling

9	tablespoons Grand Marnier
12	sugar lumps
1	orange
1	lemon
½	cup (125 g) butter
1	cup (250 ml) freshly squeezed orange juice, strained
1	tablespoon finely grated orange zest
4	tablespoons sugar, to sprinkle

Serves: 6
Preparation: 30 minutes + time to prepare the crêpes
Cooking: 15 minutes
Level: 2

■ ■ ■ *These crêpes were invented by French chef Henri Charpentier for Edward, Prince of Wales, reportedly by accident. The young chef, just 14 years old at the time, was preparing the prince's dessert when it caught fire. He thought it was ruined but, on tasting it, he realized it was delicious. The name Suzette was given in honor of the prince's guest that day.*

PINEAPPLE CRÊPE LAYER CAKE

Prepare the crêpe batter and use it to make 12 crêpes. Stack on a plate and set aside in a warm oven. • Filling: Place a crêpe on a serving dish and spread with a layer of pastry cream. Drizzle with a teaspoon of Grand Marnier and top with a little pineapple. Place another crêpe on top and repeat until all crêpes have been stacked.
• Syrup: Caramelize the sugar in a heavy-bottomed saucepan over medium-low heat. When deep gold, stir in the orange juice and simmer until reduced.
• Add the cream and bring to a boil. Simmer for 2–3 minutes, then set aside to cool. • Stir in the remaining Grand Marnier, pour over the crêpes and serve hot.

1   recipe Basic Crêpes (see page 444)

Filling & Syrup

1   recipe Vanilla Pastry Cream (see page 590)

1   cup (250 ml) Grand Marnier

12 ounces (350 g) canned pineapple rings, drained and chopped

3/4 cup (150 g) sugar

1   cup (250 ml) freshly squeezed orange juice, strained

1/3 cup (90 ml) heavy (double) cream

Serves: 6
Preparation: 25 minutes
  + time to prepare the crêpes and pastry cream
Cooking: 15 minutes
Level: 2

CRÊPES WITH CARAMELIZED APPLES

458

Prepare the crêpe batter and use it to make 12 crêpes. Stack on a plate and set aside in a warm oven. • <u>Syrup:</u> Place the apple cider, corn syrup, brown sugar, and lemon juice in a heavy-bottomed saucepan and bring to a boil. Simmer until the mixture has reduced by half, about 10 minutes. Remove from heat and stir in the butter. Set aside. • <u>Filling:</u> Melt the remaining butter in a medium frying pan over medium heat. • Add the apples and cook, stirring often, until the fruit is tender but not mushy, about 5 minutes. • Sprinkle with the sugar and simmer until caramelized and golden, about 10 minutes. Divide the crepes among 6 serving dishes. Garnish with the apple and drizzle with the syrup. • Serve immediately.

1   recipe Basic Crêpes (see page 444)

Filling

1   cup (250 ml) apple cider

¼   cup (60 ml) corn (golden) syrup

1   tablespoon brown sugar

1   tablespoon freshly squeezed lemon juice

2   tablespoons butter

Filling

2   tablespoons butter

3   firm sweet apples, such as Golden Delicious, peeled, cored, and cut into wedges

½   cup (100 g) firmly packed dark brown sugar

Serves: 6
Preparation: 30 minutes + time to prepare the crêpes
Cooking: 30 minutes
Level: 2

CRÊPES WITH BLUEBERRIES

460

Prepare the crêpe batter and use it to make 12 crêpes. Stack on a plate and set aside in a warm oven. • <u>Filling:</u> Place half the blueberries, the lemon juice and zest, sugar, ginger, and cinnamon in a heavy-bottomed saucepan. Bring to a boil over medium-high heat, stirring constantly. Simmer over low heat until the fruit has broken down and the mixture is thick, about 10 minutes. • Stir in the remaining blueberries. Cook, stirring constantly, for 1 minute. • Fold the crêpes in half and in half again to form triangles. • Melt the butter in a large frying pan over medium heat. Add the crêpes and fry until golden brown. • Serve hot with the blueberries.

1   **recipe Basic Crêpes (see page 444)**

Filling

1   **pound (500 g) fresh or frozen blueberries**

    Freshly squeezed juice and grated zest of ½ lemon

3   **tablespoons sugar**

½   **teaspoon ground ginger**

½   **teaspoon ground cinnamon**

¼   **cup (60 g) butter**

Serves: 4
Preparation: 30 minutes
   + time to prepare the crêpes
Cooking: 15 minutes
Level: 2

FRUIT-FILLED CRÊPES WITH MERINGUE TOPPING

Prepare the crêpe batter and use it to make 12 crêpes. Stack on a plate and set aside in a warm oven. • Filling: Place the pears, peaches, sugar, and butter in a heavy-bottomed saucepan. Simmer over low heat until the fruit has broken down, about 20 minutes. • Chop the fruit mixture in a food processor. Add the amaretti, egg yolk, and almond liqueur and chop until smooth. • Place a crêpe in a greased 9-inch (23-cm) ovenproof dish and spread with filling. Repeat until all the crêpes and filling are in the dish. • Beat the egg whites and confectioners' sugar in a medium bowl with an electric mixer on high speed until stiff peaks form. • Heat the preserves in a small saucepan over low heat until warm. Brush the preserves over the crêpes. Spoon the meringue over the top and smooth with the back of a spoon. • Place under a hot broiler (grill) and broil (grill) until the meringue is golden. Serve warm.

1   recipe Basic Crêpes (see page 444)

Filling

1   pound (500 g) small sweet pears, peeled and sliced

1   pound (500 g) ripe yellow peaches, peeled and sliced

½   cup (100 g) sugar

¼   cup (60 g) butter

4   ounces (125 g) amaretti cookies

1   large egg yolk

2   tablespoons almond liqueur

3   large egg whites

⅔   cup (100 g) confectioners' (icing) sugar

¼   cup (60 g) apricot preserves (jam)

Serves: 6
Preparation: 30 minutes + time to prepare the crêpes
Cooking: 30 minutes
Level: 2

CHESTNUT CRÊPES

464

Chestnut Crêpes: Combine both flours, eggs, sugar, and butter in a medium bowl. Gradually whisk in the milk. • Set aside to rest for 2 hours. • Place 1 teaspoon of extra butter in a crêpe pan or small frying pan over medium heat and warm until the butter has melted. Spoon 2 tablespoons of batter into the pan and swirl so that the batter evenly coats the base of the pan. Cook the crêpe until golden brown, about 2 minutes. Use a metal spatula to turn the crêpe and cook the other side until golden brown, about 2 minutes. • Remove from the pan and stack on a plate. Add another teaspoon of batter to the pan and cook the next crêpe in the same way. Repeat until all the batter is used. Keep the cooked crêpes in a warm oven. • Filling: Beat the cream and confectioners' sugar in a medium bowl until thick. Fold in the candied chestnuts. • Spoon 2 tablespoons of the filling onto one half of each crêpe. Fold over in half and in half again to make a triangle. Dust with confectioners' sugar. Serve immediately.

■ ■ ■ *Chestnut flour is available in some health food stores and from online suppliers. If you can't find it for this recipe, replace with the same quantity of whole-wheat (wholemeal) flour.*

Chestnut Crêpes

¾ cup (125 g) all-purpose (plain) flour

⅔ cup (100 g) chestnut flour

3 large eggs

1 tablespoon sugar

3 tablespoons butter, melted, + extra, to cook the crêpes

2 cups (500 ml) milk

Filling

1 cup (250 ml) heavy (double) cream

2 tablespoons confectioners' (icing) sugar, + extra, to dust

8 ounces (250 g) candied chestnuts (marrons glacés), chopped

Serves: 6–8
Preparation: 20 minutes
    + 2 hours to rest
Cooking: 20 minutes
Level: 2

WAFFLES WITH CHANTILLY CREAM & BERRY FRUIT

Waffles: Step 1: Beat the egg yolks and sugar in a small bowl or pitcher (jug). Pour in the milk, water, and vanilla, beating to combine. Mix the flour, baking powder, cornstarch, and salt in a medium bowl. Gradually add the milk mixture and melted butter, stirring with a wooden spoon to form a batter. • **Step 2:** Beat the egg whites in a small bowl with an electric mixer on high speed until stiff peaks form. Gently fold the whites into the batter. Cover the bowl with plastic wrap (cling film) and refrigerate for 30 minutes. • **Step 3:** Heat a waffle iron and lightly grease. Pour in 1/2 cup (125 ml) of batter and cook until golden brown and crisp, about 5 minutes. Repeat until you have eight waffles. Keep warm in a warm oven. • Chantilly Cream: **Step 4:** Beat the cream, confectioners' sugar, and vanilla in a medium bowl with an electric mixer on medium-high speed until thickened. • To serve, place two hot waffles on each serving plate. Top with berries and Chantilly Cream and serve warm.

Waffles

2   large eggs, separated

2   teaspoons sugar

3/4 cup (180 ml) milk

1/2 cup (125 ml) water

1   teaspoon vanilla extract (essence)

2   cups (300 g) all-purpose (plain) flour

1   teaspoon baking powder

2   tablespoons cornstarch (cornflour)

     Pinch of salt

1/2 cup (125 g) butter, melted

Chantilly Cream

1   cup (250 ml) heavy (double) cream

1   tablespoon confectioners' (icing) sugar

1/2 teaspoon vanilla extract (essence)

3   cups (450 g) fresh berries (raspberries, blueberries, sliced strawberries, etc)

Serves: 4
Preparation: 25 minutes
     + 30 minutes to chill
Cooking: 40 minutes
Level: 2

You will need a waffle iron to make these desserts. There are many different types of waffle iron available. If you don't already own a waffle iron we suggest you invest in a simple one with a single surface which are easier to clean than those with removeable surfaces. Some waffle irons have audible tones that tell you when the iron is hot enough to cook the batter.

1

2

1. BEAT the egg yolks and sugar. Beat in the milk, water, and vanilla. Mix the flour, baking powder, cornstarch, and salt in a medium bowl. Gradually add the milk mixture and butter.

2. BEAT the egg whites in a small bowl until stiff peaks form. Gently fold the whites into the batter. Cover the bowl and refrigerate for 30 minutes.

3

4

3. HEAT a waffle iron and grease. Pour in $1/2$ cup (125 ml) of batter and cook for 5 minutes, until golden and crisp.

4. BEAT the cream, confectioners' sugar, and vanilla in a medium bowl until a thick Chantilly Cream forms.

WAFFLES WITH BAKED PLUMS

470

Prepare the waffle batter. Cover the bowl with plastic wrap (cling film) and refrigerate for 30 minutes. • Baked Plums: Preheat the oven to 350°F (180°C/gas 4). • Place the plums cut-side down on a small baking sheet. Bake for 10 minutes, turn over, and bake for 5 more minutes. Remove from the oven and keep warm. • Heat the waffle iron and lightly grease. Pour in 1/2 cup (125 ml) of batter and cook until golden brown and crisp, about 5 minutes. Repeat until you have eight waffles. Keep warm in a warm oven. • Place two hot waffles on each serving plate, arrange two plum halves and a scoop of ice cream on top. Drizzle with maple syrup and serve.

1 recipe Waffles (see page 466)

Baked Plums

8 purple (blood) plums, halved and pitted (stoned)

4 scoops good-quality vanilla ice-cream

1/2 cup (125 ml) pure maple syrup, warmed

Serves: 4
Preparation: 25 minutes + 30 minutes to chill
Cooking: 40 minutes
Level: 2

■ ■ ■ *Serve the waffles with the homemade Vanilla Ice Cream on page 124 or Banana Ice Cream on page 130.*

CHURROS WITH CHOCOLATE SAUCE

Chocolate Sauce: Heat the water and sugar over medium heat until the sugar dissolves. Decrease the heat to low and add the chocolate, cocoa powder, and milk. Cook, stirring continuously, until the chocolate melts to form a smooth sauce. Set aside, keeping warm. • Churros: Combine the sugar, water, and butter in a large saucepan over medium heat and bring to a boil. • Stir in the flour and salt with a wooden spoon and cook until the dough comes away from the sides of the pan, about 2 minutes. • Remove from the heat and beat in the eggs, stirring continuously until incorporated. • Heat the oil in a deep-fryer or deep saucepan to 365°F (190°C). If you don't have a frying thermometer, test the oil temperature by dropping a small piece of bread into the hot oil. If the bread immediately bubbles to the surface and begins to turn golden, the oil is ready. • Spoon the dough into a pastry bag fitted with a ¹⁄₂-inch (1-cm) star tip nozzle. Pipe 4-inch (10-cm) lengths into the hot oil and fry until golden. Remove from the oil with tongs or a slotted spoon and drain on paper towels. Continue until all the dough is used. • Pour the sauce into six espresso cups and place on individual serving plates with the churros to the side and serve hot.

472

Chocolate Sauce

½ cup (125 ml) water

¼ cup (50 g) sugar

8 ounces (250 g) dark chocolate, coarsely chopped

1 tablespoon cocoa powder

¼ cup (60 ml) milk

Churros

3 tablespoons sugar

2 cups (500 ml) water

3 tablespoons butter

2½ cups (375 g) all-purpose (plain) flour

Pinch of salt

2 large eggs, lightly beaten

6 cups (1.5 liters) vegetable oil, to deep-fry

Serves: 6
Preparation: 40 minutes
Cooking: 20 minutes
Level: 2

■ PREPARING FRIED DESSERTS

Fried food need not be soggy and difficult to digest. Follow a few easy rules and you can serve crisp, light churros and other fritters. The most important rule is to make sure the oil is hot enough; the outside of the churro or fritter should "seal" on contact with the oil, so that the oil stays outside and the inside remains light.

1. HEAT the oil over medium heat to 365°F (190°C). If you don't have a thermometer, drop a piece of bread into the oil. If it bubbles to the surface and turns golden, the oil is ready.

2. FOR CHURROS pipe the dough directly into the oil. For fritter, or if not using a piping bag, lower pieces of dough carefully into the oil using a spatula or slotted spoon. Turn the churros or fritters carefully during frying to ensure even browning.

3. REMOVE the churros or fritters from the hot oil using tongs or a slotted spoon. Drain on paper towels.

CHURROS WITH CINNAMON SUGAR

Churros: Combine the brown sugar, water, and butter in a large saucepan over medium heat and bring to a boil. • Stir in the flour and salt with a wooden spoon and cook until the dough comes away from the sides of the pan, about 2 minutes. Remove from the heat and beat in the eggs and vanilla, stirring continuously until incorporated.
• Heat the oil in a deep-fryer or deep saucepan to 365°F (190°C). If you don't have a frying thermometer, test the oil temperature by dropping a small piece of bread into the hot oil. If the bread immediately bubbles to the surface and begins to turn golden, the oil is ready. • Spoon the dough into a pastry bag fitted with a ¹/₂-inch (1-cm) star tip nozzle. Pipe 4-inch (10-cm) lengths into the hot oil and fry until golden. Remove from the oil with tongs or a slotted spoon and drain on paper towels. Continue until all the dough is used. • Cinnamon Sugar: Combine the sugar and cinnamon in a small bowl, mixing well. Sprinkle over the hot cooked churros and serve immediately.

Churros

3	tablespoons brown sugar
2	cups (500 ml) water
3	tablespoons butter
2½	cups (375 g) all-purpose (plain) flour
	Pinch of salt
2	large eggs, lightly beaten
1	teaspoon vanilla extract (essence)
6	cups (1.5 liters) vegetable oil, to deep-fry

Cinnamon Sugar

½	cup (100 g) sugar
2	teaspoons ground cinnamon

Serves: 6
Preparation: 40 minutes
Cooking: 20 minutes
Level: 2

CARDAMOM FRITTERS

Mix the flour and salt in a large bowl. • Beat the egg yolks and egg white, rose water, milk, and cardamom in a large bowl with an electric mixer at medium speed until well blended. • With mixer on low speed, beat in the dry ingredients to form a smooth dough. • Turn the dough out onto a lightly floured surface and knead until smooth. • Cover with a clean kitchen towel and let stand for 2 hours. • Form into balls the size of walnuts. • Roll the balls out to $1/8$ inch (3 mm) thick and 3 inches (8 cm) in diameter. • Carefully fold the dough over, using a fork to press down the edges and to make an attractive scalloped edging to the fritters. • Cover with a kitchen towel and let rest for 5 minutes. • Heat the oil in a deep-fryer or deep saucepan to 365°F (190°C). If you don't have a frying thermometer, test the oil temperature by dropping a small piece of bread into the hot oil. If the bread immediately bubbles to the surface and begins to turn golden, the oil is ready. • Fry the fritters in batches until lightly browned all over, about 5–7 minutes per batch. • Drain well on paper towels. • Dust with the confectioners' sugar and serve hot.

$2^{2}/3$ cups (400 g) all-purpose (plain) flour

$1/4$ teaspoon salt

3 large egg yolks + 1 large egg white

$1/4$ cup (60 ml) rose water

$1/2$ cup (125 ml) milk

$1/2$ teaspoon ground cardamom

6 cups (1.5 liters) vegetable oil, to deep-fry

$1/2$ cup (75 g) confectioners' (icing) sugar, to dust

Serves: 8
Preparation: 30 minutes
+ 2 hours to rest
Cooking: 30 minutes
Level: 2

SWEET RICOTTA FRITTERS

Place the ricotta in a large bowl. Add the eggs, sugar, orange zest, vanilla, salt, baking soda, and drained raisins. Stir in the flour. Mix until smooth. Leave to rest for 1 hour. • Heat the oil in a deep-fryer or deep saucepan to 365°F (190°C). If you don't have a frying thermometer, test the oil temperature by dropping a small piece of bread into the hot oil. If the bread immediately bubbles to the surface and begins to turn golden, the oil is ready. • Scoop out tablespoonfuls of the batter and fry in batches of 6–8 until golden brown, 5–7 minutes each batch. • Drain on paper towels. • Dust with the confectioners' sugar and serve hot.

1²/₃ cups (400 g) ricotta cheese, drained

3 large eggs

¹/₃ cup (70 g) sugar

Finely grated zest of 1 orange

1 teaspoon vanilla extract (essence)

¹/₈ teaspoon salt

¹/₄ teaspoon baking soda (bicarbonate of soda)

¹/₄ cup (40 g) raisins, soaked in rum overnight

1¹/₂ cups (225 g) all-purpose (plain) flour

6 cups (1.5 liters) vegetable oil, to deep-fry

³/₄ cup (120 g) confectioners' (icing) sugar

Serves: 6
Preparation: 15 minutes + 1 hour to rest
Cooking: 20 minutes
Level: 2

SWEET RAVIOLI

Put the orange zest, candied fruit, candied peel, and butter in a food processor and blend until smooth.
• Add 2 egg yolks, one at a time, mixing well after each addition. • Mix the flour and salt in a large bowl.
• Add the remaining egg yolks and enough water to make a very stiff dough. Knead until smooth and elastic, 10–15 minutes. • Roll out the dough on a lightly floured work surface to $1/2$ inch (1 cm) thick.
• Drizzle half the melted butter over half the surface of the dough. Fold the dough over the butter and roll out again to $1/2$ inch (1 cm) thick. • Drizzle the remaining butter over half the surface of the dough. Fold the dough over the butter and roll out again to $1/2$ inch (1 cm) thick. • Fold the dough and re-roll it 4 or 5 times, until the butter is well incorporated and the dough is smooth and elastic. Roll out the dough on a lightly floured surface to $1/4$ inch (5 mm) thick.
• Place teaspoons of the fruit mixture $1^{1}/2$ inches (4 cm) apart over half the dough. Fold the remaining dough over the top and press down with your finger tips between the mounds of filling to seal. • Use a fluted pastry cutter to cut out the ravioli. Place on a floured plate. • Heat the oil in a deep-fryer or deep saucepan to 365°F (190°C). If you don't have a frying thermometer, test the oil temperature by dropping a small piece of bread into the hot oil. If the bread immediately bubbles to the surface and begins to turn golden, the oil is ready. • Fry the ravioli in batches until golden brown all over, 5–7 minutes per batch.
• Remove with a slotted spoon and drain on paper towels. • Dust with confectioners' sugar and serve hot.

Finely grated zest of 1 large orange

1 cup (150 g) chopped candied fruit

½ cup (50 g) chopped candied peel

Scant ½ cup (100 g) butter

4 large egg yolks

3 cups (450 g) all-purpose (plain) flour

½ teaspoon salt

1 cup (250 g) butter, melted

6 cups (1.5 liters) vegetable oil, to deep-fry

⅓ cup (50 g) confectioners' (icing) sugar, to dust

Serves: 12
Preparation: 45 minutes
Cooking: 30 minutes
Level: 3

RICE & APPLE FRITTERS

Cook the rice in the milk in a medium saucepan over low heat for until very tender, 30–35 minutes. If the rice begins to stick to the pan, add a little boiling water. • Remove the saucepan from the heat. Stir in the sugar, apples, eggs, rum, raisins, vanilla, and lemon zest. Add the flour and baking powder and mix well. • Heat the oil in a deep-fryer or deep saucepan to 365°F (190°C). If you don't have a frying thermometer, test the oil temperature by dropping a small piece of bread into the hot oil. If the bread immediately bubbles to the surface and begins to turn golden, the oil is ready. • Fry spoonfuls of the mixture in small batches until golden brown, 5–7 minutes each batch. • Remove the fritters with a slotted spoon and drain on paper towels. • Dust with confectioners' sugar and serve hot.

1	cup (200 g) short-grain rice
2	cups (500 ml) milk
½	cup (100 g) sugar
1	pound (500 g) apples, peeled, cored, and coarsely grated
2	large eggs, lightly beaten
2	tablespoons rum
1	tablespoon golden raisins (sultanas), soaked in warm water for 15 minutes and drained
½	teaspoon vanilla extract (essence)
	Finely grated zest of 1 lemon
⅓	cup (50 g) all-purpose (plain) flour
1	teaspoon baking powder
6	cups (1.5 liters) vegetable oil, to deep-fry
⅓	cup (50 g) confectioners' (icing) sugar, to dust

Serves: 6–8
Preparation: 20 minutes
Cooking: 15–20 minutes
Level: 1

GOLDEN RAISIN FRITTERS

486

Mix the yeast and a little of the water in a small bowl. • Add enough flour to make a firm dough. • Cover and let rise for 2 hours. • Mix the remaining water, milk, lemon zest, vanilla, salt, remaining flour, and the risen dough in a large bowl until smooth. Add the eggs and mix well. • Cover and let rise for about 2 hours. • Add the sugar and the raisins and mix well. • Heat the oil in a deep-fryer or deep saucepan to 365°F (190°C). If you don't have a frying thermometer, test the oil temperature by dropping a small piece of bread into the hot oil. If the bread immediately bubbles to the surface and begins to turn golden, the oil is ready. • Fry spoonfuls of the mixture in small batches until golden brown all over, 5–7 minutes each batch. • Remove with a slotted spoon and drain on paper towels. • Dust with the confectioners' sugar and serve hot.

1   ounce (30 g) fresh yeast or 2 (¼-ounce/ 7-g) packets active dry yeast

2   cups (500 ml) warm water

3⅓ cups (500 g) all-purpose (plain) flour

1   cup (250 ml) milk

    Finely grated zest of 1 lemon

1   teaspoon vanilla extract (essence)

¼   teaspoon salt

2   large eggs

¾   cup (150 g) sugar

    Generous ½ cup (100 g) golden raisins (sultanas)

6   cups (1.5 liters) vegetable oil, to deep-fry

4   tablespoons confectioners' (icing) sugar, to dust

Serves: 12
Preparation: 20 minutes
 + 4 hours to rise
Cooking: 20–25 minutes
Level: 2

FRITTERS WITH CITRUS SYRUP

Fritters: Heat the milk, butter, and sugar in a small saucepan over medium-low heat until the butter is melted and the sugar is dissolved. Let cool for 10 minutes then stir in the yeast. • Place the flour and salt in a small bowl. Add the egg and the yeast mixture, stirring until smooth. If the dough is too dry, add a little tepid water. • Knead on a floured work surface until smooth and elastic, about 10 minutes. • Divide the dough into pieces the size of walnuts. Place on a large plate or baking sheet in a warm place and let rise for 1 hour.
• Citrus Syrup: Place the sugar, water, lemon and orange zest, vanilla pod, and clove in a medium saucepan over low heat. Simmer until the sugar is completely dissolved. • Heat the oil in a deep-fryer or deep saucepan to 365°F (190°C). If you don't have a frying thermometer, test the oil temperature by dropping a small piece of bread into the hot oil. If the bread immediately bubbles to the surface and begins to turn golden, the oil is ready. • Fry the fritters in batches until golden brown all over, 5–7 minutes each batch. Drain on paper towels.
• Dip the fritters in the hot syrup and serve hot.

Fritters

- ¼ cup (60 ml) milk
- ¼ cup (60 g) butter, cut up
- 2 tablespoons sugar
- ½ ounce (15 g) fresh compressed yeast or 1 (¼-ounce/7-g) package active dry yeast
- ⅛ teaspoon salt
- 2 cups (300 g) all-purpose (plain) flour
- 2 large eggs, lightly beaten
- 6 cups (1.5 liters) vegetable oil, to deep-fry

Citrus Syrup

- ½ cup (100 g) sugar
- 1 cup (250 ml) water
- Zest of 1 lemon and 1 orange, in 1 long piece
- 1 vanilla pod
- 1 clove

Serves: 6–8
Preparation: 35 minutes + 1 hour to rise
Cooking: 30 minutes
Level: 3

APPLE FRITTERS

490

Combine the flour, baking powder, and salt in a large bowl. • Beat in the sugar, lemon zest, orange juice, rum, and eggs. Add the milk gradually and stir until smooth. • Stir in the raisins and apples. • Heat the oil in a deep-fryer or deep saucepan to 365°F (190°C). If you don't have a frying thermometer, test the oil temperature by dropping a small piece of bread into the hot oil. If the bread immediately bubbles to the surface and begins to turn golden, the oil is ready. • Drop scant tablespoons of the batter into the oil and fry in batches until crisp and golden brown, 5–7 minutes each batch. • Remove with a slotted spoon and drain well on paper towels. • Dust with the confectioners' sugar and serve hot.

2²/₃ cups (400 g) all-purpose (plain) flour

1 teaspoon baking powder

¼ teaspoon salt

¾ cup (150 g) sugar

Finely grated zest of 1 lemon

Freshly squeezed juice of ½ orange

2 teaspoons dark rum

2 large eggs

²/₃ cup (150 ml) milk

½ cup (90 g) golden raisins (sultanas)

1½ pounds (750 g) apples, peeled, cored, and cut into small sticks

6 cups (1.5 liters) vegetable oil, to deep-fry

⅓ cup (50 g) confectioners' (icing) sugar

Serves: 8–10
Preparation: 20 minutes
Cooking: 30 minutes
Level: 1

AMARETTI RICE FRITTERS

Place the milk in a large saucepan with the vanilla and salt. Stir in the flour and rice. • Bring to a boil over medium heat. Simmer over low heat, stirring often, until the mixture is thick and creamy and the rice is very tender, 30–35 minutes. Add a little water to the pan if the mixture becomes too thick. Remove from the heat. • Stir in the butter, half the sugar, 1 egg, and the amaretti cookies. • Turn the mixture out onto a greased work surface. Spread to $1/2$ inch (1 cm) thick. Let cool. • Cut the mixture into disks using a 3-inch (8-cm) cookie cutter. • Beat the remaining egg in a small bowl. • Put the bread crumbs on a plate. Dip the disks in the beaten egg and then in the bread crumbs, coating well. • Heat the oil in a deep-fryer or deep saucepan to 365°F (190°C). If you don't have a frying thermometer, test the oil temperature by dropping a small piece of bread into the hot oil. If the bread immediately bubbles to the surface and begins to turn golden, the oil is ready. • Fry the fritter in small batches until golden brown all over, 5–7 minutes each batch. Remove with a slotted spoon and drain on paper towels. • Sprinkle with the sugar and serve hot.

2	cups (500 ml) milk
½	teaspoon vanilla extract (essence)
¼	teaspoon salt
2	tablespoons all-purpose (plain) flour
1	cup (200 g) sticky rice
2	tablespoons butter
⅓	cup (70 g) sugar, + extra, to sprinkle
2	small eggs
½	cup (60 g) crushed amaretti cookies
½	cup (60 g) fine dry bread crumbs
6	cups (1.5 liters) vegetable oil, to deep-fry

Serves: 8
Preparation: 30 minutes
Cooking: 1 hour
Level: 2

ITALIAN CARNIVAL FRITTERS

494

Mound the flour up on a work surface and make a well in the center. Add the butter, eggs, sugar, dessert wine, salt, and orange zest. Gradually combine with the flour and knead well. The dough should be soft but hold its shape well. • Cover with a clean cloth and leave to rest for 30 minutes. • Roll out into a thin sheet using a lightly floured rolling pin. • Use a fluted pastry cutter to cut into diamonds, rectangles, and into long ribbons that can be tied loosely into knots. • Heat the oil in a deep-fryer or deep saucepan to 365°F (190°C). If you don't have a frying thermometer, test the oil temperature by dropping a small piece of bread into the hot oil. If the bread immediately bubbles to the surface and begins to turn golden, the oil is ready. • Fry the fritters a few at a time until pale golden brown, 5–7 minutes each batch. • Remove with a slotted spoon and drain on paper towels. • Dust with the confectioners' sugar and serve hot.

1²/₃ cups (250 g) all-purpose (plain) flour + ¹/₃ cup (50 g) extra

2 tablespoons butter, softened

2 large eggs

¹/₄ cup (50 g) sugar

1½ tablespoons Vin Santo or other good quality sweet dessert wine

¹/₄ teaspoon salt

1½ tablespoons finely grated orange zest

6 cups (1.5 liters) vegetable oil, to deep-fry

¹/₃ cup (50 g) confectioners' (icing) sugar, to dust

Serves: 6–8
Preparation: 30 minutes + 30 minutes to rest
Cooking: 30 minutes
Level: 2

ST. JOSEPH'S DAY FRITTERS

Bring the water, butter, sugar, salt, and lemon zest to a boil in a medium saucepan. • Add the flour all at once and stir with a wooden spoon. Continue cooking over low heat, stirring constantly, until the dough is thick and starts to come away from the sides of the saucepan. Remove from the heat and set aside to cool, about 30 minutes. • When cool, add the eggs, one at a time, beating until just blended. The dough should be soft, but not runny. • Set aside to rest for 1 hour. • Heat the oil in a deep-fryer or deep saucepan to 365°F (190°C). If you don't have a frying thermometer, test the oil temperature by dropping a small piece of bread into the hot oil. If the bread immediately bubbles to the surface and begins to turn golden, the oil is ready. • Fry teaspoons of the dough in small batches until golden brown, 5–7 minutes each batch. • Drain well on paper towels. • Dust with the confectioners' sugar and serve hot.

1	cup (250 ml) water
½	cup (125 g) butter, cut up
¼	cup (50 g) sugar
¼	teaspoon salt
	Finely grated zest of 1 lemon
2	cups (300 g) all-purpose (plain) flour
8	large eggs
6	cups (1.5 liters) vegetable oil, to deep-fry
1	cup (150 g) confectioners' (icing) sugar, to dust

Serves: 12
Preparation: 25 minutes
+ 1 hour 30 minutes
to cool and rest
Cooking: 30–35 minutes
Level: 2

■ ■ ■ *St. Joseph is the patron saint of the family and his day (March 19) is celebrated in many parts of the world with family feasts and gatherings. This recipe come from Tuscany.*

BATTERED FRESH FRUIT

Beat the eggs in a large bowl with an electric mixer at high speed until frothy. • With mixer at medium speed, beat in the flour followed by the milk. • Cover with a clean cloth and let stand in a warm place for 1 hour. • Peel the pineapple and cut the flesh into 1/2-inch (1-cm) thick slices. Cut each slice in 4. • Peel the bananas and cut in each one in four. • Stir the baking powder and vanilla into the batter. • Dip the pineapple, bananas, and apples in the batter, turning to coat well. • Heat the oil in a deep-fryer or deep saucepan to 365°F (190°C). If you don't have a frying thermometer, test the oil temperature by dropping a small piece of bread into the hot oil. If the bread immediately bubbles to the surface and begins to turn golden, the oil is ready. • Fry the fruit in batches until crisp golden brown all over, 5–7 minutes each batch. • Remove with a slotted spoon and drain well on paper towels. • Dust with the confectioners' sugar and serve hot.

3	large eggs
4	tablespoons all-purpose (plain) flour
4	cups (1 liter) milk
1	small pineapple
2	firm-ripe bananas
2	tart apples, peeled, cored, and cut into wedges
1/2	teaspoon baking powder
1	teaspoon vanilla extract (essence)
6	cups (1.5 liters) vegetable oil, to deep-fry
1/3	cup (50 g) confectioners' (icing) sugar, to dust

Serves: 6
Preparation: 30 minutes
+ 1 hour to rest
Cooking: 30 minutes
Level: 2

PEAR FRITTERS

Place the pears, sugar, and water in a medium saucepan over low heat. Simmer, stirring often, until the fruit is softened, 10–15 minutes. • Roll out the pastry on a floured surface to ¼-inch (3-mm) thick. • Use a 3-inch (8-cm) cookie cutter to cut out disks. • Brush the edges of half the pastry disks with the beaten egg. Place a little of the pear mixture in the center of each of these disks. Cover with the plain disk, pressing down on the edges to seal. • Heat the oil in a deep-fryer or deep saucepan to 365°F (190°C). If you don't have a frying thermometer, test the oil temperature by dropping a small piece of bread into the hot oil. If the bread immediately bubbles to the surface and begins to turn golden, the oil is ready. • Fry the fritters in batches until golden brown, 5–7 minutes each batch. • Remove with a slotted spoon and drain on paper towels. • Heat the apple preserves in a small saucepan. Remove from the heat and stir in the rum. • Dust the fritters with confectioners' sugar and serve hot with the apple sauce.

1 pound (500 g) firm ripe pears, peeled, cored, and cut in cubes

⅓ cup (75 g) sugar

3 tablespoons water

12 ounces (350 g) frozen puff pastry, thawed

1 large egg, lightly beaten

6 cups (1.5 liters) vegetable oil, to deep-fry

½ cup (125 g) apple preserves (jam)

1 tablespoon white rum

2 tablespoons confectioners' (icing) sugar, to dust

Serves: 6–8
Preparation: 30 minutes
Cooking: 40–45 minutes
Level: 2

PUMPKIN FRITTERS

Peel the pumpkin and remove the seeds and fibrous matter. Slice the flesh and place in a saucepan with sufficient cold water to cover. • Cook until the flesh is just tender (not too long, about 20 minutes). Drain well and press in a cloth to absorb any excess moisture. • Place in a bowl, add the white raisins, sugar, flour, baking powder, lemon zest, and salt. Mix thoroughly with a spoon and then shape into balls about the size of walnuts. • Heat the oil in a deep-fryer or deep saucepan to 365°F (190°C). If you don't have a frying thermometer, test the oil temperature by dropping a small piece of bread into the hot oil. If the bread immediately bubbles to the surface and begins to turn golden, the oil is ready. • Fry the fritters in batches until golden brown all over, 5–7 minutes each batch. • Scoop out with a slotted spoon and drain on paper towels. • Sprinkle with sugar and serve hot.

2 pounds (1 kg) pumpkin or winter squash

1 cup (180 g) seedless white raisins (sultanas), soaked in warm water for 15 minutes, drained

¼ cup (50 g) sugar

⅔ cup (100 g) all-purpose (plain) flour

1 tablespoon baking powder

Finely grated zest of 1 lemon

⅛ teaspoon salt

6 cups (1.5 liters) vegetable oil, to deep-fry

Sugar, to sprinkle

Serves: 12
Preparation: 30 minutes
Cooking: 35 minutes
Level: 2

SWEET ALMOND RAVIOLI

504

Filling: Chop the almonds in a food processor until smooth, gradually adding the sugar as you work. Add the egg and orange flower water. • Pastry: Mix both flours and salt in a large bowl. Stir in enough of the water to obtain a firm dough. • Knead the dough on a floured surface, gradually working in the lard as you knead. • Roll out the dough on a lightly floured surface to ¼ inch (3-mm) thick. • Use a 3-inch (8-cm) cookie cutter to cut out disks. • Place some almond filling at the center of each disk. Fold the pastry over the filling in half-moon shapes and seal the edges with a fork. • Heat the oil in a deep-fryer or deep saucepan to 365°F (190°C). If you don't have a frying thermometer, test the oil temperature by dropping a small piece of bread into the hot oil. If the bread immediately bubbles to the surface and begins to turn golden, the oil is ready. • Fry the fritters in batches until golden brown, 5–7 minutes each batch. • Remove with a slotted spoon and drain on paper towels. • Dust with the confectioners' sugar and serve hot.

Filling

1	pound (500 g) almonds
¾	cup (150 g) sugar
1	large egg
2	tablespoons orange flower water

Pastry

2	cups (300 g) all-purpose (plain) flour
2	cups (300 g) fine ground semolina
¼	teaspoon salt
1	cup (250 ml) warm water
3	ounces (90 g) lard, softened
6	cups (1.5 liters) vegetable oil, to deep-fry
⅓	cup (50 g) confectioners' (icing) sugar, to dust

Serves: 12
Preparation: 40 minutes
Cooking: 30–35 minutes
Level: 2

ORANGE FRITTERS

Place the yeast in a small bowl. Dissolve with 5 tablespoons of the milk. Set aside for 15 minutes. • Combine the flour and salt in a large bowl. Stir in ¹/₂ cup (100 g) of the sugar, the Cointreau, and butter. Add the eggs one at a time and mix well. • Add the yeast mixture, orange zest, and remaining milk. Mix well to obtain a fairly stiff dough. Cover and let rise in a warm place for 1 hour. • Heat the oil in a deep-fryer or deep saucepan to 365°F (190°C). If you don't have a frying thermometer, test the oil temperature by dropping a small piece of bread into the hot oil. If the bread immediately bubbles to the surface and begins to turn golden, the oil is ready. • Drop spoonfuls of the batter into the oil and fry a few at a time until golden brown, 5–7 minutes each batch. • Remove with a slotted spoon and drain on paper towels. • Sprinkle with the remaining sugar and serve hot.

1   ounce (30 g) fresh compressed yeast or 2 (¼-ounce/7-g) packages active dry yeast

1   cup (250 ml) milk, lukewarm

3¹/₃ cups (500 g) all-purpose (plain) flour

Pinch of salt

³/₄ cup (150 g) sugar

2   tablespoons Cointreau

¼   cup (60 g) butter, melted

2   large eggs

Finely grated zest of 2 oranges

6   cups (1.5 liters) vegetable oil, to deep-fry

Serves: 12
Preparation: 20 minutes
Cooking: 30–35 minutes
Level: 2

PASTRIES

HAZELNUT CREAM PUFFS WITH CHOCOLATE SAUCE

510

Preheat the oven to 400°F (200°C/gas 6). • <u>Choux Pastry:</u> **Step 1:** Bring the water and butter to a boil in a medium saucepan over low heat. • Combine the flour, sugar, and salt in a small bowl. Add to the pan, stirring constantly with a wooden spoon until the mixture comes away from the sides of the pan, about 5 minutes. • Remove from the heat and let cool for 5 minutes. • Beat the eggs in one at a time until each is fully absorbed. A glossy ball of dough will form. • **Step 2:** Line two baking sheets with parchment paper. • Fit a pastry bag with a large plain nozzle and fill with the dough. • Pipe 16 mounds about the size of a golf ball 2 inches (5 cm) apart onto the baking sheets. • Bake for 10 minutes. Decrease the oven temperature to 375°F (190°C/gas 5) and bake for 20 minutes, until puffed and golden brown. • Turn the oven off, remove the puffs and cut a slit in the side of each one. Return to the oven and leave to dry out for 10 minutes. • Transfer to a wire rack. Let cool completely. • <u>Hazelnut Cream:</u> Beat the cream in a small bowl until it begins to thicken. Add the confectioners' sugar and Frangelico and continue whipping until the cream is thick enough to hold its shape. • **Step 3:** Fit a pastry bag with a medium star-shaped nozzle and fill with cream. Pipe the cream into each puff and set aside until ready to serve. <u>Chocolate Sauce:</u> Melt the chocolate and water in a small saucepan over low heat. Add the butter and sugar and stir until the sugar has dissolved. • Place 2 cream puffs on each plate and drizzle with sauce.

Choux Pastry

1	cup (250 ml) water
⅓	cup (90 g) butter
1	cup (150 g) all-purpose (plain) flour
2	teaspoons sugar
¼	teaspoon salt
4	large eggs

Hazelnut Cream

1	cup (250 ml) light (single) cream
2	tablespoons confectioners' (icing) sugar
2	tablespoons Frangelico (hazelnut liqueur)

Chocolate Sauce

4	ounces (125 g) dark chocolate, coarsely chopped
1	tablespoon water
3	tablespoons butter
⅓	cup (70 g) superfine (caster) sugar

Serves: 6–8
Preparation: 40 minutes
  + 1 hour to cool
Cooking: 40 minutes
Level: 3

Choux pastry is made by melting butter into hot water, adding flour, and then cooking the mixture until it is smooth and not sticky. The eggs are then added one by one. The raw pastry is soft and usually piped in a pastry bag. Choux pastry rises well and is very versatile. It is used to make cream puffs and éclairs and many other light desserts.

1. BRING the water and butter to a boil in a medium saucepan over low heat. Combine the flour, sugar, and salt in a small bowl. Add to the pan, stirring constantly with a wooden spoon until the mixture comes away from the sides of the pan, about 5 minutes. Remove from the heat and let cool for 5 minutes. Beat the eggs in, one at a time, until each is fully absorbed. A glossy ball of dough will form.

2. FIT a pastry bag with a large plain nozzle and fill with the dough. Pipe 16 mounds the size of golf balls 2 inches (5 cm) apart onto the baking sheets.

3. FIT a pastry bag with a medium star nozzle and fill with cream. Pipe the cream into each puff and set aside until ready to serve.

CROQUEMBOUCHE

Preheat the oven to 350°F (180°C/gas 4). • Lightly oil 2 large baking sheets or line with parchment paper. • Prepare the choux pastry. • Spoon teaspoonfuls of the pastry into 28–30 little rounds, about the size of small walnuts, onto the baking sheets, spacing 2 inches (5 cm) apart. • Alternatively, pipe the rounds on, using a pastry bag fitted with a 1-inch (2.5-cm) plain tip. • Bake for 20–25 minutes, or until golden brown. • Make a slit in the side of each puff with a skewer to release steam. Leave to cool in the turned-off oven with the door ajar for at least 1 hour. Buttercream Filling: Mix the pudding powder with 1/3 cup (90 ml) of milk and the sugar in a small bowl until smooth. Pour the remaining 1 2/3 cups (410 ml) of milk into a saucepan, add the vanilla pod, and bring slowly to a boil. • Remove from the heat, discard the vanilla pod. Stir the pudding mixture into the milk. Stir over low heat until the pudding comes to a boil and thickens. Simmer for 1 minute, stirring constantly. Let cool. • Beat the butter with the confectioners' sugar until creamy. Fold spoonfuls of the butter mixture into the cooled pudding, making sure the butter and pudding are the same temperature. • Fit a piping bag with a small plain tip. Fill with the filling. Insert the tip into each slit and pipe some filling into each puff. As you fill the puffs, arrange them in a pyramid on a serving plate. Frosting: Melt the chocolate and butter in a double boiler over barely simmering water. • Spoon over the pyramid, letting it drizzle down the sides.

1   recipe Choux Pastry (see page 510)

Buttercream Filling

4   tablespoons vanilla pudding mix (not instant) or custard powder

2   cups (500 ml) milk

2   tablespoons sugar

1   vanilla pod, split lengthways

1   cup (250 g) butter, softened

1   cup (150 g) confectioners' (icing) sugar

Frosting

5   ounces (150 g) dark chocolate, coarsely chopped

2   tablespoons butter, diced

Serves: 10–12
Preparation: 50–60 minutes + 1 hour to cool
Cooking: 25–30 minutes
Level: 3

ICE CREAM PROFITEROLES

Preheat the oven to 350°F (180°C/gas 4). • Lightly oil 2 large baking sheets or line with parchment paper. • Prepare the choux pastry. • Fit a pastry bag with a 1-inch (2.5-cm) tip and fill the bag half-full with batter. Pipe the batter onto the baking sheet in 24 small mounds. • Bake for 20–25 minutes, or until lightly browned. • Transfer to a rack to cool. Cream Topping: Beat the cream and sugar in a medium bowl with an electric mixer at high speed until stiff. • Leave the ice cream at room temperature to soften, 10 minutes. • Cut a "lid" off the top of each cream puff. Use a teaspoon to hollow out the larger piece, if necessary. • Fill with ice cream. • Cover each puff with its lid and place on a large plate. Spoon a little cream onto the top of each cream puff. • Sprinkle with the chocolate. • Pour three-quarters of the chocolate sauce into the base of a serving plate. Arrange the cream puffs in a pyramid shape on top of the sauce. Drizzle the remaining sauce over the top.

1   recipe Choux Pastry
     (see page 510)

Cream Topping

1   cup (250 ml) heavy
     (double) cream

1   tablespoon sugar

2   cups (500 ml) firmly
     packed vanilla ice
     cream

¼   cup (30 g) milk
     chocolate, grated

1   recipe Chocolate Sauce
     (see page 472)

Serves: 8–10
Preparation: 45 minutes
     + 1 hour to cool
Cooking: 20–25 minutes
Level: 3

ALMOND & CINNAMON BAKLAVA

Baklava: Preheat the oven to 325°F (170°C/gas 3).
• Butter a 9-inch (23-cm) square baking pan. • **Step 1:** Mix the almonds, sugar, and cinnamon in a large bowl. • **Step 2:** Lay the sheets of dough out flat and cover with waxed paper and a damp kitchen towel. (This will stop them from drying out). • **Step 3:** Fit one pastry sheet in the pan and brush with butter. Fit another sheet on top and brush with butter.
• **Step 4:** Sprinkle with a little almond filling. Place another sheet on top, brush with butter, and sprinkle with filling. Repeat until all the almond mixture is used up. You should have about 12 layers of filled dough. Place the remaining sheets on top. Brush with butter. • **Step 5:** Cut the pastry into diamond shapes about 2 inches (5-cm) in length. Be sure to cut through all the layers to the bottom of the pan. • Bake for about 40 minutes, or until golden brown. • Honey Syrup: Bring the honey, water, and sugar to a boil in a saucepan over low heat until the sugar has dissolved. Add the rose water. • **Step 6:** Drizzle the syrup over the baklava after removing it from the oven. Sprinkle with the almonds. • Cool the cake completely in the pan on a rack.

Baklava

2½ cups (375 g) almonds, finely ground
¾ cup (150 g) sugar
2 teaspoons ground cinnamon
14 sheets phyllo dough, thawed if frozen
1 cup (250 g) butter, melted

Honey Syrup

1 cup (250 ml) honey
¼ cup (60 ml) water
¼ cup (50 g) sugar
1½ tablespoons rose water
2 tablespoons almonds, chopped, to decorate

Serves: 10–12
Preparation: 45 minutes
Cooking: 40 minutes
Level: 2

PREPARING BAKLAVA

Variations on this popular Middle Eastern dessert are made throughout the world. Food historians think that it may originally come from Azerbaijan, in Central Asia. Whatever its origins, there are now many versions using different combinations of nuts and syrups.

1

1. MIX the almonds, sugar, and cinnamon in a large bowl.

2

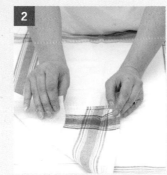

2. LAY the sheets of phyllo out flat and cover with waxed paper and a damp kitchen towel to stop them drying out.

3

3. FIT one pastry sheet in the pan and brush with butter. Fit another sheet on top and brush with butter.

4

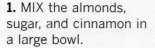

4. SPRINKLE with almond filling. Place another sheet on top. Repeat until the almond mixture is used up.

5

5. CUT into diamond shapes about 2 inches (5-cm) in length. Cut through all the layers to the bottom of the pan.

6

6. DRIZZLE the syrup over the hot baklava just after removing it from the oven. Sprinkle with the almonds.

PECAN BAKLAVA

Baklava: Preheat the oven to 350°F (180°C/gas 4).
• Butter a 9-inch (23-cm) square baking pan.
• Mix the pecans, sugar, and cinnamon in a large
bowl. • Lay the sheets of dough out flat and cover
with waxed paper and a damp kitchen towel. (This
will stop them from drying out.) • Fit one pastry
sheet in the pan and brush with butter. Fit another
sheet on top and brush with butter. • Sprinkle with
a little pecan mixture. Top with another pastry sheet
and brush with butter. Repeat until all the filling and
pastry are in the pan, finishing with a layer of phyllo
brushed with butter. • Chill in the refrigerator for
30 minutes. • Cut the pastry into diamond shapes
about 2 inches (5-cm) in length. Be sure to cut
through all the layers to the bottom of the pan.
• Drizzle with the remaining butter. • Bake for about
45 minutes, or until golden brown. • Syrup: Bring
the sugar, water, and lemon juice to a boil in a
saucepan over medium heat. Simmer for 20
minutes. • Drizzle the syrup over the hot baklava
just after removing it from the oven. • Cool the
cake completely in the pan on a rack.

Baklava

1	pound (500 g) pecans, coarsely chopped
½	cup (100 g) sugar
2	teaspoons ground cinnamon
14	sheets phyllo dough, thawed if frozen
1	cup (250 g) butter, melted

Syrup

2	cups (400 g) sugar
2	cups (500 ml) water
	Freshly squeezed juice of ½ lemon

Serves: 10–12
Preparation: 45 minutes
  + 30 minutes to chill
Cooking: 65 minutes
Level: 2

HAZELNUT, CHOCOLATE & PEAR TURNOVERS

Preheat the oven to 400°F (200°C/gas 6). • Line a large baking sheet with parchment paper. • Melt the chocolate with the cream in a small saucepan over low heat, stirring to combine. • Rub the skins off the hazelnuts using paper towels. Chop coarsely and stir into the melted chocolate. • Roll out the pastry to form two squares, each measuring 9$\frac{1}{2}$ inches (24 cm) square. • Cut each pastry sheet into quarters, creating eight squares. • Place a little of the pear in the center of each square and top with a large spoonful of the chocolate mixture. Fold the pastry over to enclose the pear in a triangle, pinch the edges to seal, and place on the prepared baking sheet. • Combine the maple syrup and water in a small cup and glaze the turnovers using a pastry brush. • Bake for 20 minutes, or until cooked through and golden. • Serve the turnovers hot with a scoop of ice cream to the side, if liked.

1   cup (180 g) dark chocolate chips

5   tablespoons heavy (double) cream

$\frac{3}{4}$ cup (120 g) hazelnuts, lightly toasted

2   ripe pears, cored and diced

2   sheets puff pastry, thawed if frozen

2   tablespoons pure maple syrup

2   teaspoons water

Vanilla ice cream, to serve (optional)

Serves: 4
Preparation: 20 minutes
Cooking: 20 minutes
Level: 1

APPLE TURNOVERS

Preheat the oven to 450°F (230°C/gas 8). • Butter a baking sheet. • Cook the apples with the apple cider, sugar, and cinnamon in a medium saucepan over low heat for 15 minutes. • Drain the apple mixture and mash with a fork until smooth. • Roll the pastry out on a lightly floured surface to ⅛ inch (3 mm) thick. Cut out four 5-inch (13-cm) rounds. • Transfer the pastry to the prepared baking sheet. Prick all over with a fork and dampen the edges with water. • Spoon the apple purée into the centers of the rounds. Fold in half and seal well. Brush the pastries with the beaten egg. • Bake for 15 minutes, or until golden brown and puffed. • Serve warm with whipped cream, if liked, and any remaining apple purée passed on the side.

6 **apples, peeled, cored, and diced**

2 **cups (500 ml) apple cider**

1 **cup (150 g) sugar**

1 **teaspoon ground cinnamon**

8 **ounces (250 g) frozen puff pastry, thawed**

1 **large egg, lightly beaten**

½ **cup (125 ml) heavy (double) cream (optional)**

Serves: 4
Preparation: 45 minutes
Cooking: 30 minutes
Level: 2

BLUEBERRY & BANANA PASTRY ROLL

Custard: Bring the cream to a boil in a small saucepan over low heat. • Beat the egg yolks and sugar in a medium bowl until pale and creamy. • Add the cream and mix well. Return the mixture to the saucepan over low heat. Stir constantly until thickened, 5–10 minutes. Remove from the heat and let cool. • Pastry Roll: Preheat the oven to 425°F (220°C/gas 7). • Set out a large baking sheet. • Roll the pastry out on a lightly floured work surface to ¼ inch (5 mm) thick. Transfer to a sheet of parchment paper. • Mix the blueberries, banana, and sugar in a large bowl. • Spread the pastry with the custard, leaving a ½-inch (1-cm) border. Spoon the fruit in an even layer on top of the custard. • Roll the pastry up, pinching the ends together. Transfer the parchment paper with the roll to the baking sheet. • Bake for 20 minutes. • Dust with the confectioners' sugar. • Bake for about 5 minutes more, or until golden brown. • Serve warm.

Custard

1   cup (250 ml) heavy (double) cream
2   large egg yolks
¼   cup (50 g) sugar

Pastry Roll

15 ounces (450 g) puff pastry
2   cups (300 g) blueberries
1   large banana, peeled and sliced
2   tablespoons sugar
2   tablespoons confectioners' (icing) sugar, to dust

Serves: 6
Preparation: 30 minutes
Cooking: 35 minutes
Level: 1

PASTRY WITH STRAWBERRIES & CREAM

Roll the pastry out into a square measuring 14 inches (35 cm). The pastry should be very thin. Cut into three equal rectangles. • Place on a dampened sheet of parchment paper and chill in the refrigerator for 3 hours. • Heat the milk and lemon zest in a medium saucepan over medium-low heat to boiling point. • Beat the egg yolks with $2/3$ cup (120 g) of sugar in a medium bowl with an electric mixer on medium-high speed until pale and creamy. Beat in the cornstarch. Gradually add the hot milk mixture, beating all the time. Return the mixture to the saucepan over low heat and, beating constantly, simmer until thickened, 5–10 minutes. Remove from the heat. Stir in the butter until melted then let cool completely. • Beat the cream until thickened then stir into the pastry cream. • Chill in the refrigerator until ready to assemble the dessert. • Preheat the oven to 375°F (190°C/gas 5). • Sprinkle the pastry with the remaining sugar. Bake until the pastry just begins to swell and rise, about 5 minutes. Cover with a wire rack and bake until pale golden brown, about 10 minutes. • Turn the oven up to 450°F (220°C/gas 8) and bake until the sugar is caramelized, 2–3 minutes. Let cool on a wire rack. • Spread the pastry with pastry cream and top with strawberries. Cut each rectangle in half and serve.

8	ounces (250 g) puff pastry
2	cups (500 ml) milk
6	large egg yolks
	Zest of 1 untreated lemon, in 1 long piece
$3/4$	cup + 2 tablespoons (180 g) sugar
$1/3$	cup (50 g) cornstarch (cornflour)
3	tablespoons butter
2	cups (500 ml) heavy (double) cream
3	cups (450 g) fresh strawberries, sliced

Serves: 6
Preparation: 30 minutes + 3 hours to chill
Cooking: 35 minutes
Level: 2

BANANA MILLEFEUILLE

Preheat the oven to 375°F (190°C/gas 5). • Butter two or three baking sheets. • Roll the pastry out on a lightly floured work surface into a large rectangle ⅛ inch (3 mm) thick. Cut into three equal-sized rectangles. • Bake for about 10 minutes, or until golden brown. If the pastry has puffed and risen, press it down with your fingertips. • Let cool completely on racks. • Bring the milk to a boil in a medium saucepan over medium heat. • Beat the egg yolks and sugar in a large bowl until pale and creamy. • Stir in the vanilla and flour. • Gradually beat in the hot milk. • Return the mixture to the saucepan and place over low heat. Bring to a boil and simmer, stirring constantly, until the custard thickens, about 5 minutes. • Remove from heat, stir in the butter, and let cool. • Peel and slice the bananas. Drizzle with the lemon juice. • Place a piece of pastry on a serving dish and spread with a third of the custard. Cover with slightly less than half the bananas and oranges. • Cover with the second piece of pastry and repeat. • Top with the remaining pastry and decorate with the remaining fruit and custard.

14 ounces (400 g) frozen puff pastry, thawed

2 cups (500 ml) milk

4 large egg yolks

½ cup (100 g) sugar

1 teaspoon vanilla extract (essence)

⅓ cup (50 g) all-purpose (plain) flour

2 tablespoons butter

3 large bananas

Freshly squeezed juice of 1 lemon

2 oranges, peeled and cut into segments

Serves: 6–8
Preparation: 20 minutes
Cooking: 20 minutes
Level: 2

MILLEFEUILLE WITH ZABAGLIONE

534

Pastry: Preheat the oven to 350°F (180°C/gas 4).
• Butter a large baking sheet. • Roll the pastry out on a floured work surface into a large rectangle ⅛ inch (3 mm) thick. Cut into three equal-sized rectangles. Brush with beaten egg and sprinkle with sugar. • Transfer to the prepared baking sheet.
• Bake for 15 minutes, or until golden brown.
• Cool completely on racks. • **Zabaglione:** Beat the egg yolks and sugar in a large bowl until pale and creamy. Add the Marsala. • Transfer to a double boiler over low heat and cook, stirring constantly, until the mixture thickens, 10–15 minutes. Do not allow it to boil. • Remove from the heat and divide between two bowls. Add the chocolate to one of the bowls and mix until melted and smooth. Let cool.
• Place one of the pastry rectangles on a serving dish and spread with the plain zabaglione. Cover with another piece of pastry and spread with the chocolate zabaglione. Cover with the remaining pastry and dust with the confectioners' sugar.

Pastry

14 ounces (400 g) fresh or frozen puff pastry, thawed if frozen

1 small egg, lightly beaten

4 tablespoons sugar

Zabaglione

6 large egg yolks

1 cup (200 g) sugar

⅔ cup (180 ml) Marsala wine

4 ounces (125 g) dark chocolate, grated

2 tablespoons confectioners' (icing) sugar, to dust

Serves: 6–8
Preparation: 30 minutes
Cooking: 25 minutes
Level: 2

PLUM & WALNUT GALETTE

Preheat the oven to 400°F (200°C/gas 6). • Line a large baking sheet with parchment paper. • Cut a 12-inch (30-cm) circle out of the pastry and place on the prepared baking sheet. • Combine the plums, brown sugar, ground almonds, cinnamon, and walnuts in a large bowl. • Place the plum mixture in the center of the pastry circle and scatter cubes of butter over the top. • Gather the edges of pastry up and fold them over to make a firm border. • Glaze the pastry by brushing it with the beaten egg and sprinkle with Demerara sugar. • Bake for 25 minutes. Decrease the temperature to 350°F (180°C/gas 4) and bake for 30 more minutes, or until the pastry is golden and the filling is bubbling. Let cool at room temperature for 10 minutes. • Beat the crème fraîche and honey in a small bowl with a wooden spoon until combined. • To serve, slice the galette into 6–8 wedges and serve with a dollop of honeyed crème fraîche.

8	ounces (250 g) puff pastry, thawed if frozen
2	pounds (1 kg) ripe red plums, pitted and quartered
3/4	cup (150 g) firmly packed light brown sugar
2	tablespoons finely ground almonds
1	teaspoon ground cinnamon
1/4	cup (30 g) walnuts, coarsely chopped
2	tablespoons butter, cubed
1	large egg, lightly beaten
1	tablespoon Demerara sugar
1	cup (250 ml) crème fraîche
3	tablespoons honey

Serves: 6–8
Preparation: 30 minutes
    + 10 minutes to cool
Cooking: 55 minutes
Level: 2

PINEAPPLE PIZZA

Preheat the oven to 400°F (200°C/gas 6). • Set out a 12-inch (30-cm) round pizza pan. • Combine the butter, $\frac{1}{4}$ cup (50 g) of sugar, and lemon juice in a saucepan over medium heat. Cook, stirring constantly, until golden brown. Add the pineapple and simmer over low heat until the mixture is almost dry, about 10 minutes. Set aside to cool. • Unroll or unfold the pastry on a lightly floured work surface and roll out to form two 14-inch (35-cm) rounds. Use one to line the pan, folding the edges over to form a raised rim. Prick all over with a fork. • Combine the pistachios, ladyfingers, and remaining $\frac{1}{4}$ cup (50 g) sugar in a food processor and process until finely chopped. • Sprinkle the pistachio mixture over the pastry. Spread with the pineapple mixture. • Cut the remaining pastry into thin strips and arrange over the pineapple in a lattice pattern. Seal the edges to the bottom crust by pinching together. Brush the pastry with the egg. Dust with the confectioners' sugar. • Bake for 20–25 minutes, or until golden brown. • Serve warm or at room temperature.

1	tablespoon butter
$\frac{1}{2}$	cup (100 g) sugar
2	tablespoons freshly squeezed lemon juice
1	fresh pineapple, weighing about 2 pounds (1 kg), peeled, tough core discarded, finely chopped
1	pound (500 g) frozen puff pastry, thawed
$\frac{3}{4}$	cup (100 g) pistachios
3	ladyfingers (sponge fingers), crumbled
1	large egg, lightly beaten
2	tablespoons confectioners' (icing) sugar, to dust

Serves: 6–8
Preparation: 40 minutes
Cooking: 20–25 minutes
Level: 2

PEAR PUFF

540

Preheat the oven to 350°F (180°C/gas 4). • Butter a large baking pan. • Drizzle the pears with the lemon juice. Use a sharp knife to make deep cuts in the pears lengthwise. Place in the baking pan, curved-side up and sprinkle with half the sugar. • Bake for 10 minutes. Drizzle with the wine. Bake for 12 minutes more. • Roll out the pastry to fit a 10-inch (25-cm) pie plate. • Bake for 10 minutes. • Add the pears, curved side up. Brush with the egg and sprinkle with the remaining sugar and the nuts. • Bake for 5–10 minutes, until the pastry is golden brown. • Serve warm or at room temperature.

4	firm-ripe pears, peeled, cored, and halved
2	tablespoons freshly squeezed lemon juice
1	cup (200 g) sugar
¼	cup (60 ml) dry white wine
8	ounces (250 g) fresh or frozen puff pastry, thawed if frozen
1	large egg, lightly beaten
½	cup (60 g) hazelnuts, lightly toasted and chopped

Serves: 4
Preparation: 35 minutes
Cooking: 25–35 minutes
Level: 2

APPLE STRUDEL

Strudel Dough: **Step 1:** Prepare the dough using the ingredients listed and following the step-by-step instructions on the facing page. • Filling: Mix the apples, almonds, hazelnuts, golden raisins, lemon zest, sugar, cinnamon, lemon juice, and rum in a large bowl. Set aside. • Preheat the oven to 375°F (190°C/gas 5). • Generously butter a large baking sheet. **Step 2:** Roll out the dough following the step-by-step instructions. • **Step 3:** Place the dough on a clean kitchen towel. Brush with melted butter and sprinkle with bread crumbs. • Spread the filling over the front half of the short side, keeping a 1$\frac{1}{2}$-inch (4-cm) border. Pick up the two nearest corners of the kitchen towel and roll up the strudel from the filled side. Fold in the top edge and sides to seal. • Position the baking sheet so that you can slip the strudel onto it. Curl the roll into a horseshoe shape if it is too big for the sheet. Brush all over with the melted butter. Place the strudel in the oven to begin baking. • **Step 4:** Glaze, Mix the cream and sugar in a small bowl. Brush the strudel two or three times during baking. • Bake for 40–45 minutes, until crisp and golden. • Leave to rest on the baking sheet for 10 minutes before carefully lifting with a spatula onto a serving dish. • Dust with confectioners' sugar and serve warm.

Strudel Dough

1½	cups (250 g) all-purpose (plain) flour
½	teaspoon salt
1	large egg
2	tablespoons sunflower oil
5	tablespoons warm water

Filling

¼	cup (60 g) butter, melted
1	cup (150 g) fine dry bread crumbs
5	large tart apples, peeled, cored, and thinly sliced
1	cup (100 g) flaked almonds
½	cup (60 g) finely chopped hazelnuts
1	cup (120 g) golden raisins (sultanas)
2	tablespoons finely grated lemon zest
½	cup (100 g) sugar
1	teaspoon cinnamon
1	tablespoon lemon juice
2	tablespoons rum

Glaze

3	tablespoons cream
2	teaspoons sugar
	Confectioners' (icing) sugar, to dust

Serves: 6–8
Preparation: 25 minutes
 + 30 minutes to rest
Cooking: 25 minutes
Level: 3

◼ PREPARING STRUDEL

Strudel is a sweet, layered pastry dessert. Nowadays it is associated with Austria, but it actually became popular in the 18th century when Austria was part of the much larger Austro-Hungarian Empire. Classic strudel is filled with apple and spices, but there are many variations. The dough is quite time-consuming to make; if you are short of time replace with phyllo dough.

Making the dough
1. Combine the flour and salt in a bowl. Beat the egg, 1 tablespoon oil, and warm water in a small bowl. Pour into the flour and mix until the dough comes away from the sides of the bowl. Turn out onto a floured board and knead until little blisters appear, about 15 minutes. Form into a disk, and cover with a cloth. Let rest for 30 minutes.

2. Sprinkle a board with flour and roll the dough out to an oblong shape. When you can't roll it any thinner, begin stretching it. Brush with the remaining oil. Dip your hands in flour and curl your fingers. Standing at the short side, lift the dough from the center with the back of your hands. Gently pull and stretch in all directions. The dough is ready when it measures 28 x 18 inches (70 x 45 cm).

543

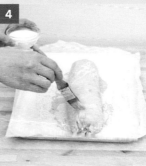

Preparing the strudel
3. Place the dough on a clean kitchen towel. Brush with melted butter and sprinkle with bread crumbs. Spread the filling over the front half of the short side, keeping a 11/2-inch (4-cm) border. Pick up the two nearest corners of the kitchen towel and roll up the strudel from the filled side. Fold in the top edge and sides to seal.

4. Glaze, mix the cream and sugar in a small bowl. Brush the strudel 2–3 times during baking.

MANGO STRUDEL

Preheat the oven to 400°F (200°C/gas 6). • Butter a large baking sheet. • Cover a work surface with a large clean cloth. • Roll the strudel pastry out very thinly on a floured work surface. It should be almost transparent (see page 543). • Transfer to the cloth and brush. • Filling: Brush the pastry with melted butter. • Mix the mangoes, sugar, lemon zest, cashew nuts, and bread crumbs in a large bowl. • Spoon the filling onto half of the pastry, leaving a wide border around the edges. Fold the end of the pastry over the filling and, using the cloth as a guide, roll the strudel up. Tuck in the ends and seal. Brush with butter and slide onto the baking sheet. • Bake for 35–45 minutes, until crisp and golden brown. • Citrus Sauce: Bring the sugar, orange juice, lemon juice, orange zest, and lemon zest to a boil in a medium saucepan over medium heat. • Simmer over low heat until the sauce becomes syrupy, about 10 minutes. • Remove from the heat and stir in the orange liqueur. • Strain the sauce into a bowl. • Serve the strudel hot or warm with the sauce passed separately.

1   recipe Strudel Dough (see page 542)

Filling

¼   cup (60 g) butter, melted

3   pounds (1.5 kg) mangoes, peeled and diced

4   tablespoons sugar

2   tablespoons finely grated lemon zest

½   cup (90 g) unsalted cashew nuts

6   tablespoons fine dry bread crumbs

Citrus Sauce

1½   cups (300 g) sugar

1   cup (250 ml) orange juice

½   cup (125 ml) freshly squeezed lemon or lime juice

2   tablespoons finely grated orange zest

2   tablespoons finely grated lemon zest

6   tablespoons orange liqueur

Serves: 10–12
Preparation: 45 minutes
Cooking: 25 minutes
Level: 1

VIENNESE FRUIT & CHOCOLATE STRUDEL

Preheat the oven to 400°F (200°C/gas 6). • Butter a large baking sheet. • Cover a work surface with a large clean cloth. • Roll the strudel pastry out very thinly on a floured work surface. It should be almost transparent (see page 543). • Transfer to the cloth and brush. • Filling: Mix the walnuts, raisins, almonds, figs, pineapple, chocolate, and cocoa in a large bowl. • Beat the sugar, egg, and butter in a medium bowl with an electric mixer at medium speed until creamy. • Brush the sugar mixture over the pastry, leaving a $1/2$-inch (1-cm) border on all sides. Gently spread with the fruit mixture, leaving a $1/2$-inch (1-cm) border. Roll the strudel up, pinching the ends together. • Carefully transfer the strudel to the prepared sheet. Gently pull it into a horseshoe shape. If the dough breaks while you are moving it, take a little dough from the end to make a patch.
• Glaze: Mix the egg yolk, sugar, and milk in a small bowl and brush over the strudel. • Bake for about 50 minutes, or until golden brown. • Slide onto a rack to cool. • Serve warm or at room temperature.

1   recipe Strudel Dough (see page 542)

Filling

1   cup (100 g) walnuts, coarsely chopped

$2/3$ cup (100 g) raisins

$1/3$ cup (40 g) flaked almonds

6   dried figs, chopped

5   canned pineapple rings, well drained and chopped

3   ounces (90 g) dark chocolate, coarsely chopped

$1/3$ (50 g) unsweetened cocoa powder

1   cup (200 g) sugar

1   large egg

$1/4$ cup (60 g) butter, melted

Glaze

1   large egg yolk

2   tablespoons sugar

1   tablespoon milk

Serves: 10-12
Preparation: 1 hour
Cooking: 50 minutes
Level: 2

BAVARIAN STRUDEL

Filling: Butter a large baking sheet. • Place the water, sugar, and ginger in a pan large enough to hold the pears. Stir over low heat until the sugar has dissolved. Increase the heat so that the liquid simmers. • Add the pears and poach until the pears can be easily pierced with a toothpick, 15–20 minutes. Let cool. • Preheat the oven to 400°F (200°C/gas 6). • Almond Cream: Process the almonds and confectioners' sugar until smooth. • Beat the butter in a large bowl with an electric mixer at medium speed until creamy. • With mixer at low speed, gradually beat in the almond mixture and flour. • Add the eggs, beating until just blended. Add the rum. • Halve the poached pears and cut out the cores. Slice each half pear thinly lengthwise and set aside. • Lay the sheets of pastry out flat and cover with waxed paper and a damp kitchen towel. (This will stop them from drying out.) • Place a sheet of pastry on the baking sheet. Brush with melted butter. Top with another sheet and brush with butter. Repeat with 4 more sheets. • Spoon the almond cream on the top layer, leaving a border. Cover with the slices of pear. Cover with 2 more pastry sheets and brush with butter. • Roll up the strudel, tucking in the ends so that the filling doesn't not come out during baking. • Bake for 10–15 minutes, or until golden brown. • Serve warm.

Filling

3	cups (750 ml water
1	cup (200 g) sugar
½	inches (4 cm) fresh ginger, peeled and sliced ½-inch (1-cm) thick
2	firm-ripe pears, peeled

Almond Cream

1	cup (90 g) flaked almonds
1	cup (150 g) confectioners' (icing) sugar
½	cup (125 g) butter
⅓	cup (50 g) all-purpose (plain) flour
2	large eggs
1	tablespoon dark rum
8	sheets phyllo pastry, thawed if frozen
½	cup (125 g) butter, melted

Serves: 6–8
Preparation: 45 minutes
Cooking: 25–35 minutes
Level: 2

PEACH & BERRY STRUDEL

Preheat the oven to 375°F (190°C/gas 5). • Butter a large baking sheet. • Chop the almonds and oats finely in a food processor. Add both sugars and the cinnamon. • Mix the peaches, raspberries, remaining cinnamon, and vanilla in a large bowl. • Lay the sheets of phyllo pastry out flat and cover with waxed paper and a damp kitchen towel. (This will stop them from drying out.) • Place a sheet of pastry on the prepared baking sheet. Brush with melted butter. Top with another sheet and brush with butter. Repeat with 4 more sheets. • Spoon the almond mixture over the top. Top with the fruit mixture. Cover with 2 more pastry sheets and brush with butter. • Roll up the strudel, tucking in the ends so that the filling doesn not come out during baking. • Bake for 30–40 minutes, until crisp and golden brown. • Serve warm.

½ cup (60 g) whole almonds, toasted

1¼ cups (120 g) old-fashioned rolled oats

½ cup (100 g) firmly packed brown sugar

¼ cup (50 g) sugar

2 teaspoons ground cinnamon

3 medium peaches, peeled, pitted, and diced

1 cup (200 g) raspberries

½ teaspoon vanilla extract (essence)

8 sheets phyllo dough, thawed if frozen

⅓ cup (90 g) butter, melted

Serves: 6–8
Preparation: 45 minutes
Cooking: 20 minutes
Level: 2

RHUBARB STRUDEL

Filling: Combine the rhubarb, orange juice, and brown sugar in a medium saucepan over medium heat. Simmer until the rhubarb is softened, 10 minutes. Drain over a bowl, reserving the juice. Let cool. • Preheat the oven to 375°F (190°C/gas 5). • Generously butter a large baking sheet. • Mix the amaretti crumbs with the golden raisins, orange zest, vanilla, and diced butter in a large bowl. Stir in the rhubarb. • To assemble, lay a sheet of phyllo pastry on a floured work surface. Brush with butter and sprinkle with wheat germ. Repeat this layering, buttering, and sprinkling with 5 sheets of phyllo. Spread half the filling over the front half, nearest to you, within 1 inch (2.5 cm) of the pastry edges. Roll it up, away from you, tucking in the sides. Using a spatula, lift the strudel onto the baking sheet, seam-side down. Brush with butter and sprinkle with wheat germ. • Use the remaining phyllo, filling, and butter to make another strudel in the same way. • Bake for 30–35 minutes, until golden and crisp. Let rest for 10 minutes. • Whip the cream with the reserved rhubarb juice, until it forms soft peaks. • Dust the strudels with confectioners' sugar and serve warm with the whipped cream.

Filling

2 pounds (1 kg) rhubarb stalks, cut into short lengths

2 tablespoons freshly squeezed orange juice

1½ cups (300 g) firmly packed light brown sugar

1 cup (150 g) crushed amaretti cookies

½ cup (75 g) golden raisins (sultanas)

Finely grated zest of 1 orange

1 teaspoon vanilla extract (essence)

2 tablespoons (30 g) butter, chilled and diced

12 sheets phyllo pastry, thawed if frozen

½ cup (125 g) butter, melted

½ cup (75 g) toasted wheat germ, to sprinkle

Confectioners' (icing) sugar, to dust

⅔ cup (150 ml) heavy (double) cream, to serve

Serves: 8
Preparation: 25 minutes
Cooking: 40–45 minutes
+ 10 minutes to rest
Level: 2

APRICOT & ALMOND STRUDEL

Preheat the oven to 350°F (180°C/gas 4). Line a 25$\frac{1}{4}$ x 17$\frac{1}{4}$-inch (65 x 45-cm) baking sheet with parchment paper. • <u>Filling:</u> Combine the apricots, ground almonds, bread crumbs, and flaked almonds in a large bowl. • Melt the apricot preserves and 2 tablespoons of butter in a small saucepan over low heat. Pour over the apricot and almond mixture and stir to combine. • To assemble the strudel, flour a clean work surface and lay out a sheet of phyllo pastry. Brush lightly with melted butter and lay another sheet on top. Repeat the process, brushing with butter in between, with another four sheets. Spread the apricot and almond filling down the center line of the pastry. Wrap the pastry around the filling. Layer the remaining pastry in the same way as before, brushing with butter in between each layer. Place the filling wrapped in phyllo down the center and wrap the pastry around the strudel, tucking in the edges. • Brush the top with melted butter and carefully transfer onto the prepared tray, placing seam-side down, and creating a horseshoe shape so it can fit. • Bake for 40 minutes, or until apricots are cooked and the pastry is crisp and golden. Let rest for 10 minutes before serving. • Serve warm with the cream.

Filling

3	pounds (1.5 kg) ripe apricots, halved, pitted, and thinly sliced
$\frac{1}{2}$	cup (50 g) ground almonds
$\frac{1}{2}$	cup (30 g) fresh bread crumbs
$\frac{1}{2}$	cup (80 g) flaked almonds, lightly toasted
$\frac{1}{4}$	cup (80 g) apricot preserves (jam)
2	tablespoons butter
12	sheets phyllo pastry, thawed if frozen
$\frac{1}{2}$	cup (125 g) butter, melted

Confectioners' (icing) sugar, to dust

1	cup (250 ml) light (single) cream, to serve

Serves: 8–10
Preparation: 25 minutes
Cooking: 40 minutes
Level: 2

APPLE & APRICOT STRUDEL

Preheat the oven to 375°F (190°C/gas 5). • Butter a large baking sheet. • Lay the phyllo pastry out flat and cover with waxed paper and a damp kitchen towel. (This will stop them from drying out.) • Lay out one sheet of pastry. Brush with melted butter. Top with another sheet and brush with butter. Repeat. Sprinkle with bread crumbs. • Mix the apples, sugar, raisins, apricots, almonds, and lemon zest and juice in a large bowl. • Gently spread the pastry sheets with half the apple mixture, leaving a 1/2-inch (1-cm) border. • Roll the strudel up, pinching the ends together. • Use a large metal spatula to transfer the strudel to the prepared baking sheet. • Brush with the remaining melted butter. Sprinkle with the sugar and cinnamon. • Repeat with the remaining three sheets of phyllo and the remaining apple mixture. • Bake for about 30 minutes, or until golden brown. • Serve warm.

6	sheets phyllo dough, thawed if frozen
1/4	cup (60 g) butter, melted
1/3	cup (50 g) fine dry bread crumbs
3	cups (300 g) apple chunks
1/2	cup (100 g) sugar
1/4	cup (40 g) raisins
1/2	cup (75 g) dried apricots, chopped
1/4	cup (30 g) almonds, coarsely chopped
1	teaspoon finely grated lemon zest
1	tablespoon freshly squeezed lemon juice
1	tablespoon sugar
1/2	teaspoon cinnamon

Serves: 4–6
Preparation: 30 minutes
Cooking: 30 minutes
Level: 2

SAVARINS &BRIOCHES

ORANGE SAVARIN WITH STRAWBERRIES

562

Savarin: **Step 1:** Stir the milk, yeast, and 1 teaspoon of sugar in a small bowl. Set aside until foamy, about 10 minutes. • **Step 2:** Combine the flour and salt in a large bowl. Stir in the yeast mixture. Add the eggs, butter, and remaining sugar and beat until well blended. Knead in the bowl using a dough hook or flat beater for 5 minutes. • **Step 3:** To knead by hand, place the dough on a floured work surface and press down. Flip the dough, pick it up, and slam it down on the surface. Repeat until smooth and pliable, about 10 minutes. • Place the dough in a clean, oiled bowl and cover with plastic wrap (cling film). Let rise until doubled in bulk, about 1 hour. • Butter a 10-inch (25-cm) savarin pan. • Punch down the dough. Place in the prepared pan, spreading it evenly. Cover with a clean cloth and let rise until almost doubled in bulk, about 30 minutes. • Preheat the oven to 375°F (190°C/gas 5). • Bake for 35–45 minutes, or until risen and golden brown. Cool the savarin in the pan for 15 minutes. Orange Syrup: Use a sharp knife to remove the zest from the orange in one long piece. • Bring the water, sugar, and orange zest to a boil in a saucepan over medium heat, stirring constantly, until the sugar has dissolved. Simmer for 8 minutes. Remove from the heat and add the rum. • Place the cake on the rack over a large plate. Spoon the syrup over the cake until it has been absorbed. Let cool completely. • Heat the preserves and rum over low heat. Spread over the savarin. Top with strawberries.

Savarin

⅓ cup (90 ml) warm (about 110°F/43°C) milk

½ ounce (15 g) fresh compressed yeast or 2 teaspoons active dry yeast

3 tablespoons sugar

2 cups (300 g) all-purpose (plain) flour

½ teaspoon salt

4 large eggs, lightly beaten

⅓ cup (90 g) butter, softened

Orange Syrup

1 large orange

2 cups (500 ml) water

1⅓ cups (250 g) sugar

1 cup (250 ml) dark rum

To Serve

⅓ cup (100 g) strawberry preserves (jam)

1 tablespoon dark rum

1 cups (150 g) fresh strawberries, halved

Serves: 6–8
Preparation: 45 minutes + 1 hour 30 minutes to rise
Cooking: 35–40 minutes
Level: 2

Jean Anthelme Brillat-Savarin (1755–1826) was a French lawyer and politician but he is best known as an epicure and food writer. His famous work, *Physiologie du goût* (The Physiology of Taste), was published in December 1825, two months before his death. This yeast cake is named in his honor.

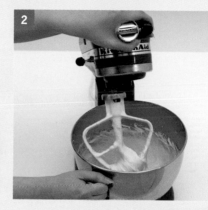

1. STIR the milk, yeast, and 1 teaspoon sugar in a small bowl. Set aside for 10 minutes, or until foamy.

2. COMBINE the flour and salt in a large bowl. Stir in the yeast mixture. Add the eggs, butter, and remaining sugar and beat until well blended. Knead in the bowl using a dough hook or flat beater for 5 minutes.

3. TO KNEAD BY HAND place the dough on a floured work surface. Flip, pick up, and slam down again. Repeat until smooth and pliable, 10 minutes.

RASPBERRY CREAM SAVARIN

Prepare the savarin dough. • Place the dough in a clean, oiled bowl and cover with plastic wrap (cling film). Let rise until doubled in bulk, about 1 hour. • Butter a 10-inch (25-cm) savarin pan. • Punch down the dough. Place in the prepared pan, spreading it evenly. Cover with a clean cloth and let rise until almost doubled in bulk, about 30 minutes. • Preheat the oven to 375°F (190°C/gas 5). • Bake for 35–45 minutes, or until golden brown. Cool the savarin in the pan for 15 minutes. • Place the savarin on a large plate and poke holes all over with a skewer. • Mix the orange juice and rum in a small bowl. Drizzle over the cake. • Fill the center of the savarin with the raspberries. • Beat the cream in a large bowl with an electric mixer at high speed until stiff. • Spoon the cream into a pastry bag and pipe in a decorative manner.

1 recipe Savarin (see page 562)

½ cup (125 ml) freshly squeezed orange juice, strained

½ cup (125 ml) dark rum

2 cups (300 g) raspberries

1 cup (250 ml) heavy (double) cream

Serves: 6–8
Preparation: 45 minutes + 1 hour 30 minutes to rise
Cooking: 35–40 minutes
Level: 2

APRICOT RUM SAVARIN

Prepare the savarin dough. • Place the dough in a clean, oiled bowl and cover with plastic wrap (cling film). Let rise until doubled in bulk, about 1 hour. • Butter a 10-inch (25-cm) tube pan. • Punch down the dough. Place in the prepared pan, spreading it evenly. Cover with a clean cloth and let rise until almost doubled in bulk, about 30 minutes. • Preheat the oven to 375°F (190°C/gas 5). • Bake for 35–45 minutes, or until golden brown. Cool the savarin in the pan for 15 minutes. Syrup: Bring: 1¼ cups (250 g) of sugar and the water to a boil in a medium saucepan. Simmer for 5 minutes. • Place the cake (still on the rack) on a large plate. Drizzle the hot syrup over the cake. Scoop up any excess syrup with a spoon and drizzle over the cake. • Drizzle with the rum. • Heat the apricot preserves in a saucepan until liquid. Pour half the hot preserves over the cake. Set aside to cool. • Repeat with the remaining preserves then set aside to cool. • Beat the cream, remaining ¼ cup (50 g) of sugar and vanilla in a medium bowl with an electric mixer at high speed until stiff. • Split the savarin in half horizontally. • Place the bottom layer on a serving plate. Spread with the cream. Place the remaining layer on top. • Decorate with the apricot halves.

1 recipe Savarin (see page 562)

Syrup

1½ cups (300 g) sugar

2 cups (500 ml) cold water

½ cup (125 ml) dark rum

1 cup (300 g) apricot preserves (jam)

1½ cups (375 ml) heavy cream

1 teaspoon vanilla extract (essence)

Canned apricot halves, to decorate

Serves: 6–8
Preparation: 1 hour
+ 1 hour 30 minutes
to rise
Cooking: 35–40 minutes
Level: 2

LEMON RUM SAVARIN

Prepare the savarin dough. • Place the dough in a clean, oiled bowl and cover with plastic wrap (cling film). Let rise until doubled in bulk, about 1 hour. • Butter a 10-inch (25-cm) tube pan. • Punch down the dough. Place in the prepared pan, spreading it evenly. Cover with a clean cloth and let rise until almost doubled in bulk, about 30 minutes. • Preheat the oven to 375°F (190°C/gas 5). • Bake for 35–45 minutes, or until golden brown. Cool the savarin in the pan for 15 minutes. Turn out onto a rack to cool. • Lemon-Rum Syrup: Bring the sugar, water, lemon zest, and cinnamon stick to a boil in a medium saucepan. • Place the cake (still on the rack) on a large plate. • Remove the cinnamon stick from the syrup. Drizzle the hot syrup over the cake. Scoop up any excess syrup with a spoon and drizzle over the cake. • Drizzle with the rum. • Heat the apricot preserves in a saucepan until liquid. Pour over the cake and set aside to cool. • Beat the cream and confectioners' sugar in a medium bowl with an electric mixer at high speed until stiff. • Spoon the cream into the center of the savarin. • Decorate with the cherries and almonds.

1	recipe Savarin (see page 562)

Lemon-Rum Syrup

1½	cups (300 g) sugar
2	cups (500 ml) cold water
2	tablespoons finely grated lemon zest
1	cinnamon stick
2	cups (500 ml) rum
½	cup (150 g) apricot preserves
1½	cups (375 ml) heavy (double) cream
⅓	cup (50 g) confectioners' (icing) sugar
	Candied (glacé) cherries and flaked almonds, to decorate

Serves: 6–8
Preparation: 1 hour + 1 hour 30 minutes to rise
Cooking: 35–40 minutes
Level: 2

PEACH SAVARIN

Prepare the savarin dough. • Place the dough in a clean, oiled bowl and cover with plastic wrap (cling film). Let rise until doubled in bulk, about 1 hour. • Butter a 10-inch (25-cm) tube pan. • Punch down the dough. Place in the prepared pan, spreading it evenly. Cover with a clean cloth and let rise until almost doubled in bulk, about 30 minutes. • Preheat the oven to 375°F (190°C/gas 5). • Bake for 35–45 minutes, or until golden brown. Cool the savarin in the pan for 15 minutes. Turn out onto a rack to cool. • Place the cake (still on the rack) on a large plate and poke holes all over with a skewer. • Mix the peach juice and rum in a small bowl. Drizzle over the cake. • Chop half the peaches coarsely. Fill the center of the savarin with the chopped peaches. • Beat the cream in a large bowl with an electric mixer at high speed until stiff. • Spoon the cream into a pastry bag and pipe in a decorative manner over the top. • Decorate with the remaining peach slices.

1	recipe Savarin (see page 562)
1	(14-ounce/400-g) can peach slices, drained (reserve the juice)
½	cup (125 ml) dark rum
1	cup (250 ml) heavy (double) cream

Serves: 6–8
Preparation: 45 minutes + 1 hour 30 minutes to rise
Cooking: 35–40 minutes
Level: 2

RUM BABAS WITH CINNAMON CREAM

Babas: Combine 1 tablespoon of the milk with the yeast and a pinch of sugar in a small bowl. Set aside in a warm place until foamy, 5 minutes. • Stir 1½ teaspoons of the flour into the yeast mixture, cover with plastic wrap (cling film) and set aside in a warm place for 45–60 minutes, until doubled in size. • Transfer the yeast mixture to a food processor fitted with a dough hook. Add the egg, the remaining 1½ teaspoons sugar, the remaining flour, and remaining 1 tablespoon milk. Process for 1–2 minutes, until a dough is formed. Add the butter and process until incorporated. • Lightly grease a large bowl. Shape the dough into a ball and add to the bowl. Cover with a clean cloth, and set in a warm place until doubled in bulk, 45–60 minutes. • Lightly butter four baba or dariole molds. • Add the raisins to the dough and "knock back" or knead for 2–3 minutes, incorporating the raisins into the dough as you knead. Divide the dough into four and place in the prepared molds, filling each one about one-third full. • Place the molds on a baking sheet, cover loosely with a clean cloth, and set in a warm place until dough has risen to the top of the molds, 30–45 minutes. • Preheat the oven to 425°F (220°C/gas 7). • Bake the babas for 12–15 minutes, until browned. Remove from the molds and place on a wire rack to cool. • Cinnamon Cream: Beat the cream with an electric mixer fitted with a whisk on high speed until thickened. Add the confectioners'

Babas

2   tablespoons warm (about 110°F/43°C) milk

½   teaspoon active dry yeast

1½ teaspoons sugar

½   cup (75 g) all-purpose (plain) flour + 1½ teaspoons

1   large egg

¼   cup (60 g) butter, softened

2   tablespoons raisins

Cinnamon Cream

¾   cup (200 ml) heavy (double) cream

2   tablespoons confectioners' (icing) sugar

1   teaspoon ground cinnamon

Rum Syrup

½   cup (100 g) sugar

¾   cup (180 ml) water

2   tablespoons freshly squeezed orange juice, strained

⅓   cup (90 ml) dark rum

Serves: 4
Preparation: 45 minutes
  + 2 hour 45 minutes
  to rise
Cooking: 12–15 minutes
Level: 2

sugar and cinnamon and beat until soft peaks form and the cream holds its shape. Set aside. <u>Rum Syrup:</u> Combine the sugar, water, and orange juice in a small saucepan over medium heat and cook until the sugar dissolves. Remove from the heat and add the rum. • Place a baking sheet under the wire rack that holds the babas. One by one, dip the warm babas into the rum syrup, let soak for 10 seconds, then return to the wire rack. • Place the babas on individual serving plates, drizzle with any remaining syrup, and place a dollop of cinnamon cream to the side.

■ ■ ■ *The name "baba" is the colloquial word for grandma or woman in many Slavic languages. Babas are a very old dessert and their origins are believed to pre-date the spread of Christianity in Europe. Records show that they were served at pagan festivals to celebrate the arrival of spring.*

FILLED RASPBERRY BRIOCHE

Step 1: Mix the yeast, 1 teaspoon of sugar, and milk in a small bowl. Set aside until frothy, 10 minutes. • Mix the flour, remaining sugar, and salt in a large bowl. • Pour in the eggs, milk, and yeast mixture. • **Step 2:** Electric Mixer: Knead the dough with a mixer fitted with a dough hook until smooth, 8–10 minutes. Beat in the butter, one piece at a time, with mixer at low speed until the dough is smooth and elastic, about 5 minutes. • **Step 3:** By Hand: Draw the flour into the eggs and yeast mixture with a plastic spatula. Mix until you have a soft dough, about 5 minutes. • Work small pieces of butter into the dough with your hands. • Knead the dough on a floured surface until smooth and elastic, 15 minutes. • **Step 4:** Form into a ball, place in an oiled bowl, and let rise until doubled in bulk, 2–3 hours. • Turn out onto a lightly floured work surface and knead for 2–3 minutes. • Return to the bowl and refrigerate overnight. • **Step 5:** Butter a 4-cup (1-liter) brioche mold. • Divide the dough into two pieces—three quarters and a quarter. • Roll the larger piece into a ball and place in the mold. Press a deep hole in the center. • Roll the smaller piece into an egg shape and press it, pointed end down, into the hole in the large ball. • Cover and let rise for 90 minutes. • Preheat the oven to 425°F (220°C/gas 7). **Step 6:** Glaze the brioche with the egg wash. Bake for 20 minutes. Decrease the oven temperature to 375°F (190°C/gas 5) and bake for 15–20 more minutes, until a skewer inserted in the center comes out clean. • Turn out of the pan and let cool on a rack. • Cut the top off the brioche and hollow out the inside. • Fill with cream and top with the raspberries.

1 ounce (30 g) compressed fresh yeast or 2 (¼-ounce/7-g) packages active dry yeast

2 tablespoons sugar

⅓ cup (90 ml) lukewarm (110°F/43°C) milk

3 cups (450 g) all-purpose (plain) flour

1 teaspoon salt

4 large eggs, beaten

¾ cup (200 g) butter, cut into small pieces and softened

Egg Wash

1 large egg yolk, lightly beaten with 1 tablespoon milk

1 recipe Chantilly Cream (see page 600)

2 cups (300 g) fresh raspberries

Serves: 6–8
Preparation: 30 minutes
+ 15 hours to rest
and rise
Cooking: 40 minutes
Level: 3

■ PREPARING BRIOCHE

Brioche is an enriched French bread. Its high egg and butter content give it a rich and tender crumb. It is often served at breakfast or as a snack, but when paired with fruit and cream, it makes a wonderful dessert.

1. MIX the yeast, 1 teaspoon of sugar, and milk. Mix the flour, remaining sugar, and salt in a bowl. Add the eggs, milk, and yeast mixture.

2. ELECTRIC MIXER: Knead with a dough hook until smooth, 8–10 minutes. Add the butter gradually until smooth and elastic, 5 minutes.

3. BY HAND: Mix with a spatula until soft, 5 minutes. Work in small pieces of butter. Knead until smooth and elastic, 15 minutes.

4. FORM into a ball and let rise until doubled in bulk, 2–3 hours. Knead for 2–3 minutes. Return to bowl and chill overnight.

5. DIVIDE the dough in two—three quarters and a quarter. Place the large piece in mold. Press a hole and fill with small piece.

6. GLAZE Glaze the brioche with the egg wash. Bake as instructed.

FRESH FRUIT PIZZA

582

Crust: Dust a large baking sheet or 15-inch (35-cm) round pizza pan with cornmeal. • Place the yeast, 1/4 cup (60 ml) water, and the sugar in a small bowl. Set aside until foamy, about 10 minutes. • Combine the flour and salt in a large bowl and make a well in the center. Stir in the yeast mixture and oil, and add as much of the remaining water as needed to make a smooth dough. • Transfer to a lightly floured surface and knead until smooth. Cover with a clean kitchen towel and let rise in a warm place until doubled in bulk, about 1 hour. • Preheat the oven to 400°F (220°C/gas 6). • Roll the dough out on a lightly floured surface into a 15-inch (35-cm) round, about 1/8 inch (3 mm) thick. Roll the dough onto the rolling pin and uncoil it onto the prepared sheet. • Topping: Mix the ricotta and mascarpone in a medium bowl. Spread the cheese mixture over the pizza dough, leaving a 1-inch (2.5-cm) border. • Stir the fruit and confectioners' sugar in a large bowl. • Spread the fruit over the pizza. • Bake for 15–20 minutes, or until the crust is crisp and the filling hot. • Serve hot or warm.

Crust

Cornmeal, to dust

1/2 ounce (15 g) compressed fresh yeast or 1 (1/4-ounce/7-g) package active dry yeast

1 1/4 cups (300 ml) lukewarm water

1 tablespoon sugar

3 cups (450 g) all-purpose flour

1/2 teaspoon salt

2 tablespoons extra-virgin olive oil

Topping

1 cup (250 g) fresh ricotta cheese

1/2 cup (125 g) mascarpone cheese

3 cups (450 g) mixed fresh blackberries, blueberries, and raspberries

1/3 cup (50 g) confectioners' (icing) sugar

Serves: 4–6
Prep: 25 minutes
  + 1 hour to rise
Cooking 15–20 minutes
Level: 2

BASIC
RECIPES

VANILLA CRÈME ANGLAISE

Step 1: Heat the milk and vanilla bean in a small saucepan over medium-low heat to simmering point. Remove from the heat. • **Step 2:** Whisk the egg yolks and sugar in a medium bowl until pale and creamy. **Step 3:** Slowly pour in one-third of the hot milk, whisking continuously. Then pour in the rest and whisk until fully combined. • **Step 4:** Pour the mixture into a clean small saucepan and cook over low heat, stirring continuously with a wooden spoon, until the mixture has thickened enough to coat the back of the spoon. • **Step 5:** Strain the custard through a fine-mesh sieve into a small pitcher (jug) for serving.

1   **cup (250 ml) milk**
½   **vanilla bean, split lengthwise**
3   **large egg yolks**
¼   **cup (50 g) sugar**

Makes: About 1½ cups (375 ml)
Preparation: 10 minutes
Cooking: 10 minutes
Level: 1

■ ■ ■ *Vanilla is the classic aroma used to flavor crème anglaise, but you can also create other flavors:*
Cinnamon Crème Anglaise: Add a stick of cinnamon to the milk as it gently heats. Remove before adding to the egg mixture.
Coffee Crème Anglaise: Dissolve 2 teaspoons of freeze-dried instant coffee granules in the milk while heating.
Chocolate Crème Anglaise: Add 2 ounces (60 g) of coarsely chopped or grated dark chocolate to the milk. Stir until dissolved as the milk heats.
Flavoring crème anglaise with liqueurs: Add 1 tablespoon of the desired liqueur to the custard after it is cooked. Grand Marnier produces a lovely orange-flavored custard.

■ PREPARING VANILLA CRÈME ANGLAISE

Vanilla Crème Anglaise is a pouring custard made with eggs, milk, sugar, and vanilla. It is not thickened with flour or cornstarch (cornflour), This custard thickens because the proteins in the egg gradually coagulate during slow cooking over low heat and constant stirring. Crème Anglaise is perfect with warm desserts such as apple pie or crisp.

1

2

3

1. HEAT the milk and vanilla bean in a small saucepan over medium-low heat, until just simmering. Remove from the heat.

2. WHISK the egg yolks and sugar in a medium bowl until pale and creamy.

3. SLOWLY POUR in one-third of the hot milk, whisking continuously. Then pour in the rest and whisk until fully combined.

4

5

4. POUR into a pan and cook over low heat, stirring continuously, until it coats the back of the spoon.

5. STRAIN the custard through a fine-mesh sieve into a small pitcher (jug) for serving.

VANILLA PASTRY CREAM

Step 1: Beat the egg yolks and sugar until pale and creamy. Beat in the cornstarch and salt. Add more or less cornstarch depending on how thick you want the pastry cream to be. • **Step 2:** Bring the milk to a boil, then stir into the egg and sugar mixture. **Step 3:** Cook over low heat until well thickened and just boiling, about 10 minutes. During the first 5 minutes of cooking time stir often with a wooden spoon. After that, stir constantly with a whisk, breaking up any lumps as they form. Gently boil for one full minute over low heat, stirring constantly. **Step 4:** Remove from the heat and stir in the vanilla (or other flavoring). If not using immediately, pour into a bowl and place a piece of plastic wrap (cling film) on the surface to stop a skin from forming.

590

5	large egg yolks
¾	cup (150 g) sugar
2–4	tablespoons cornstarch (cornflour)
	Pinch of salt
2	cups (500 ml) milk
2	teaspoons vanilla extract (essence)

Makes: About 3 cups (750 ml)
Preparation: 10 minutes
Cooking: 10–15 minutes
Level: 1

■ ■ ■ *You may flavor the custard in the following ways:*
Chocolate Pastry Cream: Add 5 ounces (150 g) of coarsely chopped or grated dark chocolate to the milk. Stir until dissolved as the milk heats.
Coffee Pastry Cream: Dissolve 1 tablespoon of instant coffee granules in the milk while heating.
Lemon Pastry Cream: Boil the finely grated zest of 1 lemon in the milk, omitting the vanilla extract. You may also add 2–3 teaspoons freshly squeezed juice to the finished custard.
Flavoring pastry cream with liqueurs: add 1–2 tablespoons of the desired liqueur to the custard after it is cooked. Grand Marnier produces a lovely orange-flavored custard.

Similar in flavor to Vanilla Crème Anglaise, Vanilla Pastry Cream is thicker because of the addition of cornstarch. Add more or less cornstarch depending on how thick you want the pastry cream to be. It is not a pouring custard but is used as a filling for millefeuille (napoleons), pastry squares, and many other cakes and desserts.

591

1. BEAT the egg yolks and sugar until pale and thick. Beat in the cornstarch.

2. BRING the milk to a boil with the salt, then stir it into the egg and sugar mixture.

3. COOK over low heat until thickened, about 10 minutes. During the first 5 minutes stir with a wooden spoon. After that, stir constantly with a whisk.

4. REMOVE from the heat and stir in the vanilla (or other flavoring).

BASIC SPONGE CAKE

592

Preheat the oven to 350°F (180°C/gas 4).
• Butter two 9-inch (23-cm) round cake pans. Line with parchment paper. • Beat the egg whites in a large bowl with an electric mixer at high speed until stiff peaks form. • Add the egg yolks and sugar and continue beating until pale and thick. Use a large rubber spatula to fold in the dry ingredients. • Bake for 15–20 minutes, or until a toothpick inserted into the center comes out clean. • Turn out onto racks and carefully remove the paper. Let cool completely.

4	large eggs, separated
¾	cup (150 g) sugar
¾	cup (120 g) cornstarch (cornflour)
2	tablespoons all-purpose (plain) flour
1	teaspoon cream of tartar
½	teaspoon baking soda (bicarbonate of soda)

Serves: 8–10
Preparation: 15 minutes
Cooking: 15–20 minutes
Level: 2

■ ■ ■ *It is very important that the eggs be at a warm room temperature. Take them out of the refrigerator several hours before you begin baking this sponge.*

ITALIAN SPONGE CAKE

594

Preheat the oven to 350°F (180°C/gas 4).
• Butter a 10-inch (25-cm) springform pan. Line
with parchment paper. • Sift the flour and salt into
a medium bowl. • Beat the egg yolks, sugar, and
lemon zest in a large bowl with an electric mixer at
high speed until pale and very thick. • Beat the egg
whites in a large bowl until stiff peaks form. • Use a
large rubber spatula to fold the dry ingredients into
the egg yolk mixture. Carefully fold in the beaten
whites. • Working quickly, spoon the batter into the
prepared pan. • Bake for 35–45 minutes, or until
springy to the touch and the cake shrinks from the
pan sides. • Cool the cake in the pan for 5 minutes.
Loosen and remove the pan sides. Invert the cake
onto a rack. Loosen and remove the pan bottom.
Carefully remove the paper. Turn the cake top-side
up and let cool completely.

1	cup (150 g) cake flour
¼	teaspoon salt
6	large eggs, separated
1¼	cups (250 g) sugar
½	tablespoon finely grated lemon zest

Serves: 8–10
Preparation: 20 minutes
Cooking: 35–45 minutes
Level: 2

■ ■ ■ *This classic Italian sponge cake contains no
butter or oil, and the leavening comes entirely from the
beaten egg whites. It is used as the basis for many
different layer cakes and desserts. You may replace the
lemon zest with vanilla extract or another flavoring of
your choice, depending on how you intend to use it.*

BASIC CHOCOLATE FROSTING

Stir the confectioners' sugar and cocoa in a double boiler. Add the butter, vanilla, and enough of the water to make a firm paste. • Stir over simmering water until the frosting is smooth and spreadable, about 3 minutes.

596

2 **cups (300 g) confectioners' (icing) sugar**
¼ **cup (30 g) unsweetened cocoa powder**
2 **tablespoons butter, softened**
1 **teaspoon vanilla extract (essence)**
  About 2 tablespoons boiling water

Makes: About 1 cup (250 ml)
Preparation: 5–10 minutes
Level: 1

RICH CHOCOLATE FROSTING

Bring the sugar and 1 cup (250 ml) of cream to a boil in a saucepan over medium heat. Boil for 1 minute, then remove from the heat. • Stir in the chocolate. • Return the saucepan to medium heat and cook, without stirring, until the mixture reaches 238°F (115°C), or the soft-ball stage. Remove from the heat. • Add the butter and vanilla, without stirring, and place the saucepan in a larger pan of cold water for 5 minutes before stirring. • Beat with a wooden spoon until the frosting begins to lose its sheen, 5–10 minutes. Immediately stir in 1 tablespoon of cream. Do not let the frosting harden too much before adding the cream. • Let stand for 3–4 minutes, then stir until smooth and spreadable consistency. Add more cream, 1 teaspoon at a time, if it is too stiff.

2   cups (400 g) sugar

1   cup (250 ml) heavy (double) cream + 1–2 tablespoons, as needed

8   ounces (250 g) dark chocolate, coarsely chopped

2   tablespoons butter

1   teaspoon vanilla extract (essence)

Makes: About 2 cups (500 ml)
Preparation: 15 minutes
Cooking: 10 minutes
Level: 2

CHANTILLY CREAM

Beat the cream in a medium bowl with an electric mixer on high speed until almost thickened. Add the confectioners' sugar and vanilla and continue beating until thickened. • Do not overbeat.

600

1   cup (250 ml) heavy (double) cream

2   tablespoons confectioners' (icing) sugar

½   teaspoon vanilla extract (essence)

Makes: About 2 cups (500 ml)
Preparation: 5 minutes
Level: 1

■ ■ ■ *These quantities will make 2 cups (500 ml) of Chantilly Cream. If you need more, double the recipe. For a light, white Chantilly Cream, make sure that the cream is well chilled before you start. Place the mixing bowl in the freezer for 10 minutes before you begin beating the cream.*

INDEX

BASIC RECIPES

CRÊPES & FRITTERS

INDEX

605